THE CRENSHAWS OF KENTUCKY

1800-1995

A GENEALOGY OF THE CRENSHAWS IN SOUTH-CENTRAL KENTUCKY, PRIMARILY THE COUNTIES OF BARREN AND METCALFE, INCLUDING THE RELATED FAMILIES OF ALLEN, ARNETT, BEARD, BIRD, BRADSHAW, DEARING, DICKEY, DUKE, FRANKLIN, GOAD, HORD, JACKSON, LOVE, MAUPIN, MITCHELL, MUNDAY, PACE, PARRISH, PEDEN, ROGERS, SLEMMONS, STOCKTON, TAYLOR, TWYMAN, WILLIAMS, AND MORE

Henry C. Peden, Jr.

HERITAGE BOOKS
2016

HERITAGE BOOKS
AN IMPRINT OF HERITAGE BOOKS, INC.

Books, CDs, and more—Worldwide

For our listing of thousands of titles see our website
at
www.HeritageBooks.com

Published 2016 by
HERITAGE BOOKS, INC.
Publishing Division
5810 Ruatan Street
Berwyn Heights, Md. 20740

Originally published by
Family Line Publications
1995

International Standard Book Numbers
Paperbound: 978-1-58549-514-6
Clothbound: 978-0-7884-6334-1

Table of Contents

Dedicated to the Memory

of

Pearl Eugenia Crenshaw Peden
(1892-1976),

daughter of
Henry Anderson Crenshaw
(1847-1907)

and wife of
William Henry Peden
(1891-1944)

of

Barren County, Kentucky

INTRODUCTION

The Crenshaws of Kentucky are descended from 33 Crenshaws (and possibly more) who had migrated at different times from Virginia to Kentucky between 1782 and 1820, or in some instances were born in Kentucky during the early part of the 19th century. Of these, only the family histories of John Crenshaw and Benjamin Crenshaw, of Barren County, Kentucky, will be covered in detail in this book. For the record, however, here are the names of those 33 Crenshaws:

BENJAMIN CRENSHAW.........Barren County............by 1801
THOMAS J. CRENSHAW........Barren County............by 1801
BENJAMIN M. CRENSHAW......Barren County............by 1801
JOHN CRENSHAW.............Barren County............by 1805
THOMPSON CRENSHAW.........Barren County............by 1805
ANDERSON CRENSHAW.........Barren County............by 1805
WALLER CRENSHAW...........Barren County............by 1805
GARLAND CRENSHAW..........Barren County............by 1805
DABNEY CRENSHAW...........Barren County............by 1805
THOMAS CRENSHAW...........Bourbon County...........by 1820
RICHARD CRENSHAW..........Bullitt County...........by 1804
BLUFORD CRENSHAW..........Bullitt County...........by 1810
COSBY CRENSHAW............Bullitt County...........by 1810
CRERTEN CRENSHAW..........Bullitt County...........by 1810
JAMES CRENSHAW............Bullitt County...........by 1810
NELSON CRENSHAW...........Bullitt County...........by 1810
OVERTON CRENSHAW..........Bullitt County...........by 1820
DAVID CRENSHAW............Fayette County...........by 1807
WILLIAM CRENSHAW..........Fayette County...........by 1810
THOMAS CRENSHAW...........Hardin County............by 1796
ABNER P. CRENSHAW.........Hardin County............by 1820
JOSEPH CRENSHAW...........Hardin County............by 1820
JOHN CRENSHAW.............Harrison County..........by 1807
THOMAS CRENSHAW...........Henderson County.........by 1820
JONER CRENSHAW............Henderson County.........by 1820
JOSEPH CRENSHAW...........Henderson County.........by 1820
J. T. CRENSHAW............Henderson County.........by 1820
THOMAS CRENSHAW...........Jefferson County.........by 1782
NICHOLAS CRENSHAW.........Montgomery County........by 1820
JOEL CRENSHAW.............Scott County.............by 1810
LEWIS CRENSHAW............Shelby County............by 1810
CORNELIUS CRENSHAW........Trigg County.............by 1819
JAMES CRENSHAW............Woodford County..........by 1791

THOMAS CRENSHAW was the first Crenshaw in Kentucky. He was in Jefferson County by December 25, 1782 when 1,456 1/2 acres of land were surveyed on Plumb Creek. [Ref: *Old Kentucky Entries and Deeds*, by Willard Rouse Jillson (1978), page 194]. Another **THOMAS CRENSHAW** left Hardin County, Kentucky, by September 30, 1796, at which time his name appeared on a long list of names in the *Kentucky Gazette* regarding land for sale to pay overdue taxes. Bullitt County was formed from Jefferson and Nelson Counties (originally in Kentucky County, Virginia) in 1796. One **RICHARD CRENSHAW** was born there in 1804 and married **MAY J. MOORE** (born 1803, Maryland). They moved to Missouri in 1832. [Ref: *Kentuckians to Missouri*, by Stuart Seely Sprague (Baltimore: Genealogical Publishing Co., 1983), page 34].

JAMES CRENSHAW was the second Crenshaw in Kentucky. He was in Woodford County by 1791, when he reported a stray mare near Boon's Creek on April 23, 1791. [Ref: *The Kentucky Gazette, 1787-1800*, by Karen Mauer Green (1983), p. 39]. "**JAMES CRENSHAW**, of the County of Kentucky, granted a power of attorney to Annanias Hall to transact business and affairs in his father's estate with brother **CHARLES CRENSHAW**, acting executor, in Louisa County, Virginia, on March 1, 1793." [Ref: *The Edward Pleasants Valentine Papers*, page 369, and *Louisa County Deed Book G:317*]. It appears that this James Crenshaw was a son of James Crenshaw and a great-great-grandson of **THOMAS J. CRENSHAW**, the progenitor. If this is the case then he and our John Crenshaw (1759-1818) were third cousins. [Ref: *The Crenshaw and Connecting Families*, by Hazel Crenshaw Wilkins (1981), page 5].

BENJAMIN CRENSHAW, the fifth Crenshaw in Kentucky, migrated to Barren County by 1801. He owned Crenshaw's Upper and Lower Mills on Beaver Creek near the road from Glasgow to Warren County. His known sons were **THOMAS J. CRENSHAW and BENJAMIN M. CRENSHAW** (but the 1810 census listed 5 sons). Their descendants will be discussed later.

JOHN CRENSHAW was the eighth Crenshaw in Kentucky. He was from Louisa County, Virginia, and was in Barren County by 1805, possibly earlier. John settled on land on the Blue Spring Creek near Knob Lick, which became part of Metcalfe County in 1860. His five sons were **THOMPSON CRENSHAW, WALLER CRENSHAW, GARLAND CRENSHAW, DABNEY CRENSHAW, and ANDERSON CRENSHAW.** [John was our ancestor and his descendants will be discussed in much more detail later. However, John was not listed in the *1810 Census of Barren County, Kentucky*, although his eldest son **THOMPSON CRENSHAW** was listed with "a wife, one son, and two daughters." **JOHN CRENSHAW** was obviously missed by the census taker because he later died in Barren County in 1818].

DAVID CRENSHAW was the fourteenth Crenshaw in Kentucky. He was in Fayette County by June, 1807, when he was a party in the suit of Hart vs. Hawkins. [Ref: *The Kentucky Gazette*, August 18, 1807].

JOHN CRENSHAW was the fifteenth Crenshaw in Kentucky. He was in Harrison County by 1807 when he witnessed the will of Susannah Chandler when it was written on October 23, 1807. He was still in Harrison County when he witnessed the will of Lewis Day when it was written June 4, 1829. [Ref: *Harrison Co. Will Books A:364 & B:467*].

BLUFORD CRENSHAW, COSBY CRENSHAW, CRERTEN CRENSHAW (his first name was obviously misspelled), **JAMES CRENSHAW, and NELSON CRENSHAW** (the latter two men's names were misspelled "Crinshaw") were all in the *1810 Census of Bullitt County, Kentucky* and, no doubt, related to one another. Their genealogy has not been researched, but in the 1810 census it was noted that Bluford was an older man and lived alone; Cosby had "a wife, three sons and two daughters"; Crerten[?] had "a wife, three sons, and 4 daughters"; James was an old man and lived alone; and Nelson had "a wife, three sons and two daughters."

JOEL CRENSHAW, the twenty-first Crenshaw (possibly earlier) in Kentucky, was the head of the household in the *1810 Census of Scott County, Kentucky*, with "a wife, three sons, and one daughter."

LEWIS CRENSHAW was the twenty-second Crenshaw in Kentucky, but an exact date of his arrival has not been determined. Therefore, he could have arrived before some of the 21 earlier Crenshaws. Lewis Crenshaw was head of household in the *1810 Census of Shelby County, Kentucky*, with "a wife, three sons, and two daughters."

WILLIAM CRENSHAW was the twenty-third Crenshaw in Kentucky. The *1810 Census of Fayette County, Kentucky*, indicates he had "a wife, three sons, and two daughters."

CORNELIUS CRENSHAW, the twenty-fourth Crenshaw in Kentucky, married Nancy Kent in Halifax County, Virginia, and came to Trigg County, Kentucky, in 1819. "He was for many years a member of the United Baptist denomination, but has afterwards associated himself with the Christian Church, and was noted for his piety and good works. Before coming to Kentucky, Cornelius served in a Virginia Company in the War of 1812, in which he was a commissioned officer stationed at Norfolk, Virginia. His son, **ROBERTSON CRENSHAW**, was born in Halifax County in September, 1816, and married **MARY FRANCES WALDEN** in Trigg County, Kentucky, in 1839. He was a member of the Christian Church and died on February 12, 1853. **THOMAS CRENSHAW**, another son of Cornelius, raised his nephew **ROBERT CRENSHAW** (son of the above named Robertson) after the death of his brother. Robert Crenshaw was born June 4, 1847, in the precinct of Roaring Springs in Trigg County, Kentucky, and became an attorney in Cadiz in 1868. He later became County Attorney in 1874 and County Judge in 1884. He also served as a School Commissioner. Robert married in 1877 to **MINNIE DABNEY**, the daughter of Judge Thomas C. Dabney, and they had six children: **Susanne Moore Crenshaw, E. Rumsey Crenshaw, Dabney H. Crenshaw, Robert Crenshaw, John W. Crenshaw, and Albert Crenshaw.**" [Ref: *A Biographical Cyclopedia of the Commonwealth of Kentucky*, compiled and published by the John M. Gresham Company, Chicago-Philadelphia (1896), pages 463-464].

ABNER P. CRENSHAW and JOSEPH CRENSHAW, the twenty-fifth and twenty-sixth Crenshaws in Kentucky, were brothers and they probably settled around Hardin County. **ABNER P. CRENSHAW** was born January 9, 1784, in Lunenburg County, Virginia, and married Philadelphia Bruce Faulk (February 20, 1791 - December 21, 1846), and they had eleven children. **JOSEPH CRENSHAW** married Mary (Lester) Smithson, widow of

Frank Smithson, and had ten children. **ABNER P. CRENSHAW and JOSEPH CRENSHAW** were sons of Revolutionary War soldier **DANIEL CRENSHAW** and his wife Nancy Dupree (born 1757, daughter of Joseph Dupree). They were second cousins to **JOHN CRENSHAW** (1759-1818) since Daniel was a son of Cornelius Crenshaw who was a brother of Nicholas Crenshaw who was the father of John Crenshaw (1759-1818). [Ref: *The Crenshaw and Connecting Families*, by Hazel Crenshaw Wilkins (1981), page 8].

The other Crenshaws (numbers 27 through 33) were the heads of household in the *1820 Census of Kentucky* as cited above, viz., **J. T. CRENSHAW, JONER CRENSHAW, JOSEPH CRENSHAW, and THOMAS CRENSHAW**, all of Henderson County, **NICHOLAS CRENSHAW** of Montgomery County, **THOMAS CRENSHAW** of Bourbon County, and **OVERTON CRENSHAW** of Bullitt County. Their relationships, if any, have not yet been determined.

When **Pearl Eugenia Crenshaw** (1892-1976), descendant of John Crenshaw (1759-1818), married to **William Henry "Will" Peden** (1891-1944) in Kentucky in 1913, our Crenshaw connection was established. For others in the Barren County area, their ancestry is from either this same John Crenshaw, or the Benjamin Crenshaw mentioned above. One should consult, in addition to the probate and land records of Virginia and Kentucky, these publications on the Crenshaw family: *The Edward Pleasants Valentine Papers*, Volume I, pages 329 to 395 (Richmond: The Valentine Museum), and *The Crenshaw and Connecting Families*, by Hazel Crenshaw Wilkins, of Gilmer, Texas (1981).

The destruction of court records of New Kent County and the very fragmentary records in King William County prevents us from obtaining a very definite outline of the early generations of the Crenshaw family. From King William County the families spread to Hanover, Louisa, Henrico, Caroline and Amelia Counties, Virginia, and then southward and westward from there. The Crenshaw name was occasionally misspelled "Cranshaw" and "Granshaw" and "Granger." Additional and corrected information is encouraged and welcomed. **Henry C. Peden, Jr.**, 707 Bedford Road, Bel Air, Maryland 21014-4424

OUR LINE OF CRENSHAWS IN VIRGINIA

THOMAS J. CRENSHAW was born in England and was granted a land patent in King William County, Virginia, on October 9, 1667, and died in 1703. He had at least three sons: John, Joseph, and Thomas. Upon his death he left the 150 acres he had received in 1667 to his eldest son **JOHN CRENSHAW**, noting if John died without children the land would go to the second son **JOSEPH CRENSHAW**. [Ref: *The Crenshaw and Connecting Families*, by Hazel Crenshaw Wilkins (1981), p. 83]. Joseph Crenshaw married Sarah --- and had eight children: William, Gideon, Joseph, Jr., Thomas, Priscilla (married ---- Duke), Hanna (married ---- Barkman), Mary (married ---- Cook), and Micajah (married Mary Ann Matthews). [Ref: *The Edward Pleasants Valentine Papers*, page 376]. Joseph Crenshaw (c1668-1757) died in Virginia.

THOMAS J. CRENSHAW, JR., youngest son of **THOMAS J. CRENSHAW**, was born in 1670 in Virginia and died there in 1730. He had a son, **WILLIAM A. CRENSHAW** (1707-1760), in Spotsylvania County, Virginia, who married ---- **ANDERSON**, a daughter of **JUDGE JOHN ANDERSON**. They had two sons, **WILLIAM A. CRENSHAW, JR.** and **NICHOLAS CRENSHAW** (who married sisters named Carr).

WILLIAM A. CRENSHAW, JR., a son of **WILLIAM A. CRENSHAW, SR.**, married **SUSANNA BROOKS CARR** and had nine children: Charles Crenshaw (1749-1814), David Crenshaw, Joel Crenshaw, Sarah Crenshaw (married William Dickson in 1796), Susanna Crenshaw (married John Burnly in 1785), Agnes Crenshaw (who married Thomas Fretwell in 1787), Jamima Crenshaw (married William Fretwell in 1789), Mary Crenshaw (married a John Crenshaw), and Nancy Crenshaw (married a Thomas Crenshaw). WILLIAM A. CRENSHAW, JR., died in 1799. Some of his descendants and related families later moved to the Carolinas.

NICHOLAS CRENSHAW, son of **WILLIAM A. CRENSHAW, SR.**, and ---- ANDERSON, was born circa 1730 and married **MARY CARR**, a sister of Susanna Brooks Carr who married William A. Crenshaw, Jr. Nicholas Crenshaw rendered patriotic service during the Revolutionary War by giving a horse to Capt. Young's militia company in Hanover County, Virginia. He also provided a supply of beef on May 24, 1782. [Ref: *Public Service Claims, Hanover County, Virginia, List I, Reel 2*, page 20, and *VA Public Service Claims, List II, Reel 2*, page 5].

NICHOLAS CRENSHAW had seven children: William Crenshaw (born March 26, 1755 and married Sarah Baker), Elizabeth Crenshaw (born March 8, 1757), **JOHN CRENSHAW** (born June 21, 1759, married **MILDRED THOMPSON**), Ann Crenshaw (born December 3, 1762), Susanna Crenshaw (born October 20, 1767), David Crenshaw (born June 6, 1771, married Frances Thompson) and, Sarah Crenshaw (born August 21, 1778). [Ref: *National Genealogical Society Quarterly*, Volume XXXII, No. 4, Dec., 1944, page 111]. John Crenshaw married Mildred Thompson, and David Crenshaw married Frances Thompson, i.e., Crenshaw brothers married Thompson sisters. David Crenshaw had four children: Garland Carr Crenshaw (1793-1837) married Susannah Shelton (1796-1840); Billy Crenshaw married Polly Edwards; Nathaniel Crenshaw married Harriet Seawell Rice; and, John Crenshaw married Betsy Parker. David died on June 17, 1831 in Sumner County, Tennessee. [Ref: *Sumner County, Tennessee, Abstracts of Will Books 1 and 2 (1788-1842)*, by Edythe Rucker Whitley, p. 53]. David Crenshaw's brother John (as noted, our ancestor) settled in Barren (now Metcalfe) County, Kentucky.

A TRIPLE CONNECTION BETWEEN THE CRENSHAWS AND THE PEDENS

Before presenting the descendants of our **JOHN CRENSHAW**, there are two other Crenshaw connections to the Peden family in Kentucky through the oldest brother of John, namely **WILLIAM CRENSHAW** (1755-1829). He married **SARAH BAKER** in Albemarle County, Virginia, and a daughter **ELIZABETH "BETSY" W. CRENSHAW** married **DAVID WATTS**, October

7, 1799. Betsey died in Barren County, Kentucky in 1851. Their son, **BENNETT S. WATTS** (November 29, 1809 - October 29, 1874) married **NANCY HAYS** (May 3, 1808 - August 5, 1878) on April 10, 1833, in Barren County, and their daughter, **SALLIE D. WATTS** (July 4, 1842 - March 18, 1880) married **EDMUND HARLIN PEDEN** (August 19, 1838 - June 4, 1914). Their son, **ELMORE "MOTE" PEDEN** (February 4, 1865 - April 6, 1941) married **JANIE TERRY ROGERS** (October 7, 1867 - August 21, 1960), and their son, **WILLIAM HENRY PEDEN** (1891-1944) married **PEARL EUGENIA CRENSHAW** (1892-1976). Also, **WILLIE FRANCIS PEDEN** married **VALERIA NELL CRENSHAW** on January 1, 1949, in Barren County. She is a daughter of **LESLIE STUART CRENSHAW** (1890-1976) and granddaughter of **ISAAC NEWTON CRENSHAW** (1855-1940). Isaac was a son of **WILLIAM A. CRENSHAW** (1830-1891) and grandson of **ANDERSON CRENSHAW** (1797-1875).

The Pedens of Kentucky descend from two Crenshaw brothers from Virginia, viz. William Crenshaw and John Crenshaw (sons of **NICHOLAS CRENSHAW** and **MARY CARR**). **WILLIAM CRENSHAW** (1755-1829) remained in Virginia, but his daughter, **BETSY CRENSHAW WATTS**, moved to Kentucky as did her uncle **JOHN CRENSHAW** (1759-1818), the brother of **WILLIAM CRENSHAW**. [Ref: The Sons of the American Revolution Supplemental Application No. 112356 on **WILLIAM CRENSHAW**, patriot, filed in 1984; and The Sons of the American Revolution Supplemental Application on **JOHN CRENSHAW**, soldier, in 1982; *Albemarle County, Virginia, Will Book No. 10*, page 173; and, *The Edward Pleasants Valentine Papers*, Volume I, pages 329 to 395, and Volume IV, pages 2249 to 2253].

No family history would be complete without an explanation of the meaning behind the family name of Crenshaw. References in this matter do not list the name as "Crenshaw," but spell it in the old English form of "Cranshaw" (as well as "Crankshaw," "Cronshaw," and "Crownshaw"). The name is derived from "Cranshaws," a location near Berwick, England. The word "Cranshaw" simply meant "the twisting or winding shaw," i. e., wood. Thus, a "Crenshaw" is "one who resides beside the small winding woods." [Ref: *British Family Names: Their Origin and Meaning*, by Henry Barber, M.D. (1903), and *A Dictionary of English and Welsh Surnames*, by Charles W. Bardsley, M.A. (1901).

The following genealogy of the Crenshaws of Kentucky covers the years from 1800 to 1995 for the Crenshaws and related families who settled in Barren and Metcalfe Counties. Thanks to Harlan and Thelma Peden, Clint and Catherine Peden, James M. Simmons, Leona H. Pace, Gail Lyons, Ray Peden, and Frances Smith for their assistance in collecting information. There will always be an incompleteness that goes with family histories. If we waited to accumulate every possible piece of data we would never get published. The waiting is over for the Crenshaws and related families. Here it is. Enjoy it.

Henry C. Peden, Jr.
April 15, 1995

CHAPTER ONE

THE DESCENDANTS OF JOHN CRENSHAW (1759-1818)

1. **JOHN CRENSHAW** (June 21, 1759 - May 1, 1818) was born in Virginia (either Louisa or Albemarle County), a son of **NICHOLAS CRENSHAW** and **MARY CARR**, and he served in the Revolutionary War. [Ref: *Historical Register of Virginians in the Revolution, 1775 to 1783*, by John H. Gwathmey, page 191, citing a petition by the officers and privates of Hanover County, Virginia, in 1782]. John married **MILDRED (MILLY) THOMPSON**, daughter of **WILLIAM THOMPSON**, who died in 1799, Albemarle County, Virginia. His will named his wife Elizabeth and these ten children: **Frances Crenshaw, Milley Crenshaw**, Roger Thompson, Nancy Thompson, Elizabeth Early, Mary Brown, Lucy Thompson, S. Brown, Wm. Thompson, and Nathaniel Thompson. [Ref: *Albemarle County Will Book No. 4*, p. 20, April Court, 1799, and *The Edward Pleasants Valentine Papers*, Vol. IV, page 329].

JOHN CRENSHAW migrated into Barren County, Kentucky, by 1805, and settled on land at Knob Lick (Antioch) which is now in Metcalfe County. In *The Times of Long Ago*, by Franklin Gorin (page 25), it states that those who settled on Beaver Creek, above the Columbia Road, including the sinks of Beaver, and surrounding country were [among others] "**JOHN GRANGER (CRENSHAW)** and **THOMPSON CRENSHAW.**" In the early days--1800 to 1804--persons carried their guns with them everywhere for protection against the Indians and wild animals. In *Kentucky Genealogy and Biography*, Vol. II, p. 80, it states "John Crenshaw arrived at this place [Barren County] on the first day of January in 1805." [Note: A brick found in the old Crenshaw house in (now) Metcalfe County had the year "1797" inscribed in it. It would appear that some of the Crenshaws came into the area and built the house prior to the arrival of the others. However, the first land records involving John Crenshaw were recorded in Barren County in 1805. The "1797" brick is, therefore, an enigma unless maybe it was done in 1805 by John's youngest son **ANDERSON CRENSHAW** (who was born in 1797) to signify his birth year rather than the year the house was built; of course, this is merely speculation on my part--HCP].

JOHN CRENSHAW received 200 acres "per an entry filed" in court on March 18, 1805, and another 200 acres "per entry filed" on April 15, 1805. [Ref: *Barren County Order Book No. 2*, pages 53-55]. On April 30, 1807, one **WILLIAM TWYMAN** sold 150 acres on Blue Spring Creek to John Crenshaw for $1,000, "lying in Barren County on the north east side of the creek, adjoining Richard Waggoner's line." [Ref: *Barren County Deed Book AA*, p. 154]. In the *1809 Tax List of Tithables in Barren County* are the following Crenshaws, all over age 21: **Benjamin Crenshaw, John Crenshaw, Thompson Crenshaw, and Waller Crenshaw.** Only John Crenshaw owned slaves, and he had 10 of them at that time. [Ref: *Traces*, Volume 16, No. 2, Summer, 1988, page 68]. Thompson and Waller were sons of John Crenshaw, while Benjamin is an undetermined relative who owned mills in western

Barren County. In 1808, John Crenshaw was among the men who were appointed by the court to lay-out a road from Walker's Mill to the town of Glasgow. [Ref: *Barren County Order Book No. 3*, page 71].

John Crenshaw's 1818 will was recorded in Barren County, Kentucky, and was copied verbatim in 1979 by Mrs. Eva Coe Peden, as follows:

> "I, **John Crenshaw**, of Kentucky State and County of Barren, being of sound mind and memory but weak in body, and well knowing that according to the Course of Human events, a dissolution of my mortal body must soon take place, and wishing to make a Just distribution of the earthly estate with which it hath please the Almighty Father of the Universe to bless me, do hereby make and ordain this as my last Will and Testament in manner and form following, to wit: My Will and Desire is that all my debts be paid punctually, and **my dearly beloved wife Milly Crenshaw** shall have the use of all my estate both real and personal during her natural life, except such property as shall be bequeathed to **my sons: Garland Crenshaw, Dabney Crenshaw; my daughter Susanna Crenshaw, & my son Anderson Crenshaw, to make them equal (previous to the general division which is to take place among all my children at my wife's decease) to Thompson Crenshaw, Lucy Twyman, Waller Crenshaw, Milley Dearing & Betsey Slemmons with respect to what they have already received of my estate** amounting to one hundred pounds each and a horse saddle and bridle, bed & furniture, cow and calf; **Lucy Twyman** has had one negro boy named Joshua at one hundred pounds, a horse saddle and bridle, bed and furniture, cow and calf; **Waller Crenshaw** has had a negro boy named Nelson at one hundred pounds, horse saddle and bridle, bed and furniture, cow & calf; **Milley Dearing** has had one hundred pounds cash, a horse saddle and bridle, bed and furniture, cow and calf. **Betsey Slemmons** has had a negro boy named Absolam at one hundred pounds, a horse saddle and bridle, bed and furniture, cow and calf, and my will and desire is that immediately after my decease, My executors deliver to my son **Garland Crenshaw** a negro boy named Overton, a horse saddle and bridle, bed and furniture, cow and calf, to make him equal with what the others before mentioned have received. My Will and desire further is that my Executors as above deliver to my son **Dabney Crenshaw** a negro boy named Edmund, a horse saddle and bridle, bed and furniture, cow & calf for the purpose last mentioned, and that said Executors as above stated deliver to my daughter **Susanna Crenshaw a** negro girl named Mary, a horse saddle and bridle, bed and furniture, cow & calf, and pay her at the general division of my Estate Two hundred dollars to make her equal to those who are first mentioned as having already received a part of my estate; and that my Executors as above stated deliver to my son **Anderson Crenshaw** a negro girl named Maria, a horse

saddle and bridle, bed and furniture, and cow and calf, and One hundred dollars to be paid at the general division of my estate to make him equal with those who have already received a part of my estate. And my will and desire further is that immediately after the decease of my dearly beloved wife **Milley Crenshaw** the balance of all my estate both real and personal shall be equally divided among all my children, to wit: **Thompson Crenshaw, Lucy Twyman, Waller Crenshaw, Milley Dearing, Betsey Slemmons, Garland Crenshaw, Dabney Crenshaw, Susanna Crenshaw, and Anderson Crenshaw**, and my will and desire is that all that part of my estate, both real and personal, which may fall to the said Milley Dearing shall be used & enjoyed by her during her life and that at her death to be equally divided among all her children, but that her present husband **George T. Dearing** is not to have, enjoy, possess nor dispose of all or any part thereof and that if he does, his acts in that respect are hereby declared null and void. And my will and desire further is that if any of my children above named shall die without an heir lawfully begotten of their body that then their part or parts of the estate shall be equally divided among the surviving legatees. And I do hereby nominate, constitute and appoint my trusty and Well beloved sons **Thompson Crenshaw, Waller Crenshaw and Garland Crenshaw** Executors of this my last Will and Testament hereby expressly publishing and declaring the foregoing as my last Will and Testament and that all others made by me are hereby annulled and revoked. Signed, Sealed and published as my last Will and Testament this 26th day of April in the year of our Lord 1818 in the presence of (Interlined before signed in 13th word Dabney Crenshaw) **Robert Field, John F. Thompson, Elizabeth Waggoner, Joel Yancey, and Betsey W. Watts**. Signed: **John Crenshaw** (seal)." [Ref: *Barren County Will Book No. 1*].

MILDRED CRENSHAW, wife of **JOHN CRENSHAW,** died on June 24, 1834, and they are buried in unmarked graves in the old Crenshaw cemetery at Knob Lick in Metcalfe County (formerly Barren County), Kentucky. They had nine children (five sons and four daughters) as follows. [My Note: Since we descend from this John Crenshaw in Kentucky, he is genealogically number "1". Thus, his children would be numbered "11" to "19," and his grandchildren would be "111" to "199," and his great-grandchildren would be numbered "1111" to "1999," etc.]

11. **THOMPSON CRENSHAW** (March 16, 1782 - May 26, 1856), the eldest son of **JOHN CRENSHAW** and **MILDRED THOMPSON,** became a captain in the Kentucky militia on July 22, 1806, and served in the War of 1812. Promoted to major during that war in 1814, his company served in the Battle of New Orleans in 1815. The statement of his military service was given in Barren County, Kentucky in 1850, as follows:

"On this 2nd day of December A.D., One Thousand Eight Hundred and Fifty, personally appeared before me, a

Justice of the Peace within and for the County and State aforesaid, **Thompson Crenshaw**, aged 68 years, a resident of the said County of Barren and State of Kentucky, who being duly sworn according to law, has declared that he is the identical **Thompson Crenshaw** who was the Captain of a company of Kentucky Militia belonging to the 45th Regiment, that he was detached as Captain as aforesaid, and took command of a company of drafted Kentucky Militia at Glasgow, Kentucky, on or about the 12th of November A.D. 1814. He states he proceeded with his company, **Samuel P. Malone** being the Lieutenant, and **Elias Button** as Ensign, by the way of Russellville, Kentucky, to the mouth of the Cumberland River, the place of Rendezvous, where he and his company were of the 20th of said month of November 1814 mustered into service for the term of six months, in the 14th Regiment of Kentucky Detached Militia commanded by **Col. Mitchison,** in the War with Great Britain declared by the United States on the 18th day of June, 1812. He further states that before said 14th Regiment left the mouth of the Cumberland River, the said **Col. Mitchison** resigned his office, and **Samuel Parker** was appointed and commissioned Colonel of said 14th Regiment, and he the said Crenshaw was appointed and commissioned Major of said Regiment. In this capacity, of Major aforesaid, he proceeded with said Regiment of Detached Kentucky Militia to New Orleans in flat boats, and continued in actual service in said war for the term of six months as Major as aforesaid, and was honorably discharged at Russellville, Kentucky, on the 20th day of May, A.D. 1815, as will appear by the muster rolls of said Regiment, he having received no written discharge. He makes this declaration for the purpose of obtaining the bounty land to which he may be entitled under the act granting bounty land to certain officers and soldiers who have been engaged in the military service of the United States passed September 28, 1850. Signed by **Thompson Crenshaw,** and certified by **W. E. Munford,** Justice of the Peace." [Ref: *Bounty Land Warrant 41813-8050, National Archives*]

The aforementioned military papers also included information that Thompson served as a captain from July 22, 1806, to December 8, 1814, and was a major from December 9, 1814, to May 20, 1815. He served at Russellville, Camp Dupree, Camp Jackson, and was in the Battle of New Orleans in 1815 under **General Andrew Jackson.** After the war he ultimately became styled **Colonel Thompson Crenshaw,** as noted in *Barren County Heritage*, by Goode, et al. (1980), page 132.

THOMPSON CRENSHAW married **MARTHA WAGGONER** on August 29, 1806, in Barren County. Her nickname was Polly or Patsy, as their marriage license gave her name as **"Miss P. Waggoner."** She died in 1836, as noted on her tombstone. On November 29, 1808, Thompson was among those ordered "to lay-out a road from the courthouse to the mouth of the Boiling Springs Branch on a direction to the Salt Works Road." [Ref: *Barren County Order Book No. 3*, page 68]. In 1816 Barren County was laid off into six districts for the purpose of appointing constables, and the 3rd District was composed of the battalion commanded by **Major Thompson Crenshaw** on October 21st, with **Martin D. Angel** appointed constable. [Ref: *Barren County Order Book No. 4*, page 126]. In February, 1818, **Thompson Crenshaw** was appointed the executor of the will of **Richard Waggoner**, deceased. [Ref: *Ibid.*, page 169]. **Thompson Crenshaw** and **H. Waggoner** were both Messengers in Mt. Zion Baptist Church in 1830 and in 1831. [Ref: *Pioneer Baptist Church Records of South Central Kentucky and the Upper Cumberland of Tennessee, 1799-1899*, by C. P. Cawthorn and M. L. Warnell (1985), page 98]. The Thompson Crenshaw Family Cemetery is located on Tick Ridge Road, Coral Hill, Barren County, Kentucky.

111. **LUCY G. CRENSHAW**, daughter of **THOMPSON CRENSHAW**, married **JOSEPH FIELD** on December 19, 1825.

1111. **SARAH D. FIELD** (January 18, 1827 - January 14, 1877) married **JAMES R. HORD** (born November 20, 1824, in Caroline County Virginia, a son of **HIRAM HORD** and **CATHERINE R. HEDGMAN**). HIRAM HORD migrated to Mercer County, Kentucky in 1833 and then Barren County in 1838. He was born in 1786 and died December 8, 1843. His wife died on June 22, 1858 in her 68th year. In 1857 **JAMES R. HORD** bought the family farm in Barren County and married **SARAH D. FIELD** (of Barren County, KY) on January 20, 1859. In the *1860 Census of Barren County, Kentucky*, **JAMES R. HORD** (age 35) was head of house with **SARAH D. HORD** (age 33) and **JANE HORD** (age 26). In 1870 they lived in the Hiseville Precinct of Barren County, and in 1877 they bought the farm near Horse Cave in Hart County, Kentucky. **JAMES R. HORD** was still living there in 1885. Sarah Hord was a life long, devoted member of the Christian Church and was buried in the Old Hord Cemetery between Hiseville and Park, KY. [Ref: *Ky. Genealogy & Biography*, Vol. I, p. 76, and *Barren County Cemeteries*, Vol. II, p. 196].

11111. **GEORGE H. HORD** (September, 1860 -) married **MARY F. ----** (born Feb., 1860) in 1883 and lived in Barren County, KY, District #4, in 1900. Occupation: Farmer. In 1910 George and family lived on Cave City Road in Hiseville District No. 4. He and Mary had 7 children and 6 were living.

In 1920 they still lived in Hiseville, KY.

111111. **LIZZIE D. HORD** (born Feb., 1884). In 1910 census her name was given as **ELIZABETH D. HORD** (unemployed).

111112. **JAMES D. HORD** (born Sept., 1886) lived in Barren County, Hiseville District No. 4, in 1910, with wife **PEARL HORD** (age 20). They had been married 1 year. Occupation: Farmer.

1111121. **MARY T. HORD** (born 1910).

111113. **KATIE P. HORD** (born Jan., 1890).

111114. **SALLIE F. HORD** (born May, 1893). In 1910 she lived with her parents and she was a telephone operator. In 1920 she also lived at home, and was apparently unemployed.

111115. **MATTIE N. HORD** (born Aug., 1897). In 1910 she lived with her parents and she was a telephone operator.

111116. **GEORGIA (GEORGIE) M. HORD** (b. 1901) was living with her parents in 1920.

111117. **TRAVIS R. HORD** (born 1905).

11112. **CATHERINE R. HORD** (born 1863) married **J. M. PERKINS**.

11113. **LUCY HORD** (born 1866).

112. **MILDRED THOMPSON**, a daughter of **THOMPSON CRENSHAW**, married **JOHN FRANKLIN** on March 1, 1831. They are not listed in the *1850 Census of Barren County, Kentucky*.

113. **NANCY CRENSHAW** (March 18, 1815 - September 28, 1884), daughter of **THOMPSON CRENSHAW**, married **WILLIAM FRANKLIN** (November 15, 1813 - September 12, 1841) on February 28, 1839. William was buried near Hartsville, Tennessee. In *Barren County Heritage*, by Goode, et al. (1980), p. 312, is the following description of the Franklin farm house: "This federal style, wooden house was built shortly after the Civil War on a portion of the **Col. Thompson Crenshaw** estate at Coral Hill. He was the father of **Nancy Crenshaw Franklin** for whose family the house was built. The "L" shape of the house was designed to include a front hall

with a stairway that apparently was carved by a native craftsman in a manner reminiscent of Bavarian folk wood carving. The parlor is on the left and the bedroom is back of this. The bedroom has doors which open to the porches on either side of this room. The second stairway is from this bedroom and leads up to the daughter's bedroom. The kitchen is the third and back room on the main floor. This, too, has doors opening to the side porch. Original hand-hewn stone steps are at this side porch." Current owners: **Mr. & Mrs. James N. (Lois Howard) Gray.** In the *1860 Census of Barren County, KY,* **NANCY FRANKLIN** (age 45) lived with her brother **HENRY A. CRENSHAW** (age 33, farmer) and her two sons, **GARLAND FRANKLIN** (age 20, farm labor) and **WILLIAM W. FRANKLIN** (age 18, farm labor) although this census does not state their relationships.

1131. **GARLAND THOMPSON FRANKLIN** (January 15, 1840, TN - November 28, 1916, KY), son of **NANCY CRENSHAW** and **WILLIAM FRANKLIN,** married **SUSAN FRANCES SAUNDERS** (Jan. 17, 1848 - April 28, 1928) and lived in the Coral Hill section of Barren County, Kentucky. She died at age 80 in Glasgow, KY. Garland died about 12 years earlier [Information contained in undated article from *The Glasgow Times*]. They were buried in the Crenshaw Family Cemetery at Coral Hill, KY. **GARLAND THOMPSON FRANKLIN** was a Union Sunday School leader at old Zion Christian Church located 2 miles northeast of Coral Hill in Barren County, Kentucky. [Ref: *South Central Ky. Historical and Genealogical Society Quarterly*, Vol. 9, No. 1 (1981), page 23]. Garland was listed as a farm laborer in the *1860 Census of Barren County*, and lived with his mother, **NANCY FRANKLIN,** brother **WILLIAM W. FRANKLIN,** and uncle **HENRY A. CRENSHAW,** farmer, in District #1. In *1870 Census of Barren County*, **GARLAND CRENSHAW** (age 29, farmer) was head of household and lived in the Hiseville Precinct. His mother **NANCY CRENSHAW** (age 55) lived with him, as did the black farmhand **JOSEPH GATEWOOD** (age 27) and his wife and children. Garland's real estate was valued at $1600 in 1870. In the *1880 Census of Barren County*, **G. T. FRANKLIN** (age 40) was household head in Hiseville District. His mother **NANCY FRANKLIN** (age 65) lived with him. In the *1910 Census of Barren County*, **GARLAND T. FRANKLIN** (age 70) was head of the household with his wife **SUSAN F. FRANKLIN** (age 62), his daughter **JULIE M. FRANKLIN** (age 24), and his son **LUTHER G. FRANKLIN** (age 20). Also boarding with them was one **HENRY T. CRENSHAW** (age 40). **GARLAND T. FRANKLIN** died testate in Barren County, and his will was probated on December 12, 1916, naming wife **S. F.**

and 2 children, **JULIA M.** and **LUTHER G. FRANKLIN.**

11311. **JULIA M. FRANKLIN** (December, 1885 -), daughter of **GARLAND T. FRANKLIN**, was a school teacher and lived with her parents in 1910. Julie married the well-known **DR. C. C. HOWARD. CARL CLIFFORD HOWARD** was born January 5, 1888, Summer Shade, KY (son of **QUEEN HOWARD** who was born in 1865 in Tennessee). [Ref: *1920 Census of Barren County, Kentucky*, Glasgow Dist. 1]. An influential and prominent physician from 1912 until his death in 1971, he founded the Maplewood Infirmary in 1914, Glasgow's first hospital, and helped establish the Community Hospital. He was a force in the establishment of State TB Hospitals, and the Howard Clinic. Dr. Howard served as Councillor of the Third Congressional District in the Kentucky State Medical Association circa 1930. [Ref: *Barren County Heritage*, by C. Goode, pages 293-299]. **MISS BESS HOWARD**, sister of **DR. C. C. HOWARD**, was the first woman elected to public office in Barren County, KY, serving as Clerk of the Court from 1925 to 1953. [*Ibid.*, pp. 159-160]. The *1910 Census of Metcalfe County, Kentucky*, listed **QUEEN HOWARD** (age 46) as head of the household in Magisterial District #3, with son **CARL C. HOWARD** (age 22), daughter **BESSIE HOWARD** (age 20), son **ROBERT L. HOWARD** (age 17) and daughter **MARY B. HOWARD** (age 15) also. In the *1920 Census of Barren County, KY*, stated **BESSIE HOWARD** (age 29, grade school teacher) and her brother **LOYD HOWARD** (age 27, laborer) lived with their father **QUEEN HOWARD** (age 55). **DR. C. C. and JULIA M. HOWARD** were not listed. **JULIA FRANKLIN HOWARD** pre-deceased her husband. Dr. Howard wrote his will on December 6, 1969, and it was probated on June 22, 1971 in Barren County. He mentioned his wife, **JULIA FRANKLIN HOWARD** (deceased), daughter **CAROLYN McKINLEY**, sister **BESS HOWARD**, daughter **MILDRED HOWARD**, daughter **LOIS GRAY**, and daughter **MARY LLOYD LESSENBERRY**. [Ref: *Barren County Wills*, 1971].

113111. **CAROLYN HOWARD** married ---- **McKINLEY.**

113112. **MILDRED HOWARD.**

113113. **LOIS HOWARD** married **JAMES NORRIS GRAY.** They reside in Coral Hill, Kentucky, on the old Crenshaw homestead that was once owned by **COL. THOMPSON CRENSHAW.**

113114. **MARY LLOYD HOWARD** married **ROBERT A. LESSENBERRY.**

11312. **LUTHER G. FRANKLIN** (May, 1890 -), son of **GARLAND T. FRANKLIN and SUSAN SAUNDERS.** In the *1920 Census of Barren County, KY,* **LUTHER G. FRANKLIN** (age 29) was head of the household in Hiseville District No. 4 with his wife **MARY E. FRANKLIN** (age 33).

113121. **SARAH F. FRANKLIN** (born 1915).

1132. **WILLIAM W. FRANKLIN** (April, 1842 -), a son of **WILLIAM FRANKLIN,** was born after his father died. He served as a Confederate soldier in the Orphan's Brigade of Barren County (1st Kentucky Brigade) in the War Between the States (Civil War, 1861-1865). [Ref: *Traces,* Vol. 10, No. 2, Spring, 1982, p. 29]. According to the *1870 Census of Barren County, KY,* **DR. FRANKLIN** lived in the Glasgow Junction Precinct with [wife] **MATTIE ----** (age 18, born in Alabama). In the *1880 Census of Barren County, KY,* **WILLIAM W. FRANKLIN** (age 38) and wife **MATTIE C. FRANKLIN** (age 28) lived in the town of Glasgow and he served as the County Court Clerk. His father was born in TN, his mother in KY, and her parents were born in AL. In 1900 **WILLIAM FRANKLIN** was a "horseler" [hostler] and his wife **MATTIE C. FRANKLIN** was born Dec. 1850. In 1910 **WILLIAM FRANKLIN** (age 68) lived in Glasgow, Kentucky, with his wife (age 59) and two daughters. His occupation was listed as "Retired Physician." They lived on East Main Street. In the *1920 Census of Barren County,* **W. W. FRANKLIN** (age 77) was head of household, with wife **MATTIE C. FRANKLIN** (age 69) and daughter **MATTIE J. FRANKLIN** (age 39). At that time they lived on West Main Street in Glasgow, KY.

11321. **MATTIE J. FRANKLIN** (born October, 1880, KY) was a Barren County school teacher in 1900.

11322. **ALINE P. FRANKLIN** (born November, 1882, KY) was a Barren County music teacher in 1900. In 1910 she worked in a millinary shop.

114. **W. T. CRENSHAW** (June 22, 1820 -), a son of **THOMPSON CRENSHAW** and **MARTHA (PATSY) WAGGONER,** became a minister. **REV. W. T. CRENSHAW** moved to either Cass or Bates County, Missouri prior to 1850. [Ref: *Kentuckians in Missouri,* by Stuart Seely Sprague (Baltimore: GPC Inc., 1983), p. 14].

115. **HENRY A. CRENSHAW** (September 4, 1825 - January 22, 1894), son of **COL. THOMPSON CRENSHAW**, married **ELIZABETH F. WOOD** (February 27, 1842 - August 10, 1927) in Barren County. One "**H. A. CRENSHAW**" was listed as a resident who lived within two miles of the Coral Hill post office in 1879. [Ref: *Barren County Heritage*, compiled by Goode et al., of the South Central Kentucky Historical & Genealogical Society in Glasgow, Kentucky (1980), page 59]. **HENRY A. CRENSHAW** was also a Sunday School leader at old Zion Christian Church circa 1870, located about two miles northeast of Coral Hill, and this Union Sunday School later met at Beaver Creek Seminary. [Ref: *South Central Kentucky Historical and Genealogical Society Quarterly*, Vol. 9, No. 1, March, 1981, page 23]. **HENRY A. CRENSHAW** wrote his will on January 17, 1894, and it was probated February 19, 1894. [Ref: *Barren County Will Book 5:179*]. Henry was buried in the Crenshaw Family Cemetery located on Tick Ridge Road in Coral Hill, Kentucky, along with other Crenshaw members, and one **JOSEPH WOOD** (1836-1906). In the *1870 Census of Barren County, KY*, **HENRY CRENSHAW** (age 44, farmer) and **ELIZABETH CRENSHAW** (age 28) lived in the Hiseville Precinct with **RICHARD CRENSHAW** (age 5), **MILDRED CRENSHAW** (age 3), and **HENRY CRENSHAW** (age 1). Henry's real estate was valued at $2500 at that time. They were also in the *1880 Census of Barren County, KY*, and had a black farm hand named **STEVEN CRENSHAW** (age 62).

1151. **WILLIAM CRENSHAW** (July 30, 1860 - July 20, 1865), a son of **HENRY A. CRENSHAW** and **ELIZABETH F. WOOD**, was buried in the Crenshaw Cemetery located on Tick Ridge Road in Coral Hill, Barren County, Kentucky.

1152. **RICHARD F. "DICK" CRENSHAW** (January 16, 1865 - December 28, 1954), son of **HENRY A. CRENSHAW**, wrote his will on April 22, 1939, and it was probated on January 22, 1955, in Barren County. He apparently never married as no wife or any children were mentioned in his will. He named: sister, **MILDRED CRENSHAW**; brothers, **JAMES G.**, **HARRY**, and **ALEXANDER CRENSHAW**; nephews **JOE** (son of deceased brother **TOM CRENSHAW**); niece **MARY** and nephew **WILLIAM** (children of deceased brother **BEN CRENSHAW**); nephews **RICHARD, CECIL, and JAMES ALLEN**, and nieces **MARY FRANCES PEMBERTON, RUBY YOUNG, and MARGARET ALLEN** (children of deceased sister **NANCY C. ALLEN**). [Ref: *Barren County Will Book 9:679*]. In the *1900 Census of Barren County*, **RICHARD F. CRENSHAW** (born January, 1865) was the head of household in District #4, and living in the household were his mother **ELIZABETH CRENSHAW** (born February, 1842), sister **MILDRED CRENSHAW** (born February, 1867), brother **BENJAMIN CRENSHAW** (born January, 1874), brother **ALEXANDER CRENSHAW** (born January, 1880), sister **NANCY CRENSHAW** (born June, 1882), brother **HARRY CRENSHAW** (born October 1885), and his uncle **J. H. WOOD** (born June 1837). In the *1910 Census of Barren County*, **RICHARD F. CRENSHAW** (age 45) was the head of the household and living with him were his mother **LIZZIEBETH F. CRENSHAW** (age 68), his sister **MILDRED E. CRENSHAW** (age 42), and his brothers **BENJAMIN CRENSHAW** (age 34) and **HARRY CRENSHAW** (age 24), plus a hired hand named **JOE PERSELL** (age 24). The census also stated that **LIZZIEBETH F. CRENSHAW** had 10 children and 8 were still living in 1910. All born in Kentucky. In the *1920 Census of Barren County*, **RICHARD F. CRENSHAW** (age 54) was the head of the household and living with him were his mother, **ELIZABETH CRENSHAW** (age 77), his sister **MILDRED CRENSHAW** (age 52), and brother **HARRY CRENSHAW** (age 33).

1153. **MILDRED E. CRENSHAW** (February 11, 1867 - November 28, 1945), daughter of **HENRY A. CRENSHAW and ELIZABETH WOOD**, was buried in the Crenshaw Family Cemetery on Tick Ridge Road at Coral Hill, Barren County, KY.

1154. **HENRY THOMPSON CRENSHAW** (May 23, 1869 - May 29, 1928), son of **HENRY A. CRENSHAW and ELIZABETH F. WOOD**, married **MINNIE A. MAYFIELD** (October 4, 1874 - October 2, 1954). "**TOM CRENSHAW**, age 59, a Coral Hill merchant, died of heart trouble. He was a splendid man, and veteran of the Spanish American War. He was the third family member to die in the past two months." [Ref: *The Glasgow Times*]. Surviving him were the following: wife, **MINNIE CRENSHAW** (formerly Mayfield); son, **JOE CRENSHAW**; daughter, **MISS ELIZABETH CRENSHAW**; brother, **R. F. CRENSHAW**, of Barren County, KY; brother, **J. G. CRENSHAW**, of Barren County, KY; brother, **HARRY CRENSHAW**, of Barren County; brother, **A. C. (ALEX) CRENSHAW**, of Smithfield, Texas; sister, **MISS MILDRED CRENSHAW**, of Coral Hill, KY. It was also noted that he was not able to attend the double funeral of his brother and sister who had died earlier: brother, **BEN CRENSHAW**, and sister **MRS. ROGER ALLEN. NANCY ALLEN**'s obituary stated that her father was Richard Crenshaw, but this is incorrect. Her father was **HENRY A. CRENSHAW** (died 1894). Richard Crenshaw was her brother. **MINNIE CRENSHAW** wrote her will on April 17, 1931, and it was probated October 20, 1954. She only mentioned her son **JOSEPH S. CRENSHAW**. [Ref: *Barren County Wills 9:642*]. Henry and Minnie were buried in the Crenshaw Cemetery located on Tick Ridge Road in Coral Hill, Kentucky, at the old Crenshaw place. In the *1910 Census of Barren*

County, **HENRY T. CRENSHAW** resided in the house of an uncle and aunt, **GARLAND T. and SUSAN FRANKLIN. MINNIE CRENSHAW** (age 34) was listed in the home of her parents **ISAAC MAYFIELD** (age 65) and **SALLIE MAYFIELD** (age 64) in 1910. **HENRY T. CRENSHAW** was head of the household in the *1920 Census of Barren County*, in Hiseville District #4.

11541. **SARAH ELIZABETH CRENSHAW**, a daughter of **HENRY T. CRENSHAW**, was born in 1913 in Virginia, according to the *1920 Census of Barren County*. Her parents and her brother Joseph were all born in Kentucky. "**ELIZABETH CRENSHAW**, only daughter of **MRS. THOMAS CRENSHAW**, married **W. H. PEDIGO** and died at age 19" [no date written on the newspaper clipping but she died in 1932] from "a complication of diseases" at the Community Hospital in Glasgow. Her mother and brother [names not stated] "survive this amiable and lovely character." [Ref: *The Glasgow Times*].

11542. **JOSEPH S. CRENSHAW** (October 23, 1915 - October 1, 1989), the only son of **HENRY THOMPSON CRENSHAW** and **MINNIE A. MAYFIELD**, wrote his will on September 5, 1977, and it was probated on October 16, 1989. He only named **RICHARD CRENSHAW**, of Munfordville (in Hart Co.). [Ref: *Barren County Will Book 16:717*]. Joe was buried in the Crenshaw Family Cemetery on Tick Ridge Road in Coral Hill, Barren County, KY.

11543. **INFANT DAUGHTER** (born and died September 5, 1918)

1155. **JOSEPH CRENSHAW** (September 28, 1871 - October 4, 1877), a son of **HENRY A. CRENSHAW and ELIZABETH F. WOOD**, was buried in the family cemetery in Coral Hill, Kentucky.

1156. **BENJAMIN MILLS CRENSHAW** (January 10, 1874 - April 11, 1928), son of **HENRY A. CRENSHAW and ELIZABETH F. WOOD**, married **EMMA PALMORE** (April 7, 1882 - August 22, 1971) and their two children were named in the will of his brother Richard (written in 1939; probated in 1955). They were listed in the *1920 Census of Barren County, Kentucky*, in Hiseville District #4. **EMMA L. CRENSHAW** wrote her will October 22, 1963, and it was probated August 28, 1971. She named MARY CRENSHAW, THE WILLIAMS FAMILY, and MRS. BENJAMIN M. CRENSHAW. [Ref: *Barren County Will Book 13:328*]. His occupation was Farmer.

11561. **MARY A. CRENSHAW**, daughter of **BENJAMIN CRENSHAW**, was born on March 15, 1919. Occupation: Teacher.

11562. **WILLIAM ANDREW CRENSHAW** (October 8, 1920 - November 12, 1959) married **AILEEN MONTGOMERY**

(May 5, 1921 -). They were buried in the Hiseville Cemetery in Barren County, Kentucky. William was injured in an automobile accident on the Campbellsville Road, 3 miles south of Lebanon, Kentucky, on November 10, 1959. The head on collision led to his death at the VA Hospital in Louisville, Kentucky on November 12, 1959. Cause of death: pneumothorax and multiple fractures of extremities and ribs. His death certificate (#59-23690) stated he was a World War II veteran, was married, was a salesman for a tractor company, and was a resident of Munfordville in Hart County, KY. His parents were Ben Crenshaw and Emma Palmore.

1157. **JAMES GARLAND CRENSHAW** (Sept. 28, 1877 - May 6, 1956), son of **HENRY A. CRENSHAW and ELIZABETH F. WOOD**, married **EMMA B. ALEXANDER** (December 27, 1885 - March 20, 1982), in Barren County, KY, a daughter of **OLIVER W. ALEXANDER** (1858-1942) and **ANNA BUSH**, of Temple Hill, KY. **JAMES G. CRENSHAW** died testate in Barren County, KY, and his will named his wife Emma and three surviving children, Henry, Ruth and Bernice. [Ref: *Barren County Will Book 10:107*]. In 1900 **JAMES G. CRENSHAW** was a boarder in the house of **JOHN W. JONES**, in District #4, where he was a merchant. In 1910 **JAMES G. CRENSHAW** was head of the household in Barren County, District #4, with his wife **EMMA CRENSHAW**. Married 7 years, they had 4 children, but only 3 living. His occupation was that of "Merchant in General Store." In the *1920 Census of Barren County*, **JAMES G. CRENSHAW** (age 43) was a wholesale merchant and lived in District No. 1 with wife **EMMA B. CRENSHAW** (age 34) and family.

11571. **ANNA CRENSHAW** (August 9, 1903 - August 23, 1907), daughter of **JAMES G. CRENSHAW and EMMA ALEXANDER**.

11572. **RUTH CRENSHAW** (June 12, 1905 - May 9, 1992), a daughter of **JAMES G. CRENSHAW and EMMA ALEXANDER**, married **PAUL HOLLOWAY** in Cave City, KY, and moved to Gary, Indiana, where she was a teacher. Ruth was buried in the Crenshaw Family Cemetery on the Tick Ridge Road in Coral Hill, Barren County, KY.

11573. **HENRY A. CRENSHAW** (February 17, 1907 - July 16, 1986), son of **JAMES GARLAND CRENSHAW and EMMA B. ALEXANDER**, died at age 79 at the T. J. Samson Community Hosp. He was survived by two sisters, **RUTH HOLLOWAY**, of Glasgow, and **BERNICE REYNOLDS**, of Cave City, and a niece, **MAYME DAVIS**, of Cave City. Funeral was by Hatcher and Saddler Funeral

Home; burial in Crenshaw Cemetery. [Ref: *Glasgow Republican*]. (A Henry A. Crenshaw lived on Rt. 3, Glasgow, Kentucky, in 1959.) **HENRY CRENSHAW** wrote his will on February 8, 1985, and it was probated on July 28, 1986, in Barren County, KY. He named sisters **BERNICE C. REYNOLDS and RUTH C. HOLLOWAY.** [Ref: *Barren County, Kentucky, Will Book 16:57*].

11574. **BERNICE CRENSHAW** (born July, 1909, Kentucky), a daughter of **JAMES G. CRENSHAW and EMMA ALEXANDER,** married (1) **TERRELL TRAVIS** (of Temple Hill, KY), in Gallatin, Tennessee, and (2) **ELLIS REYNOLDS** in Louisville, KY, where they made their home.

1158. **ALEXANDER C. CRENSHAW** (born January, 1880, KY), a son of **HENRY A. CRENSHAW** and **ELIZABETH F. WOOD,** moved to Smithfield, Texas, some time after 1900.

1159. **NANCY CRENSHAW** (June 12, 1882 - April 9, 1928), dau. of **HENRY A. CRENSHAW and ELIZABETH WOOD,** married **JOHN ROGER ALLEN** in Barren County. **NANCY (NANNIE) CRENSHAW ALLEN** died of pneumonia at the old Crenshaw home (Coral Hill). Surviving were the following (names gleaned from two different newspapers): her husband, **ROGER ALLEN;** son, **RICHARD ALLEN;** daughter, **MARY FRANCES ALLEN;** son, **CECIL ALLEN;** daughter, **RUBY ALLEN;** son, **JAMES HOWARD ALLEN;** daughter, **MARGARET ALLEN;** brother, **HENRY THOMPSON (TOM) CRENSHAW,** of Coral Hill, KY; brother, **RICHARD CRENSHAW,** of Coral Hill, KY; brother, **BENJAMIN M. CRENSHAW,** of Hiseville, KY; brother, **JAMES G. CRENSHAW,** of Temple Hill, KY [married **EMMA ALEXANDER,** daughter of Oliver]; brother, **A. C. (ALEX) CRENSHAW,** of Smithville, Texas; brother, **HARRY (HENRY) CRENSHAW,** of Bruce, KY; sister, **MISS MIT (MILDRED) CRENSHAW,** of Coral Hill, KY. One of Nancy's obituaries stated she was a daughter of the late Richard Crenshaw, but this was incorrect. **ROGER ALLEN** (March 13, 1881 - August 8, 1959) was buried in Glasgow Municipal Cemetery. He apparently married second to **MATTIE B. ----** (b. October 6, 1890) following Nancy's death. Buried next to them was one of Nancy's sons, **CECIL W. ALLEN.** [Ref: *Barren County Cemetery Records*, by Eva Coe Peden, and *The Glasgow Times* and *The Glasgow Republican* newspapers]. In the *1920 Census of Barren County, Kentucky,* they resided in Hiseville District No. 4, where **JOHN R. ALLEN** was a farmer.

11591. **RICHARD C. ALLEN** (born 1909).

11592. **MARY FRANCES ALLEN** (born 1912) married **TERRY W. PEMBERTON** (born 1908, son of **L. W. PEMBERTON**), in Scottsville, KY.

11592. **CECIL W. ALLEN** (born September 10, 1913).

11594. **RUBY ALLEN** (born 1915) married ---- **YOUNG**.

11595. **JAMES HOWARD ALLEN** (born circa 1921).

11596. **MARGARET ALLEN** (born 1926) was 19 months old at the time of her mother's death.

115-10. **HARRY CRENSHAW** (October, 1885 - 1969), son of **HENRY A. CRENSHAW**, married **MARY MARGARET** ----. Harry wrote his will on January 17, 1946, and it was probated on March 17, 1969 [Ref: *Barren County, Kentucky, Will Book 12:503*]. **MARGARET H. CRENSHAW** wrote her will on March 18, 1970, and it was probated on May 2, 1973, in Barren County, KY. She only mentioned her son, Harry. [Ref: *Barren County Will Book 14:10*]. **HARRY H. CRENSHAW** lived on Rt. 5, Glasgow, KY, in 1959.

115-10-1. **HARRY CRENSHAW.**

115-10-2. **HENDERSON CRENSHAW.**

115-10-3. **ROBERT CRENSHAW.**

115-10-4. **CHARLES CRENSHAW.**

116. **SALLY CRENSHAW** (b. 1829), daughter of **THOMPSON CRENSHAW**, married ---- **FIELD**, who apparently had died by 1850, as **SALLY FIELD** (age 21) was living in the household of her father at the time. **"R. M. FIELD"** was listed as residing within two miles of the Coral Hill post office in 1879. [Ref: *Barren County Heritage*, by C. Goode (1980), p. 59]. **R. M. FIELD** was age 73 in the *1880 Barren County Census*.

12. **LUCY CRENSHAW**, eldest daughter of **JOHN CRENSHAW and MILDRED THOMPSON**, was born on November 13, 1783, and married **WILLIAM TWYMAN**, probably in Virginia. They were not in the *1850 Census of Barren County, Kentucky* (but it is incomplete). **WILLIAM and LUCY TWYMAN** were named in June 27, 1842 deed as heirs of **JOHN CRENSHAW** [Ref: *Barren Co. Land Records*, 1842]. One **GARLAND TWYMAN** (born 1825), a probable descendant, was a distiller in Hiseville, Kentucky, in the *1880 Census of Barren County*, born in Kentucky; his parents in Virginia. **WILLIAM F. TWYMAN** (age 50) was head of household in the *1860 Census of Barren County, KY*, with **ELIZA A. TWYMAN** (age 41), **ANN E. TWYMAN** (age 15), **MARTHA TWYMAN** (age 12), **JOHN W. TWYMAN** (age 9), **GEORGE W. TWYMAN** (age 6), and **MARGARET M. TWYMAN** (age 3). They lived in District No. 1. In 1870 they had a daughter **MILDRED TWYMAN** (age 13) and a

son **HENRY TWYMAN** (age 7) also listed with them in Hiseville. W. F. **TWYMAN** (born 1809/10), a probable descendant, was a farmer (Slick Rock Precinct No. 10) in the *1880 Census of Barren County*. He and his parents were born in Virginia. There was also **WILLIAM TWYMAN** (age 54) in the *1870 Census of Barren County*, with **LUCY TWYMAN** (age 28) and **WILLIAM TWYMAN** (age 4) in the Hiseville Precinct. All born in KY. There were also Twymans in Larue County, Kentucky in 1850.

13. **WALLER CRENSHAW**, second son of **JOHN CRENSHAW and MILDRED THOMPSON**, was born May 26, 1786, in Virginia and married **NANCY HUGHES** on December 31, 1818, in Barren County, KY. They were not found in the *1850 Census of Barren County*, so their children, if any, are unknown. Also, no will or estate distribution was found in Barren County. However, a deed dated June 27, 1842, named all the heirs of **JOHN CRENSHAW**, deceased, but **WALLER CRENSHAW** was not listed. All of these heirs conveyed land to **ANDREW CRENSHAW**. His identity is not known; perhaps a son of **WALLER CRENSHAW** (deceased?). [Ref: *Barren County Land Records*, 1842]. It is also possible that ANDREW was actually ANDERSON since JOHN CRENSHAW's youngest son was named **ANDERSON CRENSHAW**. An error could have been made when abstracting the deed.

14. **MILDRED "MILLIE" CRENSHAW**, second daughter of **JOHN CRENSHAW and MILDRED THOMPSON**, was born on May 14, 1788, and married **GEORGE TWYMAN DEARING** on December 22, 1808. George served on jury duty in Barren County, Kentucky, in February, 1811, and **TWYMAN DEARING** was paid as [election?] guard in Nov., 1811. [Ref: *Barren County Order Book 3*, pp. 114, 132]. In January, 1813, **GEORGE T. DEARING** recorded his stock mark as follows: crop off right and half crop off the upper side of left ear. [Ref: *Barren County Order Book 4*, page 18]. The *1850 Census of Barren County* lists **GEORGE T. DEARING** (age 64, blacksmith born in Virginia) and **MILLY DEARING** (age 63, born Kentucky). Judging by the gaps in the years of birth, they probably had more children than those listed in the census, and it is not clear from available information that John W. was their son. **G. T. DEARING** died October 25, 1852, "of inflammation of the brain" in Glasgow, Kentucky. He was age 66, a son of **ROBERT and TABITHA DEARING** of Albemarle County, Virginia. He was also listed as a widower and blacksmith, thus indicating that his wife **MILLY CRENSHAW DEARING** had pre-deceased him between 1850 and 1852. [Ref: "Barren County Death Records" in *South Central Kentucky Historical Quarterly*, Volume I, No. 3, October, 1973, p. 13]. Note: Names of children not fully determined, so additional research is needed. A deed dated June 27, 1842, named the heirs and representatives of **JOHN CRENSHAW**, deceased, and included **GEORGE T. DEARING** and wife MILLY, plus **JOHN W. DEARING, MARY C. DEARING, ELIZA J. T. DEARING, GEORGE W. DEARING,** and **WILLIAM W. DEARING,** who

may be their children. [Ref: *Barren Co. Land Records*, 1842].

141. **JOHN WALKER DEARING** (c1809/1810 - November 10, 1861), tavernkeeper, married **NANCY ----** (November 20, 1826 - April 13, 1910). Buried in Glasgow Municipal Cemetery. (The marriage license was not found in Barren County.) The census records reveal the names of their children. In *1860 Census of Barren County* **JOHN W. DEERING** [sic] was head of household (age 50). Occupation: "Ents" [?]. At the time his real estate was valued at $1300. In the *1870 Census of Barren County*, **NANCY DEERING** [sic] was head of the house and lived in the town of Glasgow, KY. The value of her real estate was $3500 at that time and her occupation was listed as "Millinery." She was also head of household in the *1900 Census of Barren County*.

1411. **GEORGE H. DEARING** (born 1844). In 1870 his occupation was "Serving Mch. Agent." He was living with his mother in 1870.

1412. **WILLIAM A. DEARING** (born 1846). Not listed at home in the 1870 census.

1413. **ANGELINA DEARING** (born 1848). Not listed at home in the 1870 census.

1414. **SARAH M. DEARING** (born 1850). In the *1870 Census of Barren County* her age was 18 and her middle initial was "A." She lived at home with mother.

1415. **MILDRED C. DEARING** (Nov. 9, 1852 - July 4, 1906) married **---- WEBER**. In the *1860 Census of Barren County, Kentucky* her name was spelled "Mildie C." She was living at home in 1870 census, age 17. In 1900 Mildred lived with her mother in Glasgow and the census stated she was born in Nov., 1855, while her tombstone indicates it was Nov., 1852. In 1900 her occupation was listed as Dressmaker. **MILDRED C. WEBER** was buried in Glasgow Cemetery.

1416. **JOHN WALKER DEARING, JR.** (January, 1854 -) lived with his mother in both the 1880 and 1900 censuses in Glasgow, Kentucky. His occupation was a Fire Insurance Agent. As for his age, the *1880 Census of Barren County* stated he was born 1855, and the *1870 Census of Barren County* stated 1854, while the 1900 census said it was January, 1857.

1417. **WILLIS T. [F.?] DEARING** (May, 1858 -) was a travelling salesman in 1880. "Willice" lived with his mother in Glasgow, Kentucky in 1900, but his occupation was not listed at the time. In the *1920 Census of Barren County, Kentucky,* **WILLIS T. DEARING** (age 62) was a roomer in the house of a Lester Boone on East Main Street in Glasgow. His occupation: Billboard Advertiser. The 1870 census gave his middle initial as "F."

1418. **NARCISSA C. DEARING** (born 1859/60).

1419. D. **MORGAN DEARING** (January, 1862 -) worked in a carriage shop in 1880, and in 1900 was a stone mason. He married **LILLIE L. ----** (born May, 1864) in 1888 and lived in Glasgow, KY, according to the *1900 Census of Barren County*.

14191. **LAVATA M. DEARING** (born March, 1889).

14192. **CLARA M. DEARING** (born October, 1890).

14193. **LORENE DEARING** (born March, 1892).

14194. **ED M. DEARING** (born March, 1894).

14195. **ROBERT W. DEARING** (born April, 1896).

14196. **JOHN DEARING** (born August, 1897).

14197. **---- DEARING** (son, born May, 1900).

142. **POLLY DEARING** (born 1816). Polly Deering and Vicy Dearing were constituted members of Pleasant Hill Baptist Church on Carpenter's Fork of Otter Creek, Wayne County, Kentucky, June 12, 1841. [Note: This could, of course, be another "Polly Dearing." Ref: *Traces*, Volume 11, No. 3, (Fall, 1983), page 93].

143. **WILLIS DEARING** (1828-), medical doctor in 1850.

15. **ELIZABETH "BETSEY" CRENSHAW**, third daughter of **JOHN CRENSHAW and MILDRED THOMPSON**, was born on June 25, 1790 in Virginia. She married to **THOMAS WASHINGTON SLEMMONS** (son of **REV. JOHN SLEMMONS**, a Presbyterian minister) on May 5, 1812, in Barren County, Kentucky, with her father John giving his consent. In 1817, **WASHINGTON SLEMMONS** was "appointed surveyor of the road from Hamilton's Mill to opposite Benjamin Smith's, and that he with the hands to said road allotted keep the same in repair 18 feet wide." [Ref: *Barren County Order Book 4*, p. 159]. **WASHINGTON SLEMMONS** died prior to 1850, perhaps by 1835. **ELIZABETH SLEMMONS** was head of household in the *1850 Census of Barren County, Kentucky*. She was living with her son Washington in the *1860 and 1870 Censuses of Metcalfe Co.*

151. **SALLIE DEAN SLEMMONS** (February 26, 1813 -) married twice in Barren County, KY. **SALLY SLEMMONS** was married **CANDOR DAUGHERTY** on December 17, 1833, by Squire Edgar. **SARAH DOUGHERTY** [sic] married **THOMAS JONES** on Feb. 5, 1846, by H. Woods. [Ref: M. Reneau's *Marriage Records of Barren County, Kentucky, 1799-1849*, pp. 59, 148]. In the *1850 Census of Barren County, Kentucky*, **THOMAS JONES** (age 42) and **SALLY JONES** (age 37) were listed, but had no children. His occupation was House Joiner.

152. **MILLY T. SLEMMONS** (1814-), daughter of **WASHINGTON SLEMMONS**, married **ROGER THOMPSON FRANKLIN** on Jan. 22, 1835 (consent of her mother Elizabeth), Barren County, KY. One witness to the marriage was **ANDERSON CRENSHAW**. **ROGER T. FRANKLIN** (age 40, born Virginia) and **MILLEY T. FRANKLIN** (age 35, born Kentucky) are in the *1850 Census of Barren County, Kentucky*; **RODGER T. FRANKLIN** (age 52) and **MILLY T. FRANKLIN** (age 45) are in Metcalfe Co., KY, in the 1860 census; and **ROGERS T. FRANKLIN** (age 61) and **MILLY T. FRANKLIN** (age 55) are in Metcalfe Co. in 1870. **ROGER THOMPSON FRANKLIN** (May 27, 1809 - March 15, 1886) and **MILLEY T. FRANKLIN** (December 25, 1814 - no date on stone) are buried in the Franklin-Mitchell Cemetery in Metcalfe Co. [Ref: *Metcalfe County Cemeteries*, Vol. I; *1870 Census of Metcalfe Co.*, by Gladys Aitken, p. 128]. In the *1880 Census of Metcalfe County, Kentucky*, **ROGER T. FRANKLIN** (age 71) was head of household in Lafayette Magisterial District, with wife **MILLA T. FRANKLIN** (age 65), son **RICHARD G. FRANKLIN** (age 32), son **THOMPSON C. FRANKLIN** (age 25), a granddaughter **FLORENCE MITCHELL** (age 9), and a nephew named **MORTON CRENSHAW** (age 22).

1521. **JOHN W. FRANKLIN** (Dec. 2, 1835 - Sept. 30, 1862). Never married. He was buried beside his parents in the Franklin-Mitchell Cemetery, Metcalfe Co.

1522. **SARAH E. FRANKLIN** (1838 -) married **JOHN W. BEARD** (March 8, 1833 - April 28, 1900) in 1857. Census records indicate she was Tennessee born. The Beard Family Bible (owned by a **MRS. EDWARD ALEXANDER** of Knob Lick, KY, in 1963) listed the names of their nine children and was published in Eva Coe Peden's *Bible and Family Records in Barren County, Kentucky and Surrounding Areas*, Vol. I (Glasgow, KY: Privately published, n.d.). Other information on this family was taken from *Metcalfe County Cemeteries*, Volume I, page 98, and the *1870 Census of Metcalfe County, Kentucky*. In the *1880 Census of Metcalfe County, Kentucky*, **JOHN W. BEARD** (age 46) was head of the household in Lafayette Magisterial District, with his wife

SARAH E. BEARD (age 42) and family, plus a white farm worker by the name of James Webb (age 17).

15221. **FLORA B. BEARD** (born May 10, 1858) lived with her parents in 1880 and was "without occupation" in Metcalfe County.

15222. **WILLIAM T. BEARD** (born March 8, 1860) lived with his parents in 1880 and worked on the farm in Metcalfe County, Kentucky.

15223. **JAMES W. BEARD** (June 22, 1862 - Sept. 17, 1892) lived with his parents in 1880 and worked on the farm in Metcalfe Co., KY.

15224. **MARY MARTHA BEARD** (June 16, 1864 - April 7, 1963) married **EDWARD HENRY ALEXANDER** on November 16, 1881. She is buried in Shannon-Ballard Cemetery in Knob Lick, Metcalfe County, KY. In the *1880 Census of Metcalfe County* she was age 16 and lived at the home of her parents. She was "without occupation." The *1900 Census of Metcalfe County* is light and difficult to read, but Mary lived in the Antioch District. Edward was born in August, 1857, and they had been married 8 years, with one child. His mother [illegible], age 82 and a widow, also lived with them in 1900.

152241. **ELIZABETH ALEXANDER** (born September, 1882).

15225. **SUSIE MILDRED BEARD** (Sept. 16, 1866 - June 21, 1904) was buried in the Franklin-Mitchell Family Cemetery beside her father. The *1880 Census of Metcalfe County* stated she was 12 and gave the name "**MINNIE S. BEARD.**"

15226. **SARAH ALICE BEARD** (August 16, 1869 - February 9, 1916) was buried in the Franklin-Mitchell Family Cemetery beside her father. The *1880 Census of Metcalfe County* stated she was 9 and gave her name as "**ALACE BEARD.**"

15227. **WEEDEN A. BEARD** (May 4, 1872 - May 24, 1955) married **DORA M.** ---- (born May 11, 1887). Buried in the Franklin-Mitchell

Cemetery in Metcalfe County, Kentucky. In the *1910 Census of Metcalfe County,* **WEEDEN A. BEARD** (age 36) was head of the household in Knob Lick Voting Precinct, with his mother **ELIZABETH BEARD** (age 75) sister **HATTIE A. CHAPMAN** (age 32), and niece **FLORENCE CHAPMAN** (age 7), plus a white servant named **STANLEY L. PIPER.** In the *1920 Census of Metcalfe County,* **WEEDEN A. BEARD** (age 47) was head of the household in Sulphur Well District No. 2 with his wife **DORA L. BEARD** (age 32), two children, and his mother **ELIZABETH BEARD** (age 82, born Kentucky) who was a widow.

152271. **WILLIAM R. BEARD** (born 1916).

152272. **HERBERT D. BEARD** (born 1919).

15228. **N. E. BEARD** (Oct 4, 1874 - Oct 31, 1875).

15229. **HATTIE A. BEARD** (born November 5, 1877) married ---- **CHAPMAN.** In the *1910 Census of Metcalfe County, Kentucky,* she lived with her brother **WEEDEN A. BEARD** and her mother **ELIZABETH BEARD,** but her husband was not enumerated in the 1910 census.

152291. **FLORENCE CHAPMAN** (born 1903).

1523. **MARY T. FRANKLIN** (born 1840).

1524. **SUSAN FRANKLIN** (May 8, 1842 - December 20, 1915) married **J. E. MITCHELL** (July 4, 1844 - Sept. 13, 1915). Buried in the Franklin-Mitchell Cemetery. In the *1880 Census of Metcalfe County, Kentucky,* **JAMES E. MITCHELL** (age 35) was head of household in Lafayette Magisterial District with his wife **SOUSEN MITCHELL** (age 36) and their five children. In the *1910 Census of Metcalfe County, Kentucky,* **JAMES E. MITCHELL** (age 66) was head of household in Knob Lick Precinct, with wife **SUSAN MITCHELL** (age 65). They had 8 children, 6 still living, but none of them were living at home in 1910.

15241. **FLORENCE MITCHELL** (July 14, 1870 - Dec 13, 1957). Buried in Franklin-Mitchell Cem.

15242. **MILLIE MITCHELL** (1871 -).

15243. **SALLIE MITCHELL** (1873 -). She might

be the **SALLIE ROSE**, widow of **WILLIAM A. ROSE** (1867-1921) buried in the Franklin-Mitchell Cemetery in Metcalfe Co., KY. If so, her birth date was May 10, 1872, but no date of death is on the tombstone.

15244. **LILLIE MITCHELL** (1875 -).

15245. **WILLIAM T. MITCHELL** (February 16, 1879 - March 2, 1901). Buried in the Franklin-Mitchell Cemetery in Metcalfe Co., KY.

15246. **WHIT F. MITCHELL** (September 28, 1883 - December 20, 1958) married **KATE F. ----** (May 25, 1878 - December 5, 1946). Buried in the Franklin-Mitchell Family Cemetery. [Ref: *Metcalfe County Cemeteries*, p. 98]. **WHIT F. MITCHELL** (age 26) was head of the household in the *1910 Census of Metcalfe County, KY*, in Knob Lick Precinct, with his wife **KATIE MITCHELL** and family. They reportedly had 4 children, with 3 living. This census only named two children. In the *1920 Census of Metcalfe County, KY*, they lived in Sulphur Well District #2.

152461. **LLOYD MITCHELL** (born 1905).

152462. **NORA M. MITCHELL** (born 1909).

152463. **DORA L. MITCHELL** (born 1909).

152464. **RATLIFF MITCHELL** (born 1913). The Franklin-Mitchell Cemetery was copied in September, 1979, and noted that it was located on farm of **"RADCLIFF MITCHELL."** [Ref: *Metcalfe County, Kentucky Cemeteries*, Volume I, page 98].

15247-15248. **---- MITCHELL** (two names unknown), children of **JAMES and SUSAN MITCHELL.**

1525. **RICHARD G. FRANKLIN** (Oct. 5, 1844 - September 23, 1912) was buried beside his brother and parents in the Franklin-Mitchell Cem. in Metcalfe County.

1526. **WILLIAM B. FRANKLIN** (born 1848).

1527. **NANCY JANE FRANKLIN** (born 1852).

1528. **THOMPSON C. FRANKLIN** (born 1855).

153. **JOHN CRENSHAW SLEMMONS** (March 17, 1819 - July 23, 1892) married **NANCY BEARD** on April 18, 1843, Barren County, KY. She was born on July 13, 1825, and died on May 7, 1905. **NANCY BEARD** was the eldest daughter of **WILLIAM BEARD** and **---- BROCKMAN**. Her five brothers were **JOHN W. BEARD** (born March 8, 1833), **ANDREW BEARD** (born February 25, 1827), **ALBERT BEARD** (born August 1, 1829), **WILLIAM BEARD** (born February 6, 1837), and **ALEXANDER BEARD** (born January 8, 1839) and her sisters were **AELEC[?] BEARD** and **LUCY BEARD** (born February 1, 1835, and married to **ROBERT SPENCER**). Where they lived became part of Metcalfe County in 1860. In the *1880 Census of Metcalfe County, KY*, **J. C. SLEMMONS** (age 61) and **NANCY SLEMMONS** (age 54) were in the Edmonton Precinct North. **LUSEY WOODY** (age 7) was living with them and was noted by the censustaker "as one of the family." J. C. stated his father was born in Pennsylvania and his mother in Virginia. He was Kentucky born. J. C. and Nancy were buried in the Shirley Cemetery in Summer Shade, KY. [Ref: *Metcalfe County Cemeteries*, Volume I, p. 130, and *1870 Census of Metcalfe County*, by Gladys Aitken, p. 49]. In 1900 **NANCY SLEMMONS** (age 74, born July, 1825), lived with daughter **MARY S. TAYLOR** in Barren County, Kentucky. [Ref: Information on this Crenshaw-Slemmons-Taylor-Pace line was contributed by Leona Pace, of Cheyenne Wyoming, plus Eva Coe Peden's *Bible and Family Records of Barren County, Kentucky, and Surrounding Areas*, Vol. I, p. 11].

1531. **WILLIAM WASHINGTON SLEMMONS** (born January 28, 1845) married **SUSAN ELIZABETH GLASS**.

15311. **MOLLIE SLEMMONS** married **---- PAYNE**.

15312. **NANNIE SLEMMONS** married **---- WHITE**.

15313. **LOUIS SLEMMONS**.

15314. **JOHN SLEMMONS**.

15315. **AMELIA SLEMMONS** married **---- BROYLES**.

15316. **SANTFORD SLEMMONS**.

15317. **VIDA (VADA) SLEMMONS** married **---- BARTON**.

15318. **EVA LENA SLEMMONS** married **SAMUEL WESLEY JONES** and they had 8 children.

153181. **GLENNA DALE JONES** (Nov. 20, 1900 - Dec. 13, 1981).

153182. **WILLIAM IRBY JONES** (October 18, 1903 - May 15, 1904).

153183. **BERYL EBA JONES** (born October 2, 1905).

153184. **VIDA PEARL JONES** (born August 3, 1908) married first to **B. W. LUCKENBACK** and secondly to **WILBER SWANSON**.

153185. **ERNEST SAMUEL JONES** (born January 12, 1912).

153186. **EVALIN LUCILLE JONES** (born January 20, 1916).

153187. **BILLY SANTFORD JONES** (born January 2, 1921) married **OLA ----**.

1532. **MARGARET E. SLEMMONS** (born 1847, Kentucky).

1533. **MARY SUSAN "MOLLY" SLEMMONS** (January 24, 1851 - August 1, 1929) married to **JAMES WATSON TAYLOR** (March 5, 1847 - September 12, 1925), of Tenn., on March 1 or 26, 1867. Molly and James Taylor were buried in Neal's Chapel Cemetery near Lecta, Kentucky. The *1900 Census of Barren County* listed them in District No. 1, indicating they had been married 32 years, and that they had 13 children, 11 still living. **JAMES WATSON TAYLOR** was a farmer. His parents were **ABRAHAM PERRY TAYLOR** (born 1812) and **ELIZABETH CANTRELL** (born 1812). He was the 9th of 12 children. His siblings were Elizabeth Jane Taylor, Jasper Taylor, William Esau Taylor, Beady Cantrell Taylor, Sarah A. Taylor, Abel Cain "Dick" Taylor, Wilson I.(J.?) Taylor, Perry Green Taylor, Isaac Denton Taylor, Rutha Lucinda "Mary" Taylor. **ABRAHAM "ABRAM" PERRY TAYLOR** was the third of nine children born to **HENRY TAYLOR** (died June 4, 1835) and his wife **BEADY CANTRELL** (1788 - April 4, 1826). [Ref: Mrs. Leona Pace of Cheyenne, Wyoming, 1995]. They were also listed in the *1880 Census of Barren County, Kentucky*, in the Sartain Precinct, and in Glasgow District No. 1 in the *1920 Census of Barren County, Kentucky*. He was age 72 and she was age 68.

15331. **JOHN SIDNEY TAYLOR** (March 1, 1869 - January 18, 1943) married twice: first to **ADDIE BARLOW** and second to **BETTIE W.**

HARLOW (May 18, 1878 - Dec. 16, 1951). They are buried in Neal's Chapel Cemetery near Lecta in Barren County, Kentucky. In the *1920 Census of Barren County,* **JOHN S. TAYLOR** was 50 and **BETTIE H. TAYLOR** was 41.

153311. **FRED H. TAYLOR** (born 1903).

153312. **JAMES M. TAYLOR** (born 1908).

153313. **MARY F. TAYLOR** (born 1913).

153314. **JOHN W. TAYLOR** (born 1918).

15332. **MARGARET ELIZABETH TAYLOR** (March 31, 1870 - January 6, 1948) married twice, first to **WILLIAM SHIRLEY** and second to **THOMAS (TOM) W. McCLELLAN** (1870-1962) and had 9 children. Margaret and Tom were buried in the Neal's Chapel Cemetery near Lecta, Barren Co., KY. (A Masonic Emblem is mounted on his stone.)

15333. **WILLIAM ISAAC TAYLOR** (December 29, 1872 - September 8, 1906). Never married.

15334. **LELA JANE TAYLOR** (February 19, 1874 - October 28, 1953) married **STEPHEN E. GLASS** (July 12, 1873 - March 27, 1963) on Dec. 19, 1894. They were buried in the Neal's Chapel Cemetery near Lecta in Barren County, KY. The *1910 Census of Barren County, Kentucky* spelled his name **STEVEN E. GLASS**, at which time they lived in Magisterial District 1. In the *1920 Census of Barren County, KY,* **S. E. GLASS** (age 46) and wife **LELAH GLASS** (age 45) lived in Glasgow District No. 1 (with sons James G. and Willard E. Glass).

153341. **CLARA LEE GLASS** (November 7, 1895 - March 31, 1980) married **WALTER PACE** (August 31, 1886 - Nov. 26, 1944) on Dec. 25, 1914. In the *1920 Census of Barren County* they lived in Dist. 1.

1533411. **ONIE DARRELL PACE** (born Sept. 26, 1915) married **GLADYS MAUREA JONES.**

15334111. **WILMA PACE.**

15334112. **RANDAL PACE.**

15334113. **SHARON PACE.**

15334114. **SHAUNA PACE.**

15334115. **RODNEY PACE.**

1533412. **MURL RICHARDS PACE** (born June 2, 1917) married **ETHEL MARIE CARTER.**

15334121. **PENNY PACE.**

15334122. **PATTY PACE.**

15334123. **WALTER PACE.**

15334124. **PEGGY PACE.**

15334125. **WYATT PACE.**

1533413. **THELMA IRIS PACE** (born March 11, 1919) married **ROBERT WATSON TAYLOR.**

15334131. **ROBERT TAYLOR.**

15334132. **MELVIN TAYLOR.**

15334133. **WILSON TAYLOR.**

15334134. **PAUL TAYLOR.**

15334135. **LENOX TAYLOR.**

15334136. **PERRY TAYLOR.**

1533414. **DEMRY DEVON PACE** (July 14, 1920 - July 15, 1980) married **ALYNE BAILEY** on December 28, 1940.

15334141. **ILMA PACE.**

15334142. **DEMRY DEVON PACE, JR.**

15334143. **SHEILA PACE.**

1533415. **GLONDIE RUVEEZE PACE** (born Sept. 28, 1922) married **HERMAN PURSLEY** on February 28, 1942.

15334151. **ELIZABETH PURSLEY.**

15334152. **JAMES PURSLEY.**

15334153. **ACKLEY PURSLEY.**

15334154. **AVERIL PURSLEY.**

1533416. **ZELDON RANDELL PACE** (born Apr. 6, 1925) married **NINA ELIZABETH HUNT** on August 3, 1946.

15334161. **RANDELL PACE.**

15334162. **RUSSELL PACE.**

1533417. **AVERY LENOX PACE** (born June 10, 1926) married **LUELLA RUTH WANGER** on November 21, 1959.

15334171. **NANCY PACE.**

15334172. **GINA PACE.**

15334173. **WAYNE PACE.**

1533418. **GLATUS PACE** (November 19, 1928 - July 11, 1979) married **LEONA HALL** on April 30, 1949.

15334181. **ROCKY LEE PACE** (born March 28, 1954, Indianapolis, Indiana) married **LILLIAN BARNS** on April 21, 1990.

15334182. **ROXIE LEA PACE** (born Feb. 11, 1958, Indianapolis, Indiana) married **JAMES ALBERT ANDRESEN** (born April 14, 1957) on July 16, 1977.

153341821. **CRAIG ALBERT ANDRESEN** (born Feb. 12, 1981).

153341822. **MICHAEL JAMES ANDRESEN** (born Oct. 24, 1983).

153342. **JAMES G. GLASS** (born 1904).

153343. **WILLARD E. GLASS** (born 1908).

15335. **CLEAVIE TIPTON TAYLOR** (born March 7, 1876, and died in infancy sometime prior to 1880).

15336. **NANCY CORRENNA "RENY" TAYLOR** (Aug. 17, 1877- August 20, 1962) married **RUFUS I. TAYLOR**

(March 4, 1874 - May 22, 1955) on May 26, 1895, and they had 13 children. In the *1910 Census of Barren County, Kentucky*, Rufus and "Corrine" lived in the Slick Rock Precinct, and had 7 children (plus two more deceased). "Reny" (and others) are buried in the Neal's Chapel Cemetery in Lecta, Barren County, KY. The *1880 Census of Barren County, Kentucky* listed her name as **NANCY C. TAYLOR** (age 3).

153361. **WILLIAM O. TAYLOR** (born 1897).

153362. **ELLIS [?] TAYLOR** (born 1899).

153363. **VELMA LEE TAYLOR** (born 1901).

153364. **CECIL ISAAC TAYLOR** (1902-) married **RUBY A. ----** (1901-1966) and were buried in Neal's Chapel Cemetery in Barren County, KY.

153365. **BEECHER TAYLOR** (son, born 1907).

153366. **NORA SUSAN TAYLOR** (born 1909).

153367. **SALLIE MAY TAYLOR** (born 1909).

15337. **EVA L. TAYLOR** (October 25, 1879 - March 27, 1956) married **JOHN L. HARLOW** (Feb. 28, 1874 - October 28, 1953) on December 30, 1896. They were buried in Neal's Chapel Cemetery near Lecta in Barren County, Kentucky. The *1880 Census of Barren County, Kentucky*, gave her name as "Evalee" (born Dec., 1879). In the *1910 Census of Barren County* they lived on Cleveland Avenue in Glasgow, Kentucky, where John was a hardware retail merchant. In the *1920 Census of Barren County*, they lived in Temple Hill District No. 3, and her name was enumerated as **EVA L. HARLOW**.

153371. **JAMES W. HARLOW** (November 8, 1898 - January 15, 1961) married MINNIE L. ---- (Mar. 31, 1898 - Apr. 8, 1924). Buried in Neal's Chapel Cemetery. In the *1920 Census of Barren County, KY* they lived in Temple Hill Dist. #3. It gave his name as **JAMES U. HARLOW**.

1533711. **JAMES D. HARLOW** (born 1919).

153372. **LESTER E. HARLOW** (born 1901).

153373. **MARY L. HARLOW** (born 1903).

15338. **VANCE GIST TAYLOR** (October 29, 1881 - July 23, 1959) married **RUBY M. BROWNING** (September 12, 1886 - 1938) in 1905. In the *1910 Census of Barren County, KY*, they lived in Magisterial District #1. They had 3 children, but only 2 living. In the *1920 Census of Barren County, KY*, they lived in District #1 with 5 children.

153381. **EDNA E. TAYLOR** (born 1906).

153382. **LELA M. TAYLOR** (born 1909 and apparently deceased by 1920?).

153383. **CHARLES L. TAYLOR** (born 1914).

153384. **JAMES W. TAYLOR** (born 1917).

153385. **PAULINE TAYLOR** (born 1919).

15339. **LENORA TAYLOR** (June 24, 1884 - March 5, 1909) married to H. **OREM BRADLEY** and was buried next to her parents in the Neal's Chapel Cemetery in Barren County, KY.

1533-10. **NANCY ETHEL TAYLOR** (October 31, 1886 - 1970) married **JOHN SPENCER** (or John Spencer Taylor?) on November 22, 1905.

1533-11. **MAUDE TAYLOR** (September 30, 1888; died when only a few months old).

1533-12. **BEATRICE EARL TAYLOR** (July 26, 1890 - September 9, 1961) married **WALTER FRED BROWNING** (September 30, 1884 -) on December 19, 1906.

1533-12-1. **LOMA ADA BROWNING** (May 18, 1918 - December 11, 1919) was buried next to her parents in Neal's Chapel Cemetery in Barren County, Kentucky.

1533-13. **ADA PEARL TAYLOR** (March 24, 1894 - October 30, 1915). Never married.

154. **ASHER WHITEFORD SLEMMONS** (Mar. 22, 1821 - Apr. 21, 1900), son of **THOMAS WASHINGTON SLEMMONS** and **ELIZABETH CRENSHAW**,

married **MARTHA S. FRANKLIN** (Aug. 26, 1824 - Apr. 9, 1900) on March 12, 1846. He was born in Kentucky; she in Tenn. Where they lived became part of Metcalfe County in 1860. In the *1880 Census of Metcalfe County*, his name was given as **ASHBY SLEMMONS** (age 60), with wife Martha S. (age 54). They were buried in the Bagby-Slemmons-Munday Cemetery in Metcalfe Co. [Ref: *Metcalfe County Cemeteries*, Volume I].

1541. **RICHARD W. SLEMMONS** (April 10, 1847 - May 15, 1883) married **MARY C. DEPP** (July 1, 1848 - July 11, 1909) and they were buried next to his parents. After his death **MARY C. (DEPP) SLEMMONS** married **J. M. DILLON** (and her tombstone included both of these names). [Ref: *Metcalfe County Cemeteries*, Vol. I, p. 152]. **RICHARD SLEMMONS** and family lived in the "village of Edmonton" in 1880. He was "professor of school" according to the *1880 Census of Metcalfe County*.

15411. **VIRGIE J. SLEMMONS** (June 6, 1873 - April 18, 1928) married **REUBEN HENRY NUNN** (Sept. 18, 1872 - August 22, 1954) in 1901. Reuben was a banker in Hiseville, Kentucky. Virgie and Reuben are buried in the Hiseville Cemetery. In *1910 Census of Barren County, Kentucky*, **REUBEN H. NUNN** was head of household in the Hiseville District of Barren County and had been married to **VIRGIE J. NUNN** for 8 years, but they had no children. Living with them was "brother-in-law" **JAMES D. DILLON** (age 17). Reuben's occupation was Bank Cashier. In 1920 they were living in Hiseville, KY. [An abstract of her obituary is contained in Pearl Crenshaw Peden's *Scrapbook*, q.v.]

15412. **WALTER A. SLEMMONS** (born 1875).

15413. **LOU EMMA SLEMMONS** (Sept. 4, 1877 - May 14, 1953) married **ALBERT B. MAYFIELD** (Jan. 14, 1860 - October 18, 1936) who was a widower. **LOU EMMA MAYFIELD** was buried in the Summer Shade Cemetery and **A. B. MAYFIELD** was buried in the Old Randolph-Pleasant Hill Cemetery (next to his first wife) in Metcalfe County.

15414. **FANNIE SLEMMONS** (Jun 19, 1881 - Jun 9, 1969) married **REV. JOHN WILL BARTON** (Dec. 3, 1880-May 25, 1968) and resided in Edmonton, KY in 1928. John and Fannie are buried in the New Liberty Cemetery in Metcalfe Co., Kentucky.

153141. **JOHN W. BARTON** (born 1915).

15415. ---- **SLEMMONS** married **WATT A. SLEMMONS** and resided in Seattle, Washington, in 1928.

1542. **WILLIAM T. SLEMMONS** (born 1850, Kentucky).

1543. **MARY E. SLEMMONS** (born 1852/3, Kentucky).

1544. **SARAH FRANCES (FANNY) SLEMMONS** (born 1854, KY).

1545. **EMILY C. SLEMMONS** (October 2, 1859 - May 2, 1936) married **JAMES W. MUNDAY** (July 5, 1852 - May 12, 1921), son of **GEORGE W. MUNDAY** (of Virginia, but in the *1860 Census of Barren County, Kentucky*, in Dist. 1). They were buried next to her parents in Bagby-Slemmons-Munday Cemetery in Metcalfe County. In the *1900 Census of Metcalfe County, Kentucky*, **JAMES W. MUNDAY** was head of household in the west end of Magisterial District #3 with his wife **EMMA C. MUNDAY**. They had 9 children, 8 living in 1900. In the *1910 Census of Metcalfe County, Kentucky*, **JAMES W. MONDAY** (age 57) was head of household in Randolph Precinct, Magisterial District #1, with wife **EMMA C. MONDAY** (age 51) and seven children. They had 10 children with 8 still living in 1910, at which time they had been married for 28 years.

15451. **FANNIE B. MUNDAY** (born January, 1884).

15452. **RICHARD S. MUNDAY** (born September, 1885).

15453. **LILLIA [sic] MUNDAY** (born April, 1887).

15454. **WALLER W. MUNDAY** (March 13, 1889 - July 2, 1909).

15455. **GEORGE ASHER MUNDAY** (February 28, 1891 - January 4, 1919).

15456. **WILLIAM (WILLIE) OREN MUNDAY** (February 11, 1893 - January 2, 1914).

15457. **CARL T. MUNDAY** (born June, 1896).

15458. **EARL F. MUNDAY** (born October, 1898).

15459. **HERMAN O. MUNDAY** (February 24, 1903 - December 16, 1918).

154510. ---- **MUNDAY** (child deceased by 1910).

155. **GARLAND SLEMMONS** (1824, KY -), a son of **WASHINGTON**

SLEMMONS, was living at his mother's home in the *1850 Census of Barren County, Kentucky*. Occupation: Miner.

156. **WILLIAM WASHINGTON SLEMMONS** (November 5, 1825 - March 6, 1902), youngest son of **THOMAS WASHINGTON SLEMMONS**, lived in Barren County, Kentucky, with his mother and brother, **GARLAND SLEMMONS**, in the 1850 census. His occupation at the time was farmer. **WASHINGTON SLEMMONS JR.** [sic] later married **FRANCES E. ----** (born 1831, Tenn.). In the 1860 census her name was listed as **ELIZABETH F. SLEMMONS** (age 29, born KY) and Washington was then age 34. His mother, Elizabeth (age 70), was living with them in 1870 and he was a tobacco leaf dealer in Metcalfe County, Kentucky. In the *1880 Census of Metcalfe County, KY*, **WASH SLEMMONS** (age 54) and wife **FRANCES E. SLEMMONS** (age 49) lived in Edmonton Precinct North. He was born in Kentucky and his father was born in Pennsylvania; his mother in Virginia. **FRANCES E. SLEMMONS** (March 15, 1831 - September 5, 1906) and husband **WASHINGTON SLEMMONS** are buried near Dripping Springs Church in the Bagby-Slemmons-Munday Cemetery in Metcalfe Co. [Ref: *Metcalfe County Cemeteries*, Vol. I]. Also listed in this household in the 1870 census were **ELIZABETH SLEMMONS** (age 79) and **SUSAN EVANS** (age 73).

1561. **SARAH E. SLEMMONS** (born 1859).

1562. **ROBERT B. SLEMMONS** (born 1862).

1563. **SUSAN E. SLEMMONS** (born 1865).

1564. **LAURA B. SLEMMONS** (born 1867). In the *1880 Census of Metcalfe County*, **LAURA SLEMMONS** (age 13, domestic servant) was listed in the household of **G. W. THOMPSON** (age 32) and his wife **NANCY J. THOMPSON** (age 29), her cousin. They lived in Lafayette Magisterial District.

1565. **MARTHA F. SLEMMONS** (born 1870).

1566. **VICTORY W. SLEMMONS** (born 1874).

16. **GARLAND CRENSHAW**, third son of **JOHN CRENSHAW and MILDRED THOMPSON**, was born December 10, 1792, and was mentioned in his father's will in 1818 in Barren County, Kentucky, but he was not mentioned in the *1850 Census of Barren County*.

17. **DABNEY CRENSHAW** (September 29, 1794 - died by 1833/1842?), fourth son of **JOHN CRENSHAW and MILDRED THOMPSON**, married **ELIZABETH WAGGONER** on October 26, 1818, in Barren County, KY. **DABNEY CRENSHAW** was a private in Captain John Gorin's Company (later Captain Charles Harvey's Company) in 1813;

thus, serving in War of 1812. [Ref: *The Times of Long Ago*, by F. Gorin, p. 45]. Dabney may have died by May 6, 1833. A deed in Barren County named his "legal heirs" as **RICHARD W. CRENSHAW, JOHN CRENSHAW, GEORGE CRENSHAW, and SIMON BIRD** and wife (Milley). [Ref: *Barren County Land Records*, 1833]. However, another deed on June 27, 1842, named the heirs of **JOHN CRENSHAW**, deceased, and they included **DABNEY CRENSHAW** and his wife Betsy. [Ref: *Barren County Land Records*, 1842]. (Obviously, he could not be dead in 1833 and alive in 1842?) **ELIZABETH CRENSHAW** was head of household in the *1850 census of Barren County*, stating she was born in 1802 in Kentucky. However, *Barren County, Kentucky, Will Book 4:170*, stated **ELIZABETH CRENSHAW**, "widow of Thomas," [?], wrote her will on January 26, 1863, and it was probated in February, 1864, naming sons **Richard W., John, Joseph M., Dabney C., George W. Crenshaw**, and a daughter **Lucy W. Angel**. [Note: Unless the will has been abstracted in error Elizabeth was the widow of Dabney Crenshaw. She was not the widow of Thomas Crenshaw].

171. **RICHARD W. CRENSHAW** (born 1821/1822 in Kentucky) married **MARY H. MONROE**, daughter of **JAMES MONROE**, on March 19, 1844, in Barren County, Kentucky, by Rev. John McGee. Surety was **James G. Monroe**. Not enumerated in the *1850 Census of Barren County, KY*, but located in the 1860 census in District No. 2. Either he was married twice or there is an error. Richard married **N. A. ----** (born 1830, Kentucky), according to the *1860 Census of Barren County, KY*, and his mother Elizabeth (age 58) was living with them (in the 1860 census, but not in 1870 census). Richard's real estate was valued at $1200 in 1870. In the *1880 Census of Barren County, Kentucky*, **R. W. CRENSHAW** (age 56, farmer) was head of house in Cave City Magisterial District No. 2, with his son **THOMAS CRENSHAW** (age 22, labor), daughter **SARAH G. CRENSHAW** (age 20), daughter **ELIZABETH CRENSHAW** (age 19), son **RUSEAU CRENSHAW** (age 17, labor), and daughter **FANNIE CRENSHAW** (age 15). They were all born in Kentucky.

1711. **JAMES H. CRENSHAW** (born 1846).

1712. **PHOEBA (PHEBE) J. CRENSHAW** (January 17, 1848-July 1, 1919) married **J. T. COOPER** (April 6, 1845 - January 1, 1930), son of **H. M. COOPER** (b. 1813, migrated from Virginia before 1850). In the *1870 Census of Barren County*, "Phoeba" was 22 and lived with her father, Richard. In the *1880 Census of Barren County*, they resided in the Rocky Hill Precinct and living with them was his brother **J. H. COOPER** (age 36). They are buried in Walnut Hill Cemetery in Bon Ayr, KY.

17121. **G. M. COOPER** (son, born 1877).

1713. **MARTHA A. CRENSHAW** (born 1850). She was not listed at home in 1870 census.

1714. **MARY J. CRENSHAW** (born 1851/2) married **JOHN R. WILLIAMS** (born 1842/3) and they lived with her father in the 1870 census.

1715. **WILLIAM THOMAS CRENSHAW** (born 1856/7). "William T." was age 14 in 1870 census. "Thomas" was age 22 in the 1880 census.

1716. **SARAH G. CRENSHAW** (born 1859/60).

1717. **ELIZABETH CRENSHAW** (born 1860/1).

1718. **LOVELL H. ROUSEAU CRENSHAW** (born 1862/3). "Lovell H. R." wsa age 8 in 1870 census. "Ruseau" was age 17 in the 1880 census.

1719. **FRANCES (FANNIE) H. CRENSHAW** (born 1864).

172. **MILLEY T. CRENSHAW** (1823, Kentucky -) married **SIMEON G. BIRD**, a son of **THOMAS BIRD** (1788-1845), on September 13, 1841, in Barren County, Kentucky. Simeon was born in 1821 in Kentucky. The marriage was witnessed by **RICHARD W. CRENSHAW**, who was also her surety (as well as her brother), and her father **DABNEY CRENSHAW** gave his consent to their marriage. "Sim and Millie Bird" lived in the Glasgow Junction Precinct in the *1870 Census of Barren County, KY*. The value of Simeon's real estate was $40 in 1870. **THOMAS BIRD** was buried in the Walnut Hill Cemetery. There were also Birds in Washington County, Kentucky.

1721. **MATTHEW LASLEY BIRD** (born 1842) married **AMERICA ----** (born 1842) and lived in the Glasgow Junction Precinct at the time of *1880 Census of Barren County, Kentucky*.

17211. **MARTHA BIRD** (born 1867).

17212. **MARY B. BIRD** (born 1869).

17213. **MILDRED BIRD** (born 1871).

17214. **RAMSEY BIRD** (born 1873).

17215. **PERRY BIRD** (born 1875).

17216. **LELE BIRD** (daughter, born 1879).

1722. **DABNEY T. BIRD** (born 1845).
Not listed in the 1870 census.

1723. **JOANN BIRD** (born 1848).
Listed with her parents in 1870 census.

1724. **GEORGE A. BIRD** (born 1850).
Not listed in the 1870 census.

1725. **RICHARD BIRD** (born 1852).
Listed with his parents in 1870 census.

1726. **ISAAC BIRD** (born 1856).

1727. **JANE BIRD** (born 1858).

1728. **BETTY E. BIRD** (born 1860).

1729. **MARY BIRD** (born 1862).

1730. **LUCY BIRD** (born 1864).

173. **LUCY W. CRENSHAW** (born 1825, Kentucky), daughter of **DABNEY CRENSHAW**, married ---- **ANGEL**. Probably related to **MARTIN D. ANGEL** who was the constable in their district of Metcalfe County, KY in 1816, and/or **LAWRENCE ANGEL** who also lived in the area.

174. **GEORGE W. CRENSHAW** (born 1827, Kentucky).

175. **JOSEPH M. CRENSHAW**.

176. **JOHN CRENSHAW**.

177. **DABNEY C. CRENSHAW** (born 1840, Kentucky).

18. **SUSANNA "SUSAN" CRENSHAW**, youngest daughter of **JOHN CRENSHAW and MILDRED THOMPSON**, was born on March 10, 1796, and mentioned in her father's will in 1818 in Barren County, Kentucky. **SUSAN CRENSHAW** married **SAMUEL EVANS** on February 4, 1837. [Ref: *Barren County Marriage Licenses*, page 83]. This Samuel Evans must have died by 1850 because **SUSAN EVANS** (age 53, born in Virginia) was listed in the house of **ANDERSON CRENSHAW** (her brother). There was also one **SUSAN EVANS** (born 1797) in the house of **WASHINGTON SLEMMONS** in 1870 in Metcalfe County, KY, and also an **ELIZABETH SLEMMONS** (born 1791). It appears that they were both Crenshaws. **SUSAN CRENSHAW EVANS** apparently died without children. Also, a deed dated June 27, 1842, named the heirs and representatives of **JOHN CRENSHAW**, deceased, including **SAMUEL EVANS and SUSAN**

EVANS, his wife. [Ref: **Barren County Land Records**, 1842].

19. **ANDERSON CRENSHAW**, youngest son of **JOHN CRENSHAW and MILDRED THOMPSON**, was born August 10, 1797, in Louisa or Albemarle Co., Virginia. He married **ELIZABETH "BETSIE" POLSON**, a daughter of **ABSOLOM POLSON and DELILAH DAVIS**, license dated December 24, 1836 [Ref: *Barren County, Kentucky, Marriage File No. 6*]. (It appears that their first child, **WILLIAM ALBERT CRENSHAW**, was born in 1830, six years before they were married. Since I have found no prior marriage, I must assume this to be the case.) **ANDERSON CRENSHAW** was a captain in the militia, an extensive farmer in Metcalfe County, Kentucky, and lost 53 slaves during the Civil War. [Ref: *Kentucky Genealogy and Biography*, Vol. II, by Thomas Westerfield, page 80]. In the *1850 Census of Barren County* he was listed as a farmer (age 51, born in Virginia, property valued at $1,312) and the following were in his house hold: **ELIZABETH CRENSHAW** (age 45, born in Virginia), **ALBERT W. CRENSHAW** (age 19, farmer, born in Kentucky), **JAMES G. CRENSHAW** (age 12, born Kentucky), **ELIZABETH M. CRENSHAW** (age 10, born Kentucky), **THOMPSON D. CRENSHAW** (age 8, born Kentucky), **NANCY J. CRENSHAW** (age 6, born Kentucky), **HENRY A. CRENSHAW** (age 3, born Kentucky), and SUSAN EVANS (age 53, born in Virginia). In the *1860 Census of Barren County*, **ANDERSON CRENSHAW** (age 62, farmer) was head of the household with **ELIZABETH CRENSHAW** (age 56, although it looks like 36), **THOMPSON D. CRENSHAW** (age 17, although it states "Thomas S. Crenshaw," which is incorrect), **HENRY A. CRENSHAW** (age 13), and **NANCY J. CRENSHAW** (age 15, although it states "Mary J. Crenshaw," which is incorrect). The *1870 Census of Barren County* listed **ANDERSON CRENSHAW** (age 71) and **ELIZABETH CRENSHAW** (age 66), Hiseville Precinct.

191. **WILLIAM ALBERT CRENSHAW** (August 10, 1830 - May 6, 1891), the eldest son of **ANDERSON CRENSHAW and ELIZABETH POLSON**, married **HARRIET LOVE** (1829 -   ), a daughter of **WILLIAM LOVE** (born 1799) and **POLLY WITCHER** (born 1806), both of Virginia, on December 15, 1852, in Barren County, KY. The siblings of **HARRIET LOVE** were as follows: **JOHN LOVE** (born 1831), **WESLEY LOVE** (born 1833), **THOMAS LOVE** (born 1835), **DOCTOR LOVE** (1838-1923), **MARTHA LOVE** (born 1840), **HENRY LOVE** (born 1843), **EMILY LOVE** (born 1847), and **BABE LOVE** (born 1850), all born in Kentucky. William and Harriet Crenshaw are buried in the Crenshaw family cemetery in Metcalfe County, Kentucky. **WILLIAM ALBERT CRENSHAW** was a "farmer and general stock trader, owning and operating a threshing machine for 25 consecutive years. He threshed more grain than any other man in his section of Barren County. He lost five slaves in the Civil War. In politics he was formerly an old line Whig, but now affiliates with the Democratic party [1885]. He is also a member of the Baptist Church, and a member of the Masonic fraternity." [Ref: *Kentucky Genealogy & Biography*, Vol. II, page 80;

Metcalfe County Cemeteries, Volume I (1983), page 39; and *Barren County Cemeteries*, Vol. II (1981), page 50]. In the *1880 Census of Metcalfe County, Kentucky*, **WILLIAM A. CRENSHAW** (age 49) was head of household and resided in the Lafayette Magisterial District with his wife **HARRIET CRENSHAW** (age 50, born in Virginia) and seven children, plus a black farm worker named **WESLEY ESTES** (age 15). In 1900, **HARRIET CRENSHAW** (born February, 1829, VA) was head of household in the Antioch District of Metcalfe County, and listed with them was **SIMON TWYMAN**, a black farm hand.

1911. **WILLIAM A. "WILLIE" CRENSHAW** (November 3, 1853 - September 19, 1883), the eldest son of **WILLIAM A. CRENSHAW**, was buried in Crenshaw Family Cemetery in Metcalfe County, Kentucky. Occupation: Farmer.

1912. **ISAAC NEWTON "NEWT" CRENSHAW** (February 16, 1855 - June 16, 1940), second son of **WILLIAM A. CRENSHAW**, married **VELORA (VALERIA) E. PARRISH** (1866-1914), the eldest daughter of **J. E. and MARY L. PARRISH**, in 1889 in Barren County, Kentucky, and resided in the Goodnight section. Newt wrote his will on March 19, 1929, and it was probated on January 27, 1941, in Barren County, KY. Newt and Velora are buried in the Hiseville Cemetery. In his will Newt named his five children [Ref: *Barren County Will Book 8:545*]. In the *1900 Census of Barren County, Kentucky*, in District #4, **ISAAC N. CRENSHAW** (age 45), and wife **VELARA CRENSHAW** (born August, 1877 [sic], which is incorrect since she was born in 1866) were listed as having married 10 years ago. He was a farmer. In the *1910 Census of Barren County* they lived in Goodnight Precinct and the census stated they had 6 children and 5 were still living in 1910. [Ref: *Genealogy of the Pedens of Kentucky, 1756-1986*, compiled by Henry C. Peden, Jr., (1986), page 50, citing information from Valeria Crenshaw Peden].

19121. **LESLIE STUART CRENSHAW** (Nov. 1890 - 1976), of **ISAAC N. CRENSHAW and VALERIA PARRISH**, married **ANNIE PEARL COOMER** (1891 - 1969). They are buried in the Hiseville Cemetery.

191211. **INFANT SON** (b. & d. August 29, 1927).

191212. **VALERIA NELL CRENSHAW**, born April 2, 1930, in Cave City, KY, married **WILLIE FRANCIS PEDEN**, who was born on November 19, 1926, in Barren County, KY, son of **CHARLES FLEMON PEDEN and BYRD M. LYONS**.

Valerie and Willie F. Peden were married on January 1, 1949. They were named in the will of an A. P. **CRENSHAW** in Barren County in 1976.

1912121. **JUDY CAROL PEDEN.** Born April 17, 1950, and married **ROYCE PAUL PAGE** on Sept. 5, 1966.

1912122. **DONNIE LYNN PEDEN.** Born June 26, 1954, and married **CAROLYN PEARL SMITH**, July 20, 1979.

19122. **JEWELL L. CRENSHAW** (March 30, 1892 -), son of **ISAAC CRENSHAW and VALERIA PARRISH**, married **ALLIE P. ----** (born Sept. 1, 1896).

19123. **WALLER MILLS CRENSHAW** (May, 1893 -), of **ISAAC N. CRENSHAW and VALERIA PARRISH**, md. **CLARIA B. ----** (born 1896) and was listed as head of household in the *1920 Census of Barren County, KY*, Hiseville District #4.

19124. **ETTIE BIRD CRENSHAW** (Nov. 1894 -), dau. of **ISAAC N. CRENSHAW and VALERIA PARRISH**, married **JAMES ARLICE GOFF** (1889-1952) and lived in Hiseville District No. 4. In the *1920 Census of Barren County*, his sister **PAULINE B. GOFF** (age 18) lived with them. Some have spelled "Ettie" as "Eddie." The 1910 census spelled her name as "Etta B." and the 1920 census spelled it "Ettie B."

191241. **JAMES A. GOFF, JR.** (born 1913).

191242. **GLADYS GOFF** (twin, born 1913).

191243. **GOREE GOFF** (born 1915) married **HENRY CLAY ALEXANDER**, son of **O. W. ALEXANDER**, in Cave City, KY.

19125. **ALLIE P. CRENSHAW** (Sept. 1896 - 1976), son of **ISAAC N. CRENSHAW and VALERIA PARRISH**, was living with his father in *1920 Census of Barren County*. An **"A. P. CRENSHAW"** died testate (will written January 5, 1966, and probated February 20, 1976), naming these heirs (no relationships given): **CARROLL CRENSHAW, NAOMI PEDIGO, ELEANOR HARRISON, EDDIE BIRD GOFF, WILLIE F. PEDEN, VALERIE PEDEN.** [Ref: *Barren Co. Will Book 14:382*].

They are buried in the Hiseville Cemetery.

1913. **ELMORE CRENSHAW** (December 27, 1856 - December 23, 1939), third son of **WILLIAM A. CRENSHAW**, was buried in Crenshaw Family Cemetery, Metcalfe County, KY. He was not listed with his parents in 1880 census. He lived with his mother and sister Lucy in 1900. In the *1910 Census of Metcalfe County*, he was head of household in the Knob Lick Precinct, and living with him were his mother **HARRIET CRENSHAW** (age 87), his sister **LUCY SHIRLEY** (age 40), and his nephew **ALLIE L. SHIRLEY** (age 8). Both women were widows.

1914. **MELISSA CRENSHAW** (April 13, 1858 - June 14, 1943), the eldest daughter of **WILLIAM A. CRENSHAW**, married **JOSEPH C. THOMAS** (July 7, 1856 - December 13, 1912) and they were buried in the Hiseville Cemetery. The *1880 Census of Metcalfe County, Kentucky*, indicated that **MALLISSA CRENSHAW** (age 21) was living at home with her parents, and her occupation was listed as "school teaching." She was unemployed that year. In the *1900 Census of Metcalfe County* **JOSEPH C. THOMAS** was head of household in District No. 2, with wife **MELISSA THOMAS** (April, 1859 -   ). They had been married for 5 years, but had no children. Living with them was **FRANCES THOMAS** (born October, 1834), Joseph's mother, who had 8 children with 6 living. In the *1920 Census of Barren County*, **BOB CRENSHAW** (age 66) was listed as a roomer in the household of **MALISSA THOMAS** (age 63, widow) in Glasgow, KY.

1915. **WALLER CRENSHAW** (1861-1930), fourth son of **WILLIAM CRENSHAW**, married **NADINE VANZANT**, and they had two daughters. Waller was born and grew up in Hiseville of Barren County, Kentucky, and was a merchant most of his business life, for many years at Seymour and the latter years at Hiseville. He was a popular and "good merchant with a large circle of friends." He died of heart trouble at home in Goodnight, and was buried in Hiseville Cem. [Ref: *The Glasgow Times*]. (Newspaper clipping undated, but he died in 1930.)

19151. **EUGENIA CRENSHAW.**

19152. **MODIE CRENSHAW.**

1916. **MARY CRENSHAW** (1863 -   ), the second daughter of **WILLIAM ALBERT CRENSHAW and HARRIET LOVE**, was in the *1880 Census of Metcalfe County, Kentucky*, as being age 16 and "at school."

1917. **GARLAND CRENSHAW** (September 5, 1865 - September 23, 1887), fifth son of **WILLIAM A. CRENSHAW**, was buried beside his brother "Willie" in the family cemetery. In the 1880 Census of Metcalfe County, Kentucky, he was age 14 and "works on farm."

1918. **LUCY CRENSHAW** (November 8, 1869 - September 20, 1941), fourth daughter of **WILLIAM A. CRENSHAW**, married **HARVEY MILTON SHIRLEY** (August 18, 1869 - June 13, 1905). They were buried in the Crenshaw Cemetery on the Crenshaw Road in Metcalfe County. In the *1910 Census of Metcalfe County, Kentucky*, **LUCY SHIRLEY** and **ALLIE P. SHIRLEY** lived with her brother **ELMORE CRENSHAW** in the Knob Lick Precinct. However, the marriage announcement gave the name of **ALLIE P. SHIRLEY** to be **ALLIE LEWIS SHIRLEY** [?].

19181. **ALLIE LEWIS SHIRLEY** (born 1902) married **VIRGINIA WATKINS**, the daughter of **F. J. WATKINS**, of Coral Hill, on October 28, ----. [The newspaper clip was undated]. See abstract in Pearl's *Scrapbook*, q.v.

1919. **ELIZABETH "BETTIE" CRENSHAW** (October 10, 1871 - August 29, 1900), youngest daughter of **WILLIAM A. CRENSHAW**, married **ELMORE READ** on November 20, 1895. In the *1900 Census of Metcalfe County, Kentucky*, **ELMORE READ** (January, 1873 -) and wife **BETTIE READ** (born October, 1872?) lived in Antioch Dist. They had been married 4 years, with no children. Bettie died only two months after the census was enumerated. She was buried next to her parents. In the *1910 Census of Metcalfe County*, **ELMORE REID** (age 37) was head of house (Edmonton District #1) with his sisters **ALICE REID** (age 42) and **LIZZIE REID** (age 31). **ELMORE REID** was listed as widower.

192. **JAMES G. CRENSHAW**, the second son of **ANDERSON CRENSHAW** and **BETSIE POLSON**, was born in 1838 (he was age 22 in the *1850 Census of Barren County, Kentucky*, and age 22 in the *1860 Census of Metcalfe County, Kentucky*). In 1850 he was still living at home and in the 1860 census he was listed in the household of **RICHARD T. FRANKLIN** (age 28), **MARY E. FRANKLIN** (age 20), and **CHARLES FRANKLIN** (age 5 months). [Richard T. Franklin was the brother-in-law of James G. Crenshaw]. Even though the censustaker in 1870 listed **"JAMES I. CRENSHAW"** in the household of **WILLIAM POLSTON** this actually was **"JAMES G. CRENSHAW"** and his brother **HENRY CRENSHAW** was listed with him. Both were sons of **ANDERSON CRENSHAW** whose wife Elizabeth, or "Betsie," was a Polson. **JAMES G. CRENSHAW** and **R. L. CRENSHAW** operated a general store at Coral Hill (formerly Myer's Mill)

which was first started by the Jones Brothers about 1855 and operated by them for 40 years. [Ref: *Barren County Heritage*, by Cecil Goode, et al. (1980), page 265]. In the *1880 Census of Metcalfe County*, Lafayette Magisterial District, **JAMES G. CRENSHAW** (age 42) was head of household, with wife **CATHERINE H. CRENSHAW** (age 30, born in Virginia), their children, and a black farm hand named **LOUIS CRENSHAW** (age 10, born in KY). In the *1900 Census of Metcalfe County, KY*, **JAMES G. CRENSHAW** (born March, 1838) was head of household in District #2 with son **CHARLES CRENSHAW** (born October, 1872) and daughter **EMILY CRENSHAW** (born August, 1875). His wife had apparently died.

1921. **CHARLES (CHARLIE) CRENSHAW** (Oct. 6, 1872 - Feb. 7, 1955) a son of **JAMES G. and CATHERINE H. CRENSHAW**, was buried in the Charlie Crenshaw Cemetery, Metcalfe County, KY, with his wife **ETHEL PEDIGO CRENSHAW** (January 31, 1890 - April 2, 1918) and **ALLIE R. CRENSHAW** (October 17, 1932 - October 18, 1934). Charlie wrote his will September 23, 1954, and it was probated February 15, 1955, naming his only son, **REED CRENSHAW**. In the *1920 Census of Metcalfe County*, **CHARLIE CRENSHAW** (age 47) was head of household, with his son **REED CRENSHAW** (age 10) living with him; no one else was listed. At that time, they lived in Sulphur Well District #2. [Ref: *Metcalfe County Will Book 3:80*]. (Note: **CHARLES (CHARLIE) CRENSHAW** married **ETHEL PEDIGO**. In the *1920 Census of Metcalfe County* in Sulphur Well District #2, **ESTER CRENSHAW** (age 10) lived in the house of **JOHN A. PEDIGO** (born 1855) and his wife **CORNELIA A. CRENSHAW** (born 1860). Ester was their granddaughter and perhaps the daughter of Charles Crenshaw; perhaps not.)

19211. **REED CRENSHAW** (1910 -) married **BESSIE HAYES**. Her obituary gave the following data: **MRS. BESSIE HAYES CRENSHAW** (1904-1985), a resident of Knob Lick in Metcalfe County, died on February 1, 1985, at the Community Hospital [in Glasgow, KY]. Her 10 children were mentioned, plus 34 grandchildren and 14 great-grandchildren, and her sisters **IRENE THOMPSON and IVA CASSADY**. The funeral was by Butler Funeral Home with burial in Clack Cemetery. Her obituary did not state that she was the widow of **REED CRENSHAW**, but she was. [Ref: *The Glasgow Republican*, Feb., 1985].

192111. **CHARLES CRENSHAW**
Lived in Edmonton, Kentucky, in 1985.

192112. **JAMES CRENSHAW**
Lived in Knob Lick, Kentucky, in 1985.

192113. **CLAY CRENSHAW**
Lived in Anderson, Indiana, in 1985.

192114. **MARGARET CRENSHAW**, married ---- **EDLIN**, and lived in Louisville, KY, in 1985.

192115. **LILLIE CRENSHAW** married ---- **CASTEEL**, and lived in Louisville, KY, in 1985.

192116. **MARCELLA CRENSHAW** married ---- **SHAW**, and lived in Cave City, KY, in 1985.

192117. **KATHERINE CRENSHAW** married ---- **HAGAN**, and lived in Knob Lick, KY, in 1985.

192118. **EDNA CRENSHAW** married ---- **KIZZIRS**, and lived in Winfield, AL, in 1985.

192119. **DORA CRENSHAW**
Lived in Greensburg, Kentucky, in 1985.

19211-10. **ORLENE CRENSHAW** married ---- **HONEYCUTT**, and lived in Glasgow, Kentucky, in 1985.

1922. **JOSEPH CRENSHAW** (born 1875).

1923. **EMILY CRENSHAW** (born 1876).

1924. **ANDERSON CRENSHAW** (born 1878).

1925. **JAMES CRENSHAW** (1881-   ) was head of household in the *1910 Census of Metcalfe County, Kentucky* and was single. Listed with him was one hired hand named **SIDNEY PEDIGO** (age 28). **JAMES CRENSHAW** lived near **ELMORE CRENSHAW** in the Knob Lick Voting Precinct. [Note: James Crenshaw is placed here without proof positive that he was the son of James G. Crenshaw as the 1890 census is not extant].

193. **MARY ELIZABETH CRENSHAW** (April 23, 1840 - September 17, 1871), the eldest daughter of **ANDERSON CRENSHAW and BETSIE POLSON**, married in 1857 to **RICHARD T. FRANKLIN**. In the *1850 of Barren County, KY* (now Metcalfe Co.) she was listed as **ELIZABETH M. CRENSHAW**, age 10, and the 1860 census listed her as **MARY E. FRANKLIN**, age 20. She was buried in the Duff Crenshaw Cemetery in Metcalfe County, Kentucky, the only Franklin buried there. The *1870 Census of Barren County, Kentucky*, listed them in the Hiseville Precinct and gave his age as 37 (born in Tennessee) and her age as 30 (born in Kentucky). His occupation: Farmer. Also living with them at that time was **SUSAN EVANS** (age 75), and **LAURA BARTON** (age 21, black, domestic servant) and her 2 children, **HENRY BARTON** (age 1) and **MADORA BARTON** (2 months). In the *1880 Census of Metcalfe County, Kentucky*, **RICHARD T. FRANKLIN** (age 48) was head of house in Lafayette Magisterial District, with his sons **WILLIAM FRANKLIN** (age 16), **ALBERT T.**

FRANKLIN (age 13), and **ROBERT FRANKLIN** (age 10). Also living with him were **ELIZABETH CRENSHAW** (age 75), his mother-in-law, and **ELLEN E. POLSON** (age 39), his niece. As noted above, his wife, Mary Elizabeth, died in 1871, and apparently their sons Charles and James died prior to the taking of the 1880 census as they were not enumerated.

1931. **CHARLES H. FRANKLIN** (1860 -).

1932. **JAMES FRANKLIN** (1862 -).

1933. **WILLIAM FRANKLIN** (1864 -).

1934. **ROBERT FRANKLIN** (1869 -).

1935. **ALBERT T. FRANKLIN** (1872 -) was head of the household in the *1900 Census of Metcalfe County, Kentucky* (born June, 1872), with wife CATHARINE (born July, 1877) and daughters Ruby and Mary L. **ALBERT T. FRANKLIN** (age 37) was the head of the household in the *1910 Census of Metcalfe County, Kentucky*, and the name of his wife was given as **FRANCES C. ----** (age 32). They married in 1895.

19341. **RUBY A. FRANKLIN** (born March, 1896).

19342. **MARY L. FRANKLIN** (born July, 1897).

19342. **LILLIAN FRANKLIN** (born 1898/9).

19343. **MABEL F. FRANKLIN** (born 1905?).

194. **THOMPSON DAVIS CRENSHAW** (1842 -), third son of **ANDERSON CRENSHAW and BETSIE POLSON**, married to **HARRIET E. MITCHELL**. The *1860 Census of Barren County, Kentucky*, had erroneously listed his name as "**THOMAS S. CRENSHAW**" (age 17). In the *1870 Census of Metcalfe County, Kentucky*, **THOMPSON CRENSHAW** (age 37) was head of household in the Lafayette Magisterial District, with his wife **HARRIET E. CRENSHAW** (age 33, born in Kentucky), and their children. His occupation was farmer. In the *1910 Census of Metcalfe County, KY*, in Knob Lick, KY. **THOMPSON CRENSHAW** (age 67) lived with daughter **LULA BEARD**. **THOMPSON D. CRENSHAW** was listed as 78 in the *1920 Census of Metcalfe County, Kentucky* and lived in Sulphur Well District No. 2 with his daughter **LULA CRENSHAW BEARD**.

1941. **SELDON D. CRENSHAW** (1866/7 -). In the *1880 Census of Metcalfe County*, his name was spelled as **CELDON D. CRENSHAW** (age 13). Seldon was buried in Adair County, KY, according to information from a family member.

19411. **CLYDE CRENSHAW.**
Veterinarian in Columbia, Kentucky.

1942. **LUCY A. (ELLIS) CRENSHAW** (1869-1959) married **ROBERT H. BARTON** (1859-1941). In the *1920 Census of Barren County* they were living in Glasgow District #1. Also listed in this household was her brother **NOEL CRENSHAW** (age 35). The 1920 census stated she was age 48, thus born 1872, but her tombstone indicates she was born in 1869. They are buried in Glasgow Municipal Cemetery, Glasgow, KY. [If "Alice" was her middle name, thus the name "Ellis" since "Alice" and "Ellis" do sound quite a bit alike]. In the *1910 Census of Barren County*, **ROBERT H. BARTON** was head of house and lived in Glasgow, Kentucky, on North Race Street with his wife **ELLIS BARTON** (age 40), his brothers-in-law **NOAH [NOEL] CRENSHAW** (age 24) and **KING CRENSHAW** (age 21). Robert was a tobacco dealer, Noah (Noel) was a loose leaf salesman, and King was a salesman in a retail store. Robert and Ellis had been married 29 years, but they had no children. **ROBERT H. BARTON** died testate in Barren County and his will was probated on January 24, 1941, naming his brother-in-law **NOEL CRENSHAW**, sister-in-law **MRS. CORA BEARD**, nephew **DICK BARTON**, niece **EVA BARTON**, and grandniece **MARGARET CUMMINS** (the daughter of **SAM CUMMINS**), "maiden name not recalled." Her also named his wife, **ELLIS BARTON**.

1943. **GEORGE H. CRENSHAW** (1872 -) was buried in Glasgow, KY, but was not listed in *Barren County Cemetery Records* by Eva Coe Peden (2 vols.); perhaps there was no stone. He probably was the **GEORGE H. CRENSHAW** (age 37?) who was head of the household in *1910 Census of Metcalfe County*, Kentucky, Lafayette District #2, with wife **EFFE CRENSHAW** (age 30), and three children. His occupation was farmer.

19431. **LOREENA CRENSHAW** (born 1905).

19432. **BERNICE E. CRENSHAW** (born 1907).

19433. **GENEVA E. CRENSHAW** (born 1909).

1944. **HUGH A. CRENSHAW** (1874/5 - 1937) married **PEARL ----** (1880-1937). The *1880 Census of Metcalfe County, KY*, indicates Hugh was born in 1875, but his tombstone in Neal's Chapel Cemetery near Lecta, Kentucky, indicates he was born in 1871. The tombstone might be in error because his brother George was born before him and the census states he was age 8 in 1880 and Hugh was age 5. **H. A. and PEARL CRENSHAW** were listed in the *1920 Census of Barren County, Kentucky*. in the Glasgow District No. 1, with their two children: **ROY CRENSHAW**, age 14, and

LUCILE (LUCILLE) CRENSHAW, age 11. H. A. was age 48 and Pearl was age 39. **CAROL CRENSHAW** (born and died October 29, 1902), daughter of **H. A. and H. F. CRENSHAW**. Buried in Salem Church Cemetery in Barren County next to sister **NANNIE E. CRENSHAW** (1903-1904). [Note: These two infants could be the daughters of this Hugh and Pearl Crenshaw (if H. A. is for Hugh A., and H. F. should be H. P.?). This is further supported by the statement in the 1910 census that Pearl had 4 children, with only 2 living].

19441. **CAROL CRENSHAW** (born and died October 29, 1902).

19442. **NANNIE E. CRENSHAW** (Nov. 4, 1903 - June 3, 1904). Buried in Salem Cemetery near Glasgow, Kentucky.

19443. **ROY CRENSHAW** (1906 -) was living on November 8, 1981, at Route 5, Glasgow, KY, when his wife **MAYMIE G. CRENSHAW** died (age 75) at the Homewood Care Center. Her will was probated November 18, 1981, and named her husband **ROY CRENSHAW** (age 75) and family. The funeral was conducted by Hatcher and Saddler, with burial in New Salem Cemetery. [Ref: *Glasgow Republican*, and *Barren County Will Book 15:206*]. They had seven grandchildren and one great-grandchild in 1981 (no names listed).

194431. **EDNA CRENSHAW** (1928 - April 10, 1995) married **LEWIS PACE**, of Glasgow, KY.

194432. **GILBERT LLOYD CRENSHAW** (born 1932) was a resident on Route 5, Glasgow, KY, in 1959, and lived in Alabama in 1981.

194433. **MARVIN LEWIS CRENSHAW** (born 1934) was a resident of Bowling Green, KY, in 1959, and lived in California in 1981 with his wife **CAROLYN CRENSHAW**.

19444. **LUCILLE CRENSHAW** (born 1909).

1945. **LULA E. CRENSHAW** (1879 -) married **WILLIAM A. BEARD** (1875 -). In the *1920 Census of Metcalfe Co., KY*, her father, **THOMPSON D. CRENSHAW** (age 78), lived with them in Sulphur Well District No. 2. He also lived with them in 1910 (Knob Lick Precinct), but **LULA E. BEARD**'s name was then enumerated as **LULA M. BEARD**. Also living with them were her brother **HARRY B. BEARD** (age 38) and his sister **CORA M. BEARD** (age 27). William was age 36.

19451. **NINA M. BEARD** (born 1902).

19452. **HELEN BEARD** (born 1904).

19453. **WILLIAM WAYNE BEARD** (born 1912), only son of **WILLIAM BEARD and LULA CRENSHAW**, married **MARY AGNES LESSENBERRY** in Louisville, KY. "Billy Beard" lived in Knob Lick in 1972.

1946. **CORA CRENSHAW** (1882 -) married **HARRY B. BEARD** (August 26, 1876 - September 12, 1954) and lived in Sulphur Well District No. 2 at the time of the *1920 Census of Metcalfe County*. He was buried in Hiseville Cemetery, but wife **CORA CRENSHAW BEARD** was not listed. [Ref: *Barren County Cemeteries*, Volume II, page 157]. Earlier, in the 1910 census, **HARRY B. and CORA BEARD** lived with her sister Lula's family in Knob Lick, KY.

19461. **ROBERT CARL BEARD** (born 1912).

1947. **NOEL CRENSHAW** (December 25, 1884 - May 27, 1966), son of **THOMPSON D. CRENSHAW and HARRIET E. MITCHELL**, died in Barren County, KY. His will was written on November 27, 1959, and probated May 27, 1966, naming his sister **CORA BEARD**, nephew **CARL BEARD**, and sisters **LULA BEARD and ELLIS BARTON**. [Ref: *Barren County, Kentucky, Will Book 12:77*]. Noel was buried in Glasgow Municipal Cem. next to his sister **ELLIS BARTON**. He lived with her in 1920. In the *1910 Census of Barren County*, he resided with his sister's family (and brother **KING CRENSHAW**). His occupation at that time was Loose Leaf Salesman.

1948. **KING C. CRENSHAW** (March 22, 1889 - May 19, 1972), son of **THOMPSON DAVIS CRENSHAW and HARRIET E. MITCHELL**, was listed in the *1920 Census of Barren County, Kentucky*, in the house of **J. C. Jenkins** (born 1852) on Race Street in Glasgow. His occupation was "Clerk in Dry Goods Store," but King was of no relationship to this J. C. Jenkins. He is undoubtedly the same **KING CRENSHAW** who owned the reknown hotel "Buela Villa" at Sulphur Well in Metcalfe County, which he bought in 1920. The following is from an article by **Jeramey Breeding** entitled *"Remembering the Buela Villa."* **Ezekiel Neal** owned 300 acres of land on each side of the South Fork of the Little Barren River, about 20 miles northeast of Glasgow. He decided to drill for salt and in doing so he tapped a stream of water that was thought to have medicinal value and was said to cure internal disorders, stomach diseases, and nervous disorders. It contained minerals such as sulphur, iron, magnesium, and salt. In 1903 the Beula Villa Hotel was built here by **Catlett W. Thompson** (1844-1919). [Oddly enough, even though the famous sulphur well was supposed to cure stomach diseases, Thompson died of cancer of the stomach]. **Mrs. J. M. Richardson** operated the hotel until 1920 when it was sold to **KING CRENSHAW**, and he managed the hotel for almost 50 years. In 1936 the Buela Villa was the only hotel in Metcalfe County. In 1968, due to illness of **KING CRENSHAW**, the hotel was closed and was ultimately sold at auction on July 5, 1969, to Mary Fancher. Unable to meet State health requirements, the hotel closed for good 4 weeks later. The Beula Villa Hotel was a two story structure with a veranda about 10 feet wide and over 100 feet long. According to pamphlet put out by Mr. Crenshaw, the rooms were "large, well lighted and well-ventilated, all of them being outside exposure, electric-lighted and convenient to bath." The hotel was equipped with both private and public baths. There were two larger dining rooms and a garage on the hotel property that was large enough to hold several cars. The guests could drink from the sulphur well at the foot of a suspension bridge leading from the hotel. One of its best known features was its porch facilities for rest and relaxation. Two of these porches were 164 feet by 12 feet, and another was 100 feet by 20 feet. The verandas were always filled with rocking chairs. As for recreational facilities there was hunting, fishing, a pool room, a bowling alley, a dance hall, and Cook's swimming hole in the nearby Little Barren River. The rates of **KING CRENSHAW** in the 1950's were $32 for room and meal per week and $6 per day with meals included. A single meal was $2 and children under 10 could stay for half price. Meals at the Beula Villa were considered to be one of its outstanding features, with fried chicken, country ham, and vegetables from their own vegetable garden. During the Crenshaw years the hostesses were **Mrs. Carolyn Parson and Mrs. Nellie Duvall.** Perhaps the sentiment of the people who stayed there over the years can be best recalled by **Carlyle Chamberlain** who wrote the following for the each letter of "HOTEL" in 1966:

H -- Hospitality in the finest tradition of Old Kentucky exemplified in the personality of **Col. King Crenshaw.**
O -- Only place of its kind in the state, operated by him since 1920.
T -- Tables set with an abundance of wholesome food that an epicurean would delight in.
E -- Everything to make a visit enjoyable with a friendly and efficient staff.
L -- Long will this charming resort remain in our memories - a symbol of peace and happiness.

Although age, neglect, and vandalism have greatly damaged the structure itself, the memory of the Beula Villa Hotel will be with us always. [Ref: *Traces*, Vol. 15, No. 2 (1987), p. 53].

KING CRENSHAW never married. His death certificate states he was a retired hotel owner, born in Metcalfe County, KY, and was interred in the Hiseville Cemetery in Barren County, KY, on May 21, 1972, by the Butler Funeral Home of Edmonton, KY. He died at the Summit Manor Nursing Home in Columbia, Adair County, KY. The informant was **BILLY BEARD** of Knob Lick, KY. The causes of death were hypostatic pneumonia for three days and generalized arteriosclerosis/senile syndrome for 6 years.

195. **NANCY J. "NANNIE" CRENSHAW** (January 19, 1845 -), youngest daughter of **ANDERSON CRENSHAW and ELIZABETH "BETSIE" POLSON,** married **JONATHAN READ** on November 28, 1869, in Barren County. **JONATHAN READ** was born on January 5, 1826, in Barren (now Metcalfe) County, a son of **JOSEPH READ and MILLIE McINTEER.** Jonathan's first wife was **ALMEDA P. THOMPSON** (1837-1861), whom he married on December 31, 1857, and had one daughter, **NANNIE I. READ.** His second wife was **NANCY J. CRENSHAW.** In addition to farming and merchandising pursuits, **JONATHAN READ** was postmaster at Knob Lick in Metcalfe County, Kentucky, for many years commencing around 1859 and continuing to at least 1885. He was often called upon to act as an administrator of estates and guardian of minors. In politics he was a Democrat. [Ref: *Kentucky Genealogy and Biography,* Volume II, page 94]. The *1860 Census of Barren County, Kentucky,* erroneously listed her name as "**MARY J. CRENSHAW**" (age 15). In the *1880 Census of Metcalfe County, Kentucky,* **JOHNATHAN READ** (age 54) was head of household in the Lafayette Magisterial District, with his wife **NANCY J. READ** (age 35) and family plus **SMITH H. READ** (age 44), his brother, and **VIOLA WREN** (age 23), a boarder (and teacher).

1951. **JOSEPH A. READ** (born 1871).

1952. **ELIZZEE READ** (died young).

1953. **MINNIE READ** (born 1875).

1954. **JAMES A. READ** (born 1877).

196. **HENRY ANDERSON CRENSHAW** (March 16, 1847 - April 16, 1907), youngest child of **ANDERSON CRENSHAW and ELIZABETH "BETSIE" POLSON,** was born in Barren (now Metcalfe) County, KY. Henry married **MARTHA ALICE EMBREE** (January 2, 1856 - June 25, 1922), a daughter of **RICHARD EMBREE** (1819-1875) and **LETHA ANN DAVIS** (1825-1898) on October 25, 1872, in Metcalfe County, KY. The siblings of Martha Alice Embree were: **ELLEN ELIZABETH EMBREE** (1852-1918), who married **WILLIAM HENRY LAMBIRTH** (1849-1892); **WILLIAM M. EMBREE; MARY C. "MOLLIE" EMBREE** (1858-1936), who married to **FRANK TOLBERT ROYSE** (1858-1896); **NANCY L. EMBREE; SUSAN F. EMBREE; VIRGINIA ANN "GINNY" EMBREE** (1867-1936), who married ---- **THOMPSON;** and, **RICHARD ALBERT EMBREE** (1870-1907) who married **ANN CLAY** (1880-1908). **HENRY ANDERSON CRENSHAW** was

a well-respected community man and church leader all of his life. He died of complications from being bitten in the chest by his horse. His wife, **MARTHA ALICE CRENSHAW**, died on June 3, 1922, from "a mental condition that caused her to refuse food, thereby starving to death." A possible contributing factor was a condition known as "erysipelas," which is an infection with streptococci. [Ref: *Commonwealth of Kentucky, Certificate of Death No. 16510, Metcalfe County*]. The informant at the time of her death was **MARY ALICE JACKSON**, of Hiseville, Kentucky, and the undertaker was Mayfield S. Foster, of Hiseville, KY. (Death certificates were not required at the time of the death of **HENRY ANDERSON CRENSHAW** in 1907.) They were buried in the old Crenshaw family cemetery at Knob Lick in Metcalfe County, Kentucky, on Blue Spring Creek, site of the original home of **JOHN CRENSHAW**. [Ref: *Metcalfe Co. Cemeteries*, Vol. I, p. 91]. In the *1880 Census of Metcalfe County*, **HENRY A. CRENSHAW** (age 32) was head of household in Lafayette Magisterial District with his wife **MARTHA A. CRENSHAW** (age 22) and their children. In the *1900 Census of Metcalfe County*, **HENRY A. CRENSHAW** (born March, 1847) was head of household in Antioch District with his wife **MARTHA A. CRENSHAW** (born June, 1856), and children. They had 9 children, all were living and all born in Kentucky. In the *1920 Census of Metcalfe County*, **ALICE CRENSHAW**, widow, (age 63), was head of household with **NANNIE THOMPSON**, sister, (age 57), and **MARIE SMITH**, niece (age 7), living with her in Sulphur Well Dist. #2. Census was enumerated on Jan. 29, 1920. (As might be expected, earlier censuses gave different dates.)

1961. **FLORENCE ANN CRENSHAW** (August, 1873 -   ), daughter of **HENRY ANDERSON CRENSHAW and MARTHA ALICE EMBREE**, was married 6 times: (1) **EPHRAM LOVE**; (2) **--- GERALDS**; (3) **JOHN O. BOGIE**; (4) **---- GOFF**; (5) **CARL "JACK" SHIVE**; divorced and re-married (6) **CARL "JACK" SHIVE**. Husbands Geralds and Bogie were killed by horses (separate accidents). She had two children by Love. The *1900 Census of Metcalfe County, Kentucky*, in the Randolph Magisterial District, listed **EPHRAM LOVE** (born January, 1861) as head of household, with his wife **FALARNCE [FLORENCE] LOVE** (born Aug. 1873) and daughter **MARY A. LOVE** (born July, 1893). **FLORENCE SHIVE** is buried in Horse Cave, Hart County, Kentucky [Ref: Information from **FRANCES SMITH**, of Glasgow, KY, 1995]. In the *1920 Census of Barren County, Kentucky*, **JOHN O. BOGIE** (age 40), wife **FLORENCE A. BOGIE** (age 44), and stepson **JOHN H. LOVE** (age 18) lived in Hiseville District No. 4, where John Bogie was unemployed and John Love was a house painter.

19611. **MARY ALICE LOVE** (July 11, 1893 -   ) daughter of **EPHRAM LOVE** and **FLORENCE ANN CRENSHAW**, married **WILLIAM RUDOLPH "WILLIE" JACKSON** (September 14, 1891 - August, 1985) of Barren County, Kentucky, In the *1920 Census of Barren County, Kentucky*, **WILLIAM R. JACKSON** (age 24), wife **MARY A. JACKSON** (age 23), and son **GLEN L. JACKSON** (age 1 year and 5 months) lived in Hiseville District #4, where **WILLIAM R. JACKSON** worked as a hardware salesman.

196111. **GLEN LOVE JACKSON** (born September 27, 1918 - died in an automobile accident).

196112. **WILLIAM COURTNEY JACKSON** (born August 5, 1928) married **JOYCE TRIPLETT**.

1961121. **KATRINA JACKSON**.

1961122. **MARK JACKSON**.

196113. **MARGIE ANN JACKSON** (December 15, 1931 - 1989) married 3 times: (1) ---- **HOWELL**; (2) ---- **HALL**; and, (3) **BARK CLAY**.

1961131. **MICHAEL LOVE HOWELL** (born May 26, 1955).

1961132. **WILLIAM TIMOTHY HOWELL** (born August, 1957).

196114. **AMANDA FRANCES JACKSON** (born September 24, 1933) married **RAY JOHN SMITH** (June 10, 1925 - May 1, 1985), Glasgow, Kentucky.

1961141. **MARY LISA SMITH** (born May 5, 1959) married (1) ---- **GOSSETT** and (2) **JEFF HOLMAN**.

19611411. **CAINE JACKSON GOSSETT** (born 1986).

196115. **RALPH DEPP JACKSON** (born July 11, 1939) married **GAIL FARRIS**.

1961151. **RALPH FARRIS JACKSON** (born 1965)

1961152. **GLENN SHELTON JACKSON** (born 1969)

196116. **HARRY EPHRAM JACKSON** (born January 31, 1941) married **SANDRA SMITH**.

1961161. **CINDY JACKSON** (born 1965).

1961162. **MICHELLE JACKSON** (born 1967).

19612. **JOHN HENRY LOVE** (1901 -), son of **EPHRAM LOVE** and **FLORENCE ANN CRENSHAW**, was living with his mother and his stepfather, **JOHN O. BOGIE**, in the

1920 Census of Barren County, Kentucky, at which time he was age 18 and worked as a house painter.

196121. **JOHN HENRY LOVE, JR.** (born about 1925) married **MARTHA FREEMAN**.

1961211. **ELIZABETH ANN LOVE.** (Deceased; date unknown)

1961212. **HENRY LOVE.**

1961213. **JERRY LOVE.**

1961214. **RONNIE JOE LOVE.**

1961215. **DWIGHT LOVE.**

1961216. **CAROLYN LOVE.**

1962. **RICHARD EMBREE CRENSHAW** (September, 1875 -), son of **HENRY ANDERSON CRENSHAW and MARTHA ALICE EMBREE**, married ---- and had a son, ---- (names unknown). They moved to Kansas. The *1880 and 1900 Censuses of Metcalfe County, KY*, both listed **RICHARD E. CRENSHAW** as living in the home of his parents.

1963. **NANNIE ELIZABETH CRENSHAW** (Jan. 14, 1878 - July 10, 1903), the second daughter of **HENRY ANDERSON CRENSHAW and MARTHA ALICE EMBREE**, married **THOMAS A. LAMBIRTH** (December 7, 1870 - October 31, 1942). They were buried in the old Crenshaw family cemetery at Knob Lick, Metcalfe County, Kentucky. In the *1900 Census of Metcalfe County*, **THOMAS A. LAMBIRTH** was head of household in the Antioch District, with wife **NANCY E. LAMBIRTH**, son Henry R., and daughter Elizabeth Lambirth.

19631. **HENRY R. LAMBIRTH** (born February, 1898).

18632. **ELIZABETH LAMBIRTH** (born January, 1900).

19633. **HAZEL VERN LAMBIRTH** (Nov. 19, 1901 - Dec. 8. 1930) was buried next to her parents in Metcalfe Co., KY.

19634. **ALMA LAMBIRTH** (born 1903) was listed in the household of **WILLIAM H. PEDEN** and **PEARL E. CRENSHAW** in the *1920 Census of Barren County, Kentucky*. She was her niece. **ALMA LAMBIRTH** married **EUGENE B. RAY**, of Indianapolis.

1964. **HENRY EMMITT CRENSHAW** (January, 1880 -), second son of **HENRY ANDERSON CRENSHAW and MARTHA ALICE EMBREE**, married **MURDIS** ---- and they lived in Sherman, Texas. No children. The *1880 Census of Metcalfe County, Kentucky* indicated he was born in February and the 1900 census indicated January.

1965. **CHARLES ELZIE "DOC" CRENSHAW** (May 8, 1882 - Feb. 20, 1961), the second son of **HENRY ANDERSON CRENSHAW and MARTHA ALICE EMBREE**, married **ELLA ----** and lived in California. He was a resident of Visalia, and was buried in that cemetery. A pallbearer at his funeral was his nephew, **EWELL PEDEN**, a son of his youngest sister, **PEARL EUGENIA CRENSHAW PEDEN**.

1966. **FRANK E. CRENSHAW** (January 21, 1885 - December 22, 1912), the fourth son of **HENRY ANDERSON CRENSHAW and MARTHA ALICE EMBREE**, died of pneumonia in Kentucky. Frank never married. In the *1910 Census of Metcalfe County, KY*, in the Knob Lick Precinct, **FRANK E. CRENSHAW** (age 25) was head of household, and living with him were his mother **ALICE CRENSHAW** (age 54), his sister **CARRIE E. CRENSHAW** (age 22), his brother **GEORGE D. CRENSHAW** (age 20), his sister **PEARL E. CRENSHAW** (age 17), and his niece **ALICE A. LAMBIRTH** (age 7). The census stated that **ALICE CRENSHAW** was a widow and she had 9 children, of which 8 were still living in 1910 in Metcalfe County, KY.

1967. **CARRIE E. CRENSHAW** (August 12, 1887 - February 19, 1916), the third daughter of **HENRY ANDERSON CRENSHAW and MARTHA ALICE EMBREE**, married **D. S. SMITH**. He may have been the **DANIEL S. SMITH** (born 1877), a son of **SIDNEY SMITH**, who lived near the Metcalfe Lambirths and Crenshaws in 1880. Unfortunately, the specifics are lacking at this writing, but there are Smiths in *Pearl E. Peden's Scrapbook*, q. v. Carrie was buried in the Duff Crenshaw Cemetery in Metcalfe County, Kentucky, and she was the only Smith buried there. Since **CARRIE E. CRENSHAW** was still single in 1910 and died only 6 years later, she may not have had any children. She was "dressmaker at home" in *1910 Census of Metcalfe County*.

1968. **GEORGE DUFF CRENSHAW** (January 18, 1890 - November 14, 1955), the youngest son of **HENRY ANDERSON CRENSHAW and MARTHA ALICE EMBREE**, married **LESSIE FREEMAN** (October 16, 1892 - April 17, 1950). Duff died testate. His will only mentioned his wife's grave, the Antioch Church and **REV. AND MRS. V. A. JONES, and A. R. FREEMAN**. [Ref: *Metcalfe County, Ky., Will Book 3:83*]. He and his children are buried in the Duff Crenshaw Cemetery on the land originally settled by John Crenshaw around 1805. In the *1920 Census of Metcalfe County*, **GEORGE D. CRENSHAW**, farmer, was head of house with wife **LESSIE CRENSHAW** (age 27), son **GEORGE H. CRENSHAW** (age 1 year and 7 months) and **GEORGE FREEMAN**, his brother-in-law (age 29). They lived in Sulphur Well District #2. Census was enumerated on January 29, 1920.

19681. **GEORGE HENRY CRENSHAW** (May 3, 1918 - December 8, 1947) the son of **GEORGE DUFF CRENSHAW**, committed suicide by shooting himself in the head with a shotgun. George H. was buried next to his parents in Metcalfe County, KY.

19682. **JENNIE ELIZABETH CRENSHAW** (February 12, 1925 - April 19, 1925). Buried near her parents in Metcalfe County.

1969. **PEARL EUGENIA CRENSHAW** (September 7, 1892 - October 15, 1976) was the youngest child of **HENRY ANDERSON CRENSHAW and MARTHA ALICE EMBREE.** Born at Knob Lick in Metcalfe County, KY., she married **WILLIAM HENRY "WILL" PEDEN** (Oct. 13, 1891 - Feb. 24, 1944), only son of **ELMORE "MOTE" PEDEN** (1865-1941) and **JANIE TERRY ROGERS** (1867-1960), and grandson of **EDMUND HARLIN PEDEN** (1838-1914) and **SARAH D. WATTS** (1842-1880), and **CHARLES BAGBY ROGERS** (1840-1919) and **SARAH MOSS FORBIS** (1843-1921). SARAH D. WATTS was a daughter of **BENNETT S. WATTS** (1809-1874) and **NANCY HAYES** (1808-1878), and a granddaughter of **DAVID WATTS** and **ELIZABETH CRENSHAW** (d. 1851). Will and Pearl obtained a marriage license in Wayne County, Kentucky, and were married on December 29, 1913. Their marriage was recorded in Barren County, Kentucky. They were separated around 1934. Pearl kept a scrapbook of newspaper clippings from 1913 to 1944, which has been copied and included in this book since they contain lots of information on the family, friends and acquaintances from this time period which may be of interest to the family. Will Peden was a prominent tobacco farmer and mule logger in the years prior to the Great Depression. He subsequently lost three farms after the Crash of 1929, including the beautiful Weldon place (once called "Adairland") in the Goodnight area in northern Barren County. Only the family farm in the Lecta-Coral Hill section remained in the family. Will also operated the Blue Goose tavern (known in those times as a "roadhouse") located on Hwy. 31E, northeast of Glasgow, Kentucky. With the county voting itself dry in 1936, the Blue Goose was finally shutdown in January, 1942 (as were several other roadhouses). By this time Will and Pearl had divorced. **WILL PEDEN** died of heart block and cirrhosis of the liver on February 24, 1944. The funeral director was A. F. Crow, of Glasgow, Kentucky. The informant was his mother, **MRS. JANIE PEDEN**, of Route 2, Cave City, Kentucky. [Ref: *Commonwealth of Kentucky, Death Certificate No. 3351*, in Barren County, Kentucky; *Heart of the Barrens*, by Cecil E. Goode (1986), pp. 106-107; *Barren County Heritage*, by Cecil E. Goode, et al. (1980), p. 278; *Genealogy of the Pedens of Kentucky, 1756-1986*, by Henry C. Peden, Jr. (1986), pp. 92-94]. **PEARL EUGENIA CRENSHAW PEDEN** died at the Johnson Nursing Home in Glasgow, Kentucky, on October 15, 1976, of respiratory arrest, cerebral thrombosis and advanced generalized arteriosclerosis. A mistake on her death certificate gave her mother's name as Alice Emory, but it is "Embree" (sometimes spelled Embry). Pearl was buried in Glasgow Municipal Cemetery. The funeral director was Hatcher and Saddler, Glasgow, Kentucky. The informant was **MARY PEDEN**, of Glasgow. [Ref: *Commonwealth of Kentucky Death Certificate No. 116-76-22758*, dated October 15, 1976, Barren County, KY]. (Additional information on the Pedens is compiled in the book

Genealogy of the Pedens of Kentucky 1756-1986, by Henry Clint Peden, Jr., grandson of William Henry Peden and Pearl Eugenia Crenshaw. Book is available in many genealogical libraries.)

19691. **WILLIAM CLYDE PEDEN** (October 14, 1914 - July 30, 1977), eldest son of **WILLIAM HENRY PEDEN and PEARL E. CRENSHAW**, married **LEONA MORGAN** (1915-1962), a daughter of **HENRY MORGAN and MATTIE RABON WILLIAMS**. Clyde died of cancer in Glasgow, Kentucky and was buried in the Neal's Chapel Cemetery in the Lecta section of Barren County, Kentucky.

196911. **WILLIAM CLYDE PEDEN, JR.** (March 8, 1935, KY - June 10, 1991, TX, eldest son of **CLYDE PEDEN**) married (1) **PATSY LOUISE CARTER** in 1953, (2) **PATTY SUE COX** in 1963, and (3) **CAROL ANN KEMP**, daughter of **WILLIAM A. KEMP and MILDRED HAPP**, in 1969. Billy had two sons by each wife. Some of the family lives in Gilmer, Texas. He died of cancer and is buried in Glasgow, Kentucky.

1969111. **WILLIAM STANLEY PEDEN** (born 1955).

1969112. **CHARLES STEVEN PEDEN** (born 1958).

1969113. **WILLIAM ANTHONY PEDEN** (born 1964).

1969114. **JEFFREY SCOTT PEDEN** (born 1966) married **SAMMI JO BYRD** on June 23, 1984, in Metcalfe County, Kentucky.

1969115. **WILLIAM CURTISS PEDEN** (b. March 14, 1971).

1969116. **MITCHELL EUGENE PEDEN** (b. March 17, 1974).

196912. **AUBREY ALLEN PEDEN** (Nov. 8, 1937 - Dec. 4, 1937).

196913. **EUGENIA RABON PEDEN** (born March 27, 1939, KY) married **SETH THOMAS GROCE**, son of **TAYLOR ROBERT GROCE and CATHERINE DUGARD**, on December 23, 1955. Genie and Seth reside in Barren County, Kentucky.

1969131. **THOMAS ALLEN GROCE** (b. September 6, 1957) married **TAMARA KAY SIMMONS**, daughter of **DELMER SIMMONS**, on August 12, 1978.

1969132. **GARY LAWRENCE GROCE** (born April 11, 1964) married **MELISSA FAY GARRETT**, daughter of **CARL R. GARRETT**, on September 15, 1984.

196914. **LESLIE FRANK PEDEN** (born December 3, 1940, KY) married **SHIRLEY JEAN TAYLOR** (born July 30, 1941, daughter of **WILLIAM TAYLOR and RUIE PEARL HURT**) on July 11, 1959. Frank and Shirley reside in Glasgow, Kentucky.

1969141. **MARLA JO PEDEN** (born October 30, 1964) married **KEITH WOOD** on August 3, 1985.

1969142. **DONNA SUE PEDEN** (born August 3, 1958).

196915. **SHELBY RAY PEDEN** (born November 25, 1942, KY) married **KAREN SUE MAYES** (born on June 20, 1945, daughter of **JOHN T. MAYES and GLADYS NICHOLS**, of Virden, Illinois), in Macoupin County, Illinois, on December 21, 1961. Ray and Karen reside in Gladewater, Texas.

1969151. **BEVERLEY JEAN PEDEN** (b. November 25, 1962 in Charleston, South Carolina) married to **DANIEL RAY VESS**, in Perrysville, Ohio, on July 3, 1981. Beverley and Dan reside in Fort Walton Beach, Florida.

19691511. **JAMIN RAY VESS** (born March 5, 1983, in Milton, Florida).

19691512. **TIA DANIELLE VESS** (born July 12, 1986, in Pensacola, Florida).

1969152. **CONNIE SUE PEDEN** (born April 15, 1966) married **CARL RILEY JACKSON** on June 23, 1984, in Smithwick, Texas.

19691521. **CARL RILEY JACKSON II** (born Dec. 16, 1985, Austin, Texas).

19691522. **CHRISTOPHER WAYNE JACKSON** (born April 25, 1989, Austin, Texas).

19691523. **CHARLES LEVI JACKSON** (born June 9, 1992, Austin, Texas).

1969153. **KENNETH RAY PEDEN** (born March 5, 1969) married **NENA LYNETTE HINES** in Longview, Texas, on December 31, 1986.

19691531. **BRADLEY RAY PEDEN** (born July 25, 1987, Longview, Texas).

19691532. **ELIZABETH CHRISTINE PEDEN** (born Feb. 8, 1989, Longview, Texas).

19691533. **ALEXANDER SCOTT PEDEN** (born

May 2, 1992, Shreveport, LA).

196916. **HENRY LEE PEDEN** (born February 18, 1944, KY) married (1) **PEGGY COX**, and (2) **SANDRA HOUCHENS**.

1969161. **TERESA FAYE PEDEN** (born 1965) married **JOHN R. RIDDLE, JR.**, son of **JOHN RIDDLE and PHILLIS ----**, on October 30, 1982.

19691611. **DANIEL LEROY RIDDLE** (born July 21, 1983).

1969162. **KAREN LEE PEDEN** (born September 26, 1970). married ---- **CONNER**.

196917. **JAMES MAXIE PEDEN** (born January 6, 1946, Kentucky) married **CHERRY FAY BRADSHAW** (born June 14, 1949, a daughter of **TEVIE JOHN BRADSHAW II** (1914-1978) and **JESSIE GOODE**) on March 20, 1965, Barren County, KY.

1969171. **BOBBI DAWN PEDEN** (born November 2, 1966) married **JEFFREY EDWARDS** on July 9, 1982.

19691711. **TRINITY JADE EDWARDS** (born January 5, 1982).

19691712. **MORGAN TURNER EDWARDS** (born 1985).

1969172. **JAMA MONIK PEDEN** (born February 26, 1973). Student at Western Kentucky University.

1969173. **JIMMY ROSCOE PEDEN** (born March 8, 1977).

196918. **DOROTHY FAYE PEDEN** (born April 3, 1948, Kentucky) married **JESSE ROSCOE BRADSHAW** (born April 18, 1944, son of **TEVIE JOHN BRADSHAW II** (1914-1978) and wife **JESSIE GOODE**) in 1963. Faye and J. R. Bradshaw live in Temple Hill, Barren County, Kentucky.

1969181. **TINA LYNN BRADSHAW** (born July 13, 1964) married **WAYNE THOMAS HALL** (born Nov. 14, 1958) on December 2, 1982. Tina and Tom live in Frankfort, Kentucky, where Tom is a preacher in the Church of Christ.

19691811. **SUMMER CHANTE HALL** (born October 28, 1983).

19691812. **JENILYN HALL** (born August 16, 1985).

1969182. **KEVIN DALE BRADSHAW** (born July 19, 1965)

married **BETH HODGES** (born Nov. 30, 1965) on May 18, 1985.

19691821. **CHELSIE TATE BRADSHAW** (born January 26, 1988).

19691822. **COLBY NASH BRADSHAW** (born July 30, 1989).

1969183. **MICHELLE DENISE BRADSHAW** (born April 4, 1968) married **TODD CLEMMONS**; divorced.

19691831. **JOSHUA TODD CLEMMONS** (born September 14, 1988).

1969184. **JENNIFER JILL BRADSHAW** (born June 20, 1975).

19692. **MARY EUGENIA PEDEN** (March 11, 1916 - October 7, 1994), the eldest daughter of **WILLIAM H. PEDEN and PEARL E. CRENSHAW**, was married twice: (1) **SHELBY STEVENS**; (2) **MARVIN SHELLEY**. Divorced twice. No children. Mary died of cancer in Bowling Green, Kentucky and she was buried in the Glasgow Municipal Cemetery. Her will was probated in Barren County, Kentucky.

19693. **KATHLEEN PEDEN** (November 18, 1917 - February 4, 1920), the second daughter of **WILLIAM H. PEDEN and PEARL E. CRENSHAW**, was buried in Glasgow Municipal Cem. in Glasgow, Kentucky.

19694. **DORTHY DEPP PEDEN** (April 3, 1919 - December 16, 1988), third daughter of **WILLIAM H. PEDEN and PEARL E. CRENSHAW**, was married twice: (1) **ORLIN ROLLIN "DOC" FROEDGE** in 1939; and, (2) **PAUL JEFFERSON GOAD**, in 1946; both from Kentucky. Dorthy lived in Lake Placid, Florida for 16 years before her death in Arcadia, Florida. She died of cancer and was buried in the Oak Hill Cemetery in Lake Placid, Florida. [Ref: Obituaries in *The Lake Placid The News-Sun*, December 18, 1988, and *The Glasgow Republican*, December 22, 1988].

196941. **DON TRAVIS FROEDGE** (born January 17, 1943, KY) married twice: (1) **MARY MARSHA RIDDLE** in 1967, no children, divorced; (2) **MONICA CLAIRE KASICK** (born January 6, 1955) married November 24, 1990. D. T. and Monica reside in Glasgow, Kentucky.

1969411. **MAXWELL TRAVIS FROEDGE** (b. April 27, 1993).

1969412. **---- FROEDGE** (son expected in April, 1995).

196942. **PAULA GAIL GOAD** (born November 3, 1946, Kentucky) married **ROGER DOUGLAS LYONS** (born June 2, 1943) on July 4, 1964, in Barren County, Kentucky.

1969421. **ROGER DOUGLAS LYONS, JR.** (born April 9, 1966) married twice: (1) **TRACY LEE PEDIGO** on June 15, 1991; and, (2) **MELISSA THOMAS** on March 25, 1995.

1969422. **GREGORY ALLEN LYONS** (born July 10, 1967).

1969423. **SONYA BETH LYONS** (born April 16, 1971).

196943. **LARRY DEPP GOAD** (born August 18, 1948) married **WANDA WILLIAMS**; divorced.

1969431. **KIMBERLY DAWN GOAD** (born May 13, 1971).

1969432. **LARRY TIMOTHY GOAD** (born June 21, 1974).

196944. **BONNIE RAE GOAD** (born July 23, 1949, KY) married (1) **LARRY DELK**, (2) **PHILIP JOLLY**, (3) **---- STEWART**, and (4) **DONALD DRIGGERS**. Lives in Lake Placid, Fla.

1969441. **KRISTIE RAE DRIGGERS** (born March 3, 1972).

1969442. **MITZI DAWN DRIGGERS** (b. January 26, 1980).

1969443. **HARDIE DONALD DRIGGERS** (b. Sept. 23, 1981).

196945. **JO ANN GOAD** (born January 30, 1951) married (1) **--- PAYNE**, and (2) **DONNY SANDERS THOMAS**, November, 1984.

1969451. **MELISSA GAIL PAYNE** (born March 16, 1970) married **ANTHONY VERNON**.

19694511. **HAILEY PAIGE VERNON** (born November 20, 1992).

1969452. **JAMES FRANK PAYNE** (born August 20, 1971).

1969453. **TIFFANY JO THOMAS** (born May 4, 1988).

196946. **PAUL JEFFERSON GOAD, JR.** (born November 7, 1956).

1969461. **WINDY NATALIE GOAD** (born August 17, 1980).

1969462. **PAUL JEFFERSON GOAD III** (b. Mar. 19, 1982).

19695. **HENRY CLINT PEDEN** (born May 30, 1921, in Barren County, KY, on the old Foster place near Lecta), second son of **WILLIAM HENRY "WILL" PEDEN and PEARL EUGENIA CRENSHAW**, married **MARY CATHERINE FRANK** (born May 19, 1926, in Baltimore County, MD, the daughter of **WALTER REMINGTON FRANK** (1894-1960) and **RUBY NORRIS CADLE** (1898-1960), of Baltimore and Harford Counties respectively. Clint and Catherine married on June 14, 1942, in Elkton, Cecil County, Maryland. Clint is a retired truck driver and a U. S. Army veteran who served in World War II. They live near Kearneysville, Jefferson Co., West Virginia.

196951. **CAROL ANN PEDEN** (born March 16, 1943, Baltimore, MD, the eldest daughter of **HENRY CLINT PEDEN and MARY CATHERINE FRANK**) married (1) **LOYNEL DELMORE WILLIAMS** (born April 15, 1936, Greenbrier Co., West Va., son of **LOYNEL NEWTON WILLIAMS and IVA BELLE MORRISON**), on December 1, 1962, in Baltimore County, Maryland; divorced, July, 1974; md. (2) **ARTHUR WAYNE MICHAEL** (b. May 9, 1939, a son of **GROVER and OPAL MICHAEL**), on June 21, 1975, Baltimore County, Maryland. They reside in Middle River, Baltimore County, Maryland.

1969511. **REBECCA LYNN WILLIAMS** (born July 5, 1964) married **RONALD LEE SANZONE** (born August 19, 1963, in Baltimore, MD) on June 9, 1983. They reside in Harford County, Maryland.

19695111. **RONALD LEE SANZONE, JR.** (born November 30, 1990, Baltimore, MD)

19695112. **ROBERT LUKAS SANZONE.** (born August 29, 1993, Baltimore, MD)

1969512. **CYNTHIA ANN WILLIAMS** (b. September 6, 1968) married **DONALD LEE MEINSCHEIN** (b. July 28, 1960) on November 15, 1986, Baltimore, MD.

19695121. **BRYAN JAMES MEINSCHEIN.** (born July 11, 1991, Baltimore County, MD)

196952. **HENRY CLINT PEDEN, JR.** (born November 4, 1946, at old Franklin Square Hospital, Baltimore, Maryland, son of **HENRY CLINT PEDEN and MARY CATHERINE FRANK**) married **VERONICA ANN CLARKE** (born January 30, 1950, the daughter of **GERALD LUKE CLARKE** (1909-1982) and **VERONICA MARY PAPSA** (1912-   ), on July 11, 1970, at St. Mary's Star of the Sea Church, Baltimore, MD. Hank served in the U. S. Air Force (1966-1970, Staff Sergeant) and was in Cam Rahn Bay, Vietnam, in 1968. He later earned a master's degree from Towson State University (near Baltimore), and is certified by the National Board for the Certification of Genealogists. Hank and Roni reside in Bel Air, Harford County, MD.

1969521. **HENRY CLINT PEDEN III** (b. January 27, 1971).

196953. **LINDA MARLENE PEDEN** (born May 25, 1949, Maryland), a daughter of **HENRY CLINT PEDEN and MARY CATHERINE FRANK**, married **RICHARD ANDREW NOLL** on December 5,

1970. Reside in Mt. Washington, Baltimore, Maryland.

1969531. **DANIELLE RENEE NOLL** (born July 31, 1972). Graduate of George Washington University.

1969532. **MICHELLE MAREE NOLL** (born March 24, 1975). Student at Tulane University in Louisiana.

1969533. **LYNNELLE MARLENE NOLL** (born March 7, 1978).

1969534. **WILLIAM PEDEN NOLL** (born Sept. 22, 1984).

19696. **EWELL ELMORE "DUGAN" PEDEN** (born December 5, 1924), third son of **WILLIAM HENRY PEDEN and PEARL EUGENIA CRENSHAW**, was married thrice: (1) **JEAN SAVIEU**, (2) **CORDELIA EATMON**, and, (3) **M. SALLEY A. ----**. He had two children by his second wife Cordelia, and three by his third wife, Salley. From Barren County, Kentucky, he moved to Fresno, California, where he has been a businessman for the past forty years. Dugan is a U. S. Army veteran and served in World War II.

196961. **THERESA YVONNE PEDEN** (born October 26, 1948, KY) married (1) **BLAINE SNAVELY**, and they had a son; and, married (2) **JAMES CARLISLE**. Divorced twice. Theresa resides in Fresno, California.

1969611. **CHAD DUGAN BLAINE SNAVELY** (b. July 14, 1972)

196962. **EWELL CLAYTON PEDEN** (born September 10, 1950, KY) married twice (and divorced twice) in California.

1969621. **DUGAN JASON PEDEN** (born in October, 1970).

1969622. **MARK A. PEDEN** (born in February, 1975).

196963. **HARVEY KYLE PEDEN** (born February 4, 1986).

196964. **KRYSTAL HAVEN PEDEN** (born May 4, 1987).

196965. **WILL TRAVIS PEDEN** (born April 5, 1990).

19697. **HARLAN CHARLES PEDEN** (born January 3, 1927, KY), fourth son of **WILLIAM HENRY "WILL" PEDEN and PEARL EUGENIA CRENSHAW**, married **THELMA BEATRICE CRABTREE** (born on November 22, 1931, daughter of **CHARLIE CRABTREE and ELIZABETH ELLEN HOWELL**) on June 2, 1951 in Jeffersonville, Indiana. Harlan is a retired teacher from the Kentucky School System, having received his degree from Western Kentucky University. He also served in the U. S. Army. Harlan and Thelma reside in Lecta, Kentucky.

196971. **HARLAN CHARLES PEDEN II** (born August 3, 1952, KY) married **GEORGE ANN ROGERS** (born August 14, 1953, a daughter of **DORIS EVERETT ROGERS and EVELYN GOODWIN**) on June 29, 1975, in Hopkinsville, Christian County, Kentucky. Harlan is a school teacher and earned his master's degree from the University of Kentucky. Ann earned her doctorate from the University of Alabama and teaches at the University of Kentucky. Harlan and Ann reside in Lexington, Fayette Co., Kentucky.

1969711. **HARLAN CHARLES PEDEN** III (b. April 13, 1982)

196972. **PAMELA ANN PEDEN** (born November 13, 1953, Kentucky) married **RANDY BROWN NALLY** (born November 12, 1950) on August 10, 1974, in Webster County, Kentucky. Pam and Randy reside near Dixon in Webster County, Kentucky. Randy is a veteran of the Vietnam War.

1969721. **HEATHER DAWN NALLY** (born March 26, 1976).

1969722. **NICHOLAS RICE NALLY** (born March 17, 1979).

196973. **JANICE DELL PEDEN** (born February 20, 1957, KY) married **RICKEY LEE BROWN** (born March 7, 1953) on January 5, 1976, in Shawneetown, Illinois. Janice and Rickey reside near Dixon, Webster County, KY.

1969731. **MANDY LEE BROWN** (born February 17, 1977).

196974. **SCOTT TALBOT PEDEN** (born November 4, 1963, KY) married **MARCIE LYNETTE ATWELL** (born April 1, 1971, daughter of **DANNY ATWELL and PATRICIA POINTER**) on December 26, 1992, at Park Methodist Church. He has a master's degree from Western Kentucky University. Scott and Marcie reside in Lecta, Barren Co., KY.

196975. **VAN JASON PEDEN** (born January 10, 1969, Kentucky) married **JONI CAROL WADDELL** (born March 12, 1974, daughter of **J. C. WADDELL and NORMA RUTH NUNN**, of Metcalfe County, Kentucky) on December 29, 1990, at the Coral Hill Church of Christ. He received a bachelor's degree from Western Kentucky University. Jason and Joni reside in Three Springs, Kentucky. They are expecting their first child in May, 1995.

19698. **CLAYTON LOUIS PEDEN** (born June 12, 1930, KY), youngest son of **WILLIAM HENRY "WILL" PEDEN and PEARL EUGENIA CRENSHAW**, married **HELENE BARBARA KOPP** (born December 10, 1937, the daughter of **GABRIEL JOHN KOPP and HELEN LOUISE WARREN** of Tacoma, Washington) on September 30, 1955, in Tacoma, and resides in Lecta-Coral Hill section of Barren County, KY. Clayton is a U. S. Air Force veteran of the Korean War, a tobacco farmer, and an accomplished guitarist and artist. The former owner of Peden's Curiosity Shop in Glasgow, KY,

Clayton is currently constructing Dogwood Valley, an open air entertainment theatre near Coral Hill, Barren Co., KY.

196981. **PATRICIA LYNN PEDEN** (born August 27, 1956, KY) married **JOSEPH THEODORE WINLOCK III** in 1974. Divorced; no children. She lives in California.

196982. **SANDRA LEE PEDEN** (born September 26, 1958, KY) married (1) **JIMMY MOONEY**, (2) **MICHAEL THOMAS**, and (3) **BOYD DAVIS**. They live in Barren County.

1969821. **DANIEL HEATH MOONEY** (born May, 1978).

196983. **BRUCE WAYNE PEDEN** (twin, born July 9, 1962, KY) married **LINDA GAYLE DEVASHER** (born on January 13, 1961, daughter of **WILLIAM A. DEVASHER and SHIRLEY MARR**) on July 31, 1982. Bruce and Linda live in the Lecta-Coral Hill section of Barren Co., KY.

1969831. **BRADLEY WAYNE PEDEN** (born Feb. 24, 1989).

1969832. **LAURA GALE PEDEN** (born March 28, 1991).

196984. **BRIAN LOUIS PEDEN** (twin, born July 9, 1962, KY) married **JANET SMITH** (born July 5, 1963), who had two sons by a previous marriage, Ben and Brad Wood. They were married July 11, 1993, but subsequently divorced. Brian lives in Barren County, Kentucky.

196985. **DON CLAYTON PEDEN** (born October 26, 1964, KY) married **CYNTHIA ANNE BAGBY** (born August 30, 1963, daughter of **ROBERT FRANKLIN BAGBY and CATHERINE ARABELLE BOWLES**) on May 16, 1986, in Glasgow, KY. Don and Cynthia live in Barren County, Kentucky.

1969851. **WESLEY CLAY PEDEN** (born July 20, 1989).

1969852. **TREVOR BENJAMIN PEDEN** (born Oct. 13, 1992).

196986. **MICHAEL TRAVIS PEDEN** (born July 12, 1970) married **TINA LYNN KERR** on June 12, 1993. Mike and Tina live in the Lecta-Coral Hill section of Barren Co., KY.

196987. **ANTHONY DEAN PEDEN** (born January 26, 1977, KY).

CHAPTER TWO

THE DESCENDANTS OF BENJAMIN CRENSHAW (c1745-1828)

2. **BENJAMIN CRENSHAW** (c1745-1828) was in Barren County by 1801 when his son, **BENJAMIN MILLS CRENSHAW**, was born (as noted in the census of 1850 when Benjamin Mills Crenshaw said he was born in Kentucky). Franklin Gorin also states in *The Times of Long Ago* that Benjamin Crenshaw was "an old pioneer of Barren County" (page 119). He owned two mills west of Glasgow on Beaver Creek that had been once owned by Simeon Buford and which were originally owned by Killian Kreek at the time of the creation of Barren County in 1799. In August, 1808, Benjamin Crenshaw applied for "a new road for traveling to and from the neighborhood of Henry Hailey's to the said Crenshaw's Lower Mill on Beaver Creek, beginning at said mill to intersect the road leading from the courthouse to Amos' Ferry, said proposed road being within Barren County." [Ref: *Barren County Order Book No. 3*, pp. 60, 63, 67, 83, 102, 105]. **BENJAMIN CRENSHAW** was listed in the 1809 Barren County List of Tithables and he owned no slaves. [Ref: *Traces*, Volume 16, No. 2, Summer, 1988, p. 68]. In July, 1811, he was appointed surveyor (overseer) of the road from his Lower Mill to the courthouse and to keep the same road in repair 18 feet wide. [Ref: *Barren County Order Book No. 3*, p. 121]. This matter over a proper road was in court for a number of years. Subsequent entries in the county's order books constantly refer to this issue through April, 1813, when the matter of "Benjamin Crenshaw's (formerly Buford's) Mill was still under review by the court over the issue of the new road's direction." [Ref: *Barren County Order Book No. 4*, page 25]. In August, 1814, the Court ordered the lines and corners of Benjamin Crenshaw's land to be re-marked. [Ref: *Ibid.*, page 56].

BENJAMIN CRENSHAW wrote his will on February 26, 1828, and he apparently died before July, 1828, when it was probated in Barren County. He named his wife **TABITHA CRENSHAW**, son **THOMAS CRENSHAW** and his heirs and his present wife, son **BENJAMIN MILLS CRENSHAW** and his heirs, son-in-law **GEORGE DUKE** and his heirs, and son-in-law **FLEMING SHORT** and his heirs. (It should be pointed out that the *1810 Census of Barren County* stated that there were 5 young boys (probably his sons), but only two were named in his will in 1828.) His inventory and estate sale were in December, 1828. [Ref: *Barren County Will Book No. 2*, pp. 417, 591, 593]. In *Barren County Cemeteries*, Vol. I, page 6, it states that a **BENJAMIN CRENSHAW**, aged 70, died on November 26, 1925 [sic]. Buried beside him are **TABITHA CRENSHAW** (died in 1841, "supposedly aged 90 years old") and one **WILLIAM W. CRENSHAW** (January 4, 1836 - November 8, 1842), [grandson?]. They are all buried in the Old Short Family Cemetery near the Glasgow Airport and Mt. Tabor Church Cemetery. Not all the stones in this cemetery are legible, and also buried there are Fleming Short and wife Elizabeth Short, Pamelia Parrish, Harriet H. Wade (1830-1848), and Ann Eliza Thompson Wade (died in 1898). In all likelihood this Benjamin Crenshaw (c1745-1828) was also buried in this cemetery.

The relationship between Benjamin Crenshaw (c1745-1828) and our John Crenshaw (1759-1818) has not been determined, but in reviewing records in colonial Virginia it was discovered that they were both in Louisa County around the same time. This is known because of the above mentioned tombstone inscriptions and the following item from the land records: "**BENJAMIN CRENSHAW JR. AND TABITHA, HIS WIFE,** OF LOUISA COUNTY" sold land on south fork of Fork Creek (on Pamunkey River, in Trinity Parish) in Louisa County, 845 acres, "whereon he formerly lived, to Hastings Mark on June 9, 1800, it being the same land purchased by said Crenshaw from William Price as by deed dated November 26, 1786." [Ref: *Louisa Co. Deed Book J:33*, and *The Edward Pleasants Valentine Papers*, Vol. I, p. 368, 371]. He was likely the son of **BENJAMIN CRENSHAW, AND WIFE ELIZABETH,** OF GOOCHLAND COUNTY, Virginia, who also sold 365 acres on Fork Creek in Louisa County to William Isbell on April 13, 1789. [Ref: *Louisa Co. Deed Book F:408*, and *The Edward Pleasants Valentine Papers*, p. 369]. The ancestry of Benjamin Crenshaw ends here as it is uncertain who his parents were and this line is not discussed in *Crenshaws and Connecting Families* by Hazel Crenshaw Wilkins (1981). [**My Note:** As for his descendants I have the following information, which is quite incomplete at this time. Their family line begins with the No. "2" since our Crenshaw family line has been assigned the No. "1" as I explained earlier].

BENJAMIN CRENSHAW JR. (c1745-1828), of Louisa County, Virginia, son of **BENJAMIN AND ELIZABETH CRENSHAW,** sold his land in Virginia in 1799 and moved to Kentucky, settling in western Barren County, where he owned two mills (noted earlier). He married **TABITHA ----** prior to migrating to Kentucky, and they had at least two sons and two daughters, namely Thomas, Benjamin, Nancy, and Elizabeth. One Benjamin Crenshaw was active in the Mt. Tabor Baptist Church, and at their March, 1819, meeting, the minutes recorded that "**BENJAMIN CRENSHAW,** formerly a member of this church, came forward with such a recantation as met general approbation. He was then restored to the fellowship of the church." [Ref: *Heart of the Barrens*, by Cecil E. Goode (1986), page 86]. **BENJAMIN CRENSHAW** died in 1828 and his wife Tabitha died in 1841. As noted earlier, they had 4 children.

21. **NANCY CRENSHAW** (1767, Virginia -), the eldest daughter of **BENJAMIN and TABITHA CRENSHAW,** married **GEORGE DUKE** and had children at the advanced age of 53. [Ref: *Kentucky Genealogy and Biography*, Vol. I, page 88]. In the *1850 Census of Barren County, Kentucky*, **NANCY DUKE** (age 83, born Virginia) lived in the house of **THOMAS T. DUKE** (age 43, born Virginia) in 1850. **GEORGE DUKE** was a member of the Mt. Tabor Baptist Church in 1811, and **NANCY DUKE** was baptized there in August, 1819, as was **SALLY CRENSHAW and THOMAS CRENSHAW.** [Ref: *Pioneer Baptist Church Records of South-Central Kentucky and Upper Cumberland of Tennessee, 1799-1899*, by C. P. Cawthorn and N. L. Warnell (1985), pp. 78-79]. **GEORGE DUKE** was a native of Virginia and one of the earliest pioneers in Barren County, Kentucky. He was a veteran of the War of 1812 and a member of the Baptist

Church. [Ref: *Ky. Genealogy and Biography*, Vol. II, p. 129]. **GEORGE DUKE** died testate in Barren County and his will which was written on January 7, 1847 (with codicils on January 28, 1848, and July 25, 1849) was probated in October term, 1849. He was a wealthy man, owning many slaves, a lot of land and personal property, plus stock in a local turnpike company. He named his wife **NANCY DUKE**, sons **ALBERT DUKE** and **FOUNTAIN DUKE**, and daughters **ELIZABETH PARRISH, SARAH ANN MIDDLETON, POLLY PARRISH, and TABITHA DICKEY**. The aforementioned **THOMAS T. DUKE** was not mentioned. Therefore, since all the children of George Duke are unidentified, it is assumed that another was **COSBY DUKE**. There undoubtedly were others not shown here.

211. **MARY (POLLY) DUKE** married **FLEMING T. PARRISH** in 1827 and died on October 17, 1858. Fleming T. was born on December 3, 1800/1, and died on February 11, 1846. His parents, **PARKS (PARKES) PARRISH and ELIZABETH TISDELL (or TISDALE)**, of Louisa or Hanover County, Virginia, migrated to Kentucky in 1817. **FLEMING T. PARRISH** was buried in Parrish Cemetery at Goodnight in Barren County, KY. Mary was 43 (or 44) in 1850. The heirs of **PARKS PARRISH** are named in an equity case in Barren County, Kentucky, filed March 21, 1831 (Case No. 520), noting that he and his wife have deceased and their heirs petitioned the court to sell his land and divide it equally among them. [Ref: *Traces*, Vol. 12, No. 3 (Fall, 1984), p. 84].

2111. **SARILDA MAGDALEN PARRISH**, the daughter of Fleming Parrish and Mary Duke, married **WADDY W. THOMPSON** on November 14, 1847, in Barren County, Kentucky. Surety: **ALBERT DUKE**. [It should be noted that Waddy and Sarilda were not found in the 1850 or 1860 census records for Barren and Metcalfe Counties, Kentucky].

2112. **HENRY C. PARRISH** (June 13, 1831 -), son of Fleming T. Parrish and Mary Duke, married **FANNY DUFF**, youngest daughter of **HUBBARD DUFF** (October 3, 1793 - 1845), of Virginia, and **SARAH DRANE** (Nov. 9, 1796 - April 2, 1843, a daughter of **ANTHONY and CATHERINE DRANE**, of Maryland) on Sept. 10, 1856. Hubbard and Sarah Duff are buried in the Parrish Cemetery at Goodnight in Barren County, KY. [Ref: *Barren County Cemeteries*, Volume II, by Eva Coe Peden (1981), p. 189]. **HENRY C. PARRISH and wife FANNY DUFF** lived near Horse Cave in Hart County, Kentucky, but they are not in the Parrish Cemetery at Goodnight where her parents are buried.

One "H. C. PARRISH" was a Messenger of the Salem Baptist Church in Barren County in 1856, and was not listed again until 1888. [Ref: *The Pioneer Baptist Church Records of South-Central Kentucky and Upper Cumberland of Tennessee, 1799-1899*, by C. P. Cawthorn and N. L. Warnell (1985), page 110]. In the *1860 Census of Barren County*, **HY. C. PARRISH** (age 29) was head of household in District No. 1, with **FANNIE PARRISH** (age 21), **GEORGE D. PARRISH** (age 3), and **FLORENCE B. PARRISH** (age 1), along with two others named Thomas Wilson (age 23, merchant) and Elisha Budwell (age 47, saddler) listed with them. In the *1870 Census of Barren County*, Henry Parrish and family lived in the Cave City Precinct. His real estate was valued at $7500 in 1870.

21121. **GEORGE D. PARRISH** (born 1857/8).

21122. **FLORENCE B. PARRISH** (June 10, 1859 - July 8, 1893) married **W. PERRY SUMMERS** (1855-). Florence was buried in the Summers Cemetery east of Hiseville on the Barren-Metcalfe County line, but there was no tombstone there for Perry. [Ref: *Barren County Cemeteries*, Vol. I]

211221. **BETTIE F. SUMMERS** (October 25, 1892 -July 19, 1893)

21123. **MARY MAUD PARRISH** (born 1861).

21124. **S. CORINNE PARRISH** (born 1863).

21125. **ADDIE C. PARRISH.**

2113. **GEORGE W. PARRISH** (August, 1840 -). In 1860, George was a farm laborer (age 19) in Barren County, KY, and was listed in the census with **BURREL THOMPSON** (age 21), **JOHN TWYMAN** (age 35), **SARAH C. TWYMAN** (age 27), **WILLIAM R. TWYMAN** (age 4 1/2), and **FANNY E. TWYMAN** (age 3) in Glasgow District No. 1. He married **MARTHA ----** (born 1847, KY), and they lived in Cave City Magisterial Dist. 2 in the *1880 Census of Barren County, KY*. In 1900 George was a farmer in Barren County's District No. 4 with his wife **MATTIE PARRISH** (born July, 1846), whom he married in 1872. **RICHARD J. MUNFORD** boarded with them in 1900.

The 1900 census also stated that George and Mattie had 6 children; only 4 were living.

21131. **ELIZABETH M. PARRISH** (born Dec. 1873) married ---- **COLEMAN** in 1898. Lizzie was living with her parents in 1900.

21132. **OSCAR L. PARRISH** (December 6, 1874 - July 2, 1901) married **SUSIE D. WALTON** (August 25, 1876 - August 10, 1908) in 1899. They lived with his parents in the *1900 Census of Barren County*. They are buried in Hiseville Cemetery.

21133. **ALLIE PARRISH** (daughter, born 1878).

21134. **MILTON PARRISH** (born December, 1882).

212. **THOMAS T. DUKE** (1807/8 -) married twice: (1) **ANN E. CURD** on May 14, 1835; and (2) **ELVIRA MALONE** on October 16, 1849. Elvira was age 37 in the *1850 Census of Barren County, KY*. Thomas' mother, **NANCY DUKE** (age 83, born in Virginia), lived with them. **THOMAS T. DUKE** once owned the land that the town of Cave City, Kentucky, is now situated on. [Ref: *Traces*, Volume 16, No. 3 (Fall, 1988), page 107].

2121. **NANCY J. DUKE** (born 1836).

2122. **BENJAMIN B. DUKE** (September 4, 1837 - June 25, 1919) married **ANNIE R. WHITE** on January 20, 1882, in Barren County, but his first wife was **JENNIE C. ----** (April 28, 1836 - September 12, 1888). He was a Messenger in the Salem Baptist Church from 1874 to 1887. An 1877 entry listed the name as "**B. B. DUKE, JR.**" His name was actually Benjamin B. Duke, Sr. [Ref: Cawthorn and Warnell, *loc. cit.*] In the *1860 Census of Barren County, KY*, **BENJAMIN DUKE** (age 22, clerk) was listed in the household of **C. ROBERTS**, merchant. Ben married **JENNEY C. ----** (born 1839). They lived in Cave City Precinct in the *1870 Census of Barren County, Kentucky*, and in the Cave City Magisterial District No. 2 in the *1880 Census of Barren County*. **BENJAMIN B. DUKE** (age 72) and second wife **ANN R. DUKE** (age 64) were listed in the *1910 Census of Barren County*, Cave City District 6, indicating they had been married 18 years.

They were buried in the Duke Cemetery near Cave City, off Route 685 to Goodnight, KY.

21221. **ANNA (ANNIE) M. DUKE** (born 1866).

21222. **JAMES P. DUKE** (born 1869).

21223. **THOMAS J. DUKE** (born July, 1872) married **LOUREIDE TAYLOR** (March 10, 1879 - December 16, 1913) in 1896. They lived near Cave City in 1900.

212231. **BENJAMIN (BENNIE) BELL DUKE** (born April, 1898).

212232. **LUCY MAYME DUKE** (born 1900).

21224. **JOHN H. DUKE** (Aug. 6, 1873 - Sept. 9, 1906) married **J. W. ----** and they were buried in Duke Cemetery near Cave City.

212241. **LAURA C. DUKE** (Jan. 16, 1901 - June 16, 1907)

212242. **INFANT DAUGHTER** (born and died Oct. 12, 1905)

21225. **BENJAMIN B. DUKE, JR.** (Sept. 25, 1875- May 19, 1955) married **LIZZIE B. ----** b. August 11, 1879) in 1897. Lived in Cave City Precinct No. 6 at the time of the *1920 Census of Barren County, Kentucky*. **BEN B. DUKE** was a farmer. They are buried in Cave City Cemetery.

212251. **ANNIE MAE DUKE** (Aug. 30, 1898- June 25, 1946) married **SAMUEL B. DICKEY** (1886-1945) and were buried in Cave City Cemetery.

212252. **DOVIE W. DUKE** (June 6, 1901 - March 4, 1926) married **C. W. WILLIAMS** and died giving birth. Buried in Cave City Cemetery.

2122521. **JULIA E. WILLIAMS** (died at birth on March 2, 1926).

21226. **PATTIE B. DUKE** (September 10, 1878 - November 4, 1881).

21227. **JENNIE M. DUKE** (December 4, 1882 - July 14, 1900).

2123. **JESSE T. DUKE** (born 1842).

2124. **WILLIAM T. DUKE** (March 18, 1846 - March 29, 1928) married **ELIZABETH R. ----** (March 10, 1851 - May 27, 1924). They were buried in Smiths Grove Cemetery in Warren County, KY. [Ref: *South Central Kentucky Historical and Genealogical Society Quarterly*, Volume 5, No. 4, January, 1978, pages 112-114].

21241. **BENJAMIN OSCAR DUKE** (May 19, 1874 - March 9, 1911) was buried in Smiths Grove Cemetery next to his parents. He might have married to **DELILA ----** (1884-1963) who is buried next to him and **CHARLES WHITLOW DUKE** (1911-1913).

21242. **ADDIE DUKE** (August 19, 1875 - Sept. 1, 1956) married **---- TUCKER**, and she was buried in the Smiths Grove Cemetery.

21243. **HALLIE H. DUKE** (1877-1964) was buried in the Smiths Grove Cemetery.

21244. **ERNEST PAYTON DUKE** (October 17, 1879-October 23, 1902) was buried in Smiths Grove Cemetery in Warren County, KY.

21245. **ROYAL A. DUKE** (November 18, 1883 - March 10, 1884) was buried in Smiths Grove Cemetery in Warren County, KY.

21246. **ARCHIE DEAN DUKE** (May 8, 1885-Nov. 7, 1887) was buried in Smiths Grove Cem.

21247. **DAISY E. DUKE** (May 22, 1895 - July 22, 1895) was buried in Smiths Grove Cem.

213. **ELIZABETH DUKE** (1809-1855) married **PARKS T. PARRISH** on March 30, 1831, in Barren County. The surety was **GEORGE DUKE**. In the *1850 Census of Barren County* it states that Parks was age 50 (born 1800, Virginia) and his occupation was miner, with property valued at $5,000. **ELIZABETH PARRISH** was age 41 (born 1809). **PARKES (PARKS) T. PARRISH**, a son of **PARKES (PARKS) PARRISH and ELIZABETH TISDELL (or TISDALE)**, came to Barren County with his parents in 1817. In 1850 he "started for California in company with a party

of some thirty of his neighbors--of which he was selected captain--to seek a fortune. From Missouri the party accomplished all of the long journey on foot across the great American desert. Immediately they engaged in mining, reaped a rich harvest, and continued the same until his death October 2, 1850. He was buried upon the wharf at San Francisco where his remains still rest. He was a veteran of the War of 1812, having entered service in his 15th year. He and wife were life-long members of the Baptist Church." **PARKS T. PARRISH** was born in 1799 and died in 1850, and his wife, **ELIZABETH DUKE PARRISH**, died September 1, 1855, in her 47th year, in Barren Co., Kentucky. Her father, **GEORGE DUKE**, was a veteran of the War of 1812 (in Virginia), an early pioneer of Barren County, Kentucky, and a member of the Baptist Church. [Ref: *Kentucky Genealogy and Biography*, Vol. II, page 129; *South Central Kentucky Historical and Genealogial Society Quarterly*, Vol. 9, No. 2, p. 83]

2131. **ELIZABETH A. PARRISH** (born 1832, Kentucky) married **DR. EDMUND SHACKLEFORD** (born 1822) and they were living with her parents in the *1850 Census of Barren County, Kentucky*. In 1860 they lived in District No. 2. This census gave his age as 42 and hers as 27, and spelled his name "Edmd. Shacelford."

21311. **ROBERTA SHACKLEFORD** (born 1855).

21312. **ELIZABETH SHACKLEFORD** (born 1857).

2132. **BENJAMIN MILLS PARRISH** (August 23, 1836 -), a son of **PARKES T. PARRISH and ELIZABETH DUKE**, was born in Barren County, Kentucky, near the Hart County line. "He was educated at Urania College in Glasgow, Kentucky, where he was a very successful tobacco grower and dealer. He married **ELIZABETH E. HARE** (b. February 8, 1839, in Green County, Kentucky, a daughter of **WILLIAM HARE and NANCY MAXEY**) on Aug. 26, 1857. **B. MILLS PARRISH** was elected in 1877 to represent Barren County in the Lower House of the Kentucky Legislature. He was a member of the Masonic fraternity, and a member of the Christian Church; in politics, a Democrat. He had been three times a candidate for tobacco inspector at Louisville--a position which pays about $8,000 per annum--and was each time only beaten by one vote." [Ref: *Kentucky Genealogy and Biography*, Volume II, page 129]. In *1860*

Census of Barren County, B. **MILLS PARRISH** (age 24, farmer) was head of household in District No. 1, with **ELIZABETH E. PARRISH** (age 22) and **WILLIAM W. PARRISH** (age 1). Also listed was a **FRANCES PARRISH** (age 44, overseer). In 1870 he was a farmer in the Cave City Precinct of Barren County; real estate valued at $17,500. In the *1880 Census of Barren County*, his home included one R. J. **MUNFORD** (age 32, cousin, male) and a number of black labors/servants.

21321. **WILLIAM W. PARRISH** (born 1859).

21322. **EDMOND P. PARRISH** (born 1861).

21323. **CHARLES M. PARRISH** (born 1863).

21324. **ROBERT BURKE PARRISH** (born 1868).

21325. **JENNIE ROBERTA PARRISH** (born 1871).

2133. **N. ROBERTA PARRISH** (born 1841, Kentucky).

214. **COSBY DUKE**, possible son of **GEORGE DUKE and NANCY CRENSHAW**, wrote his will in Barren County, KY, on July 9, 1839 and it was probated in December, 1845. [Ref: *South Central Kentucky Historical Quarterly*, Volume 4, No. 3, October, 1976, page 63]. Since he pre-deceased George Duke, Cosby is not named in his will which was probated in Barren County in 1849.

2141. **JOHN E. DUKE** (born 1819) married **MARTHA ----** (born 1822) and lived in District No. 2 in *1860 Census of Barren County, KY*. **FOUNTAIN DUKE** (age 45) was also listed in his house. **MARTHA DUKE** died prior to the 1870 census, and John (age 63) was head of household in *1880 Census of Barren County* with youngest children, John (age 20) and Diana (age 17).

21411. **SARAH M. DUKE** (born 1847).

21412. **MARY J. DUKE** (born 1849).

21413. **JAMES C. DUKE** (born 1851).

21414. **ROBERT E. DUKE** (born 1854) married **PAULINE L. ----** (born 1855). They lived in Cave City District No. 6 in the *1920 Census of Barren County*.

21415. **E. A. DUKE** (daughter, born 1857). She was not listed in 1870 census.

21416. **JOHN A. DUKE** (born 1859).

21417. **DIANA T. DUKE** (born 1862).

2142. **THOMAS DUKE**, married **NANCY ----**.

21121. NANCY JANE DUKE.

215. **SARAH ANN DUKE**, daughter of **GEORGE DUKE and NANCY CRENSHAW**, was married to **GEORGE T. MIDDLETON** on June 11, 1835, by Rev. Jacob Lock, in Barren Co. She was named in her father's will in 1849. In the *1850 Census of Barren County*, George was age 35 (born 1815) and Sarah was age 38 (born 1812).

2151. **JAMES MIDDLETON** (born 1838). He may be the **GEORGE J. MIDDLETON** (August 12, 1836-June 5, 1904) who is buried in the Cave City Cemetery beside **TABITHA TUCKER.**

2152. **TABITHA MIDDLETON** (December 9, 1842 - October 3, 1919) married **---- TUCKER.** She was buried in Cave City Cemetery.

21521. **GEORGE T. TUCKER** (1893-1966) married **HELEN M. ----** (1893-1968). Buried in the Cave City Cemetery.

2153. **FOUNTAIN MIDDLETON** (born 1846).

2154. **NANCY MIDDLETON** (born 1849).

216. **FOUNTAIN DUKE** (October 1, 1814 - May 9, 1851), a son of GEORGE DUKE and NANCY CRENSHAW, was named in his father's will in Barren County, Kentucky, in October, 1849. In the *1850 Census of Barren County*, **FOUNTAIN DUKE** was age 35, a farmer, and lived alone. However, he had married **SARAH MARTIN** (December 31, 1818 - May 30, 1843), daughter of **CHARLES and POLLY MARTIN**, on October 30, 1838. All were buried in the Martin Cemetery west of Glasgow, Barren County, KY. [Ref: *Barren County Cemeteries*, Vol. II, page 125].

2161. **MARY DUKE** (Sept. 13, 1839 - Feb. 1, 1840).

217. **ALBERT DUKE** (1819-   ), son of **GEORGE DUKE and NANCY CRENSHAW**, was age 31 in the *1850 Census of Barren County*. He was single and living alone at the time.

In 1870 **ALBERT DUKE** (age 53) was listed in the Cave City Precinct as head of household and listed with him were **TABITHA DICKEY** (age 50), **CYRUS DICKEY** (age 26), **ELEANE DICKEY** (age 25), **GEORGE D. DICKEY** (age 20), and **HELLEN DICKEY** (age 17). The census taker indicated that **ALBERT DUKE**, a farmer, was blind.

218. **TABITHA A. DUKE** (1820-1906), daughter of **GEORGE DUKE and NANCY CRENSHAW**, married **ELISHA DICKEY** on May 23, 1842. Her father gave his permission to marry. [Ref: Martha Reneau's *Barren County Marriages*, page 67]. Elisha was considerably older than Tabitha, as the *1850 Census of Barren County* gave his age as 64 and hers as 30, thus born in 1786 and 1820 respectively. Elisha had children almost the same age as Tabitha. In the *1870 Census of Barren County* she lived with her brother Albert and had at least four children. **TABITHA A. DICKEY** is buried in Cave City Cemetery.

2181. **CYRUS DICKEY** (July 22, 1844 - Feb. 17, 1890). He was buried in the Cave City Cemetery.

2182. **ELEANE (ELEANA) DICKEY** (born 1846).

2183. **GEORGE DUKE DICKEY** (1850-1925) married BEATRICE ---- (1861-1952). They were buried in the Cave City Cemetery. The names of all their children are unknown.

21831. **LERA DICKEY** (1879-1964) married **SAMUEL B. DAVIS** (1876-1935).

21832. **GEORGE BURNICE DICKEY** (July 15, 1894 - Dec. 20, 1918).

2184. **HELLEN (HELEN) E. DICKEY** (1853-1931), married ---- **MURRELL** in Barren County, KY. She was buried in the Cave City Cemetery. Buried nearby is **EARLE DICKEY** (1897-1969).

21841. **ALBERT DUKE MURRELL** (1878-1935). He is buried beside his mother.

22. **THOMAS CRENSHAW**, a son of **BENJAMIN and TABITHA CRENSHAW**, was appointed "surveyor of the road from Warner Clark's to the east end of John McFerran's lane in Barren County, and to keep the road in repair 30 feet wide," on October 17, 1814, and April 21, 1817. [Ref: *Barren County Order Book No. 4*, pages 61, 142, 143]. **THOMAS CRENSHAW** married twice (first wife name unknown) and his second wife was

named **AGNES PERMELIA SHORT**. They were married on January 6, 1825, with Benjamin Mills Crenshaw as surety. Thomas died around January, 1827, and **PAMELIA AGNESS CRENSHAW** married **HENRY G. WADE** on December 17, 1827. However, the Barren County Court indicates a **SALLY CRENSHAW**, widow of of **THOMAS CRENSHAW**, died in December, 1828. [Ref: *Barren County Will Book 2*, pages 532, 533, 561, 573, 574, 596]. Obviously, this is quite difficult to explain especially when a **SALLY CRENSHAW** (born 1799) married **DAVID LOCKE** in 1831. See information under "*Unidentified Crenshaws*," q.v. **HENRY WADE** also died soon after because **AGNES PAMELEA WADE** wrote her own consent to marry to **ROBERT PARRISH** in Barren County. This marriage occurred on November 17, 1835. She seems to have had a daughter **HARRIET H. WADE** (1830-1848). **AGNES PERMELIA SHORT CRENSHAW WADE PARRISH** died by 1849 since **ROBERT PARRISH** married Agnes' sister Tabitha. This family line needs more research, and I may have confused two men named Thomas Crenshaw who died near the same time. **SALLY CRENSHAW and THOMAS CRENSHAW** were baptized into the Mt. Tabor Baptist Church in August, 1819. [Ref: Cawthorn & Warnell, *loc. cit.*] Somewhere from all this there seems to be at least these descendants (children, I believe) of the above marriages (and undoubtedly more), as follows. (See information under **AGNESS PERMELIA SHORT**, #232, q.v.)

221. **HARRIET H. WADE** (1830-1848).

222. **FLEMING PARRISH** (born 1837).

223. **PERMELA PARRISH** (born 1840).

224. **MARY PARRISH** (born 1842).

Since **THOMAS CRENSHAW** died in December, 1828, and **SALLY CRENSHAW** was a widow at a young age, she was probably the **SALLY CRENSHAW** who married **DAVID LOCK** on October 20, 1831. [Ref: Reneau's *Barren County Marriage Licenses*, p. 161). In the *1850 Census of Barren County*, was found **DAVID LOCK**, age 59 (born 1791, Kentucky, a waggoner), and **SALLY LOCK**, age 51 (born 1799, Kentucky), with the following children:
LUANN LOCK, age 16 (born 1834, Kentucky)
HELEN LOCK, age 12 (born 1838, Kentucky)
WILLIAM LOCK, age 8 (born 1842, Kentucky)

23. **ELIZABETH CRENSHAW**, daughter of **BENJAMIN and TABITHA CRENSHAW**, married **FLEMMING SHORT**. They are buried in unmarked graves in the Old Short Family Cemetery in Barren County, Kentucky. "Brother Flemming Short" was a member of Mt. Tabor Baptist Church in a 1810 listing of members, and "Flem Short" was a Messenger in 1840. [Ref: *Heart of the Barrens*, by Cecil E. Goode, page 89,

and *Pioneer Baptist Church Records of South Central Ky. and the Upper Cumberland of Tennessee, 1799-1899*, p. 78]. **FLEMING SHORT** was listed in the *1850 Barren County Census* as being age 69 (born 1781, Virginia), with **MARTHA SHORT** (age 68, born Virginia) and **SALLY GADBERRY** (age 73, born Virginia), but **ELIZABETH SHORT**, his wife, was not listed. It appears that **ELIZABETH CRENSHAW SHORT** died by 1848 as **FLEMING SHORT** married **MARTHA GADBERRY** on October 5, 1848 so she would be the Martha Short listed in 1850 census. **MARTHA G. SHORT** was born in 1782 and died May 20, 1856, in Barren County where Fleming owned Short's Mill. [Ref: "Famous Barren County Clock," in *South Central Kentucky Historical Qtrly.*, Vol. 3, No. 3, Oct., 1975, pp. 9-11]. In the *1860 Census of Barren County*, **"FLEMG. SHORTT"** (age 80, born Virginia) lived alone. Occupation: "Pleasure." FLEMMING SHORT wrote his will on September 19, 1856, in Barren County (codicils on February 19, 1857 and May 16, 1861 and May 19, 1861) and it was probated in February, 1863. It named his four daughters and his grandchildren.

231. **ELIZA ANN SHORT** (Aug. 14, 1804 - Jan. 12, 1875), daughter of **FLEMMING SHORT and ELIZABETH CRENSHAW**, married **JAMES S. ARNETT** on October 17, 1822, in Barren County. One witness was **B. MILLS CRENSHAW**. **JAMES ARNETT** (Nov. 15, 1795 - Sept. 6, 1854) was a native of Lincoln County, Kentucky, and he was buried in the Mayfield Cemetery in Barren County. **ELIZA ARNETT** was buried in the Arnett Cemetery on the Edmonton Road about six miles from Glasgow, KY. The *1850 Census of Barren County* listed **JAMES ARNETT**, age 55 (born 1795, Kentucky), **ELIZA ANN ARNETT**, age 46 (born 1804, Virginia), and their children (all of whom were born in Kentucky). In the *1860 Census of Barren County*, **ELIZA ARNETT** (age 55) was head of household in District No. 1 with **WILLIAM ARNETT** (age 27), **ELIZABETH ARNETT** (age 21) and **ANN ELIZA ARNETT** (age 14) with her. [Ref: Data contained in queries in the *Quarterly of the South Central Ky. Hist. and Gene. Society*, Volume 5, No. 1, April, 1977, p. 24, and Vol. 11, No. 1 (Spring, 1983), page 44, by **MRS. HELEN W. BISHOP**, of Cleveland, Tennessee, plus the clock article by **LEONA ARNETT MURRAY**, published in 1909 in Franklin, Kentucky's *Franklin Favorite*, and in *Kentucky Genealogy & Biography*, Vol. II, p. 105]. In the *1870 Census of Barren County*, **ELIZA ARNETT** (age 63) was head of household in the Hiseville Precinct, and **ELIZABETH ARNETT** (age 45), **ELIZA WILLIAMS** (age 24), **ARTHUR WILLIAMS** (age 1), and **WILLIAM ARNETT** (age 35, farmer) lived with her.

2311. **SAMUEL P. S. ARNETT** (January 20, 1824 - Feb. 20, 1895) married **MARY BLAKE PEDIGO** (May 11, 1831 - November 27, 1908) at the home of her father, **JOHN PATTERSON PEDIGO**, on December 26, 1854, in Barren County, KY. In the *1860 Census of Barren County*, **SAMUEL ARNETT** (age 36) was head of house in Dist. #1, with **MARY B. ARNETT** (age 29), **THEODORE ARNETT** (age 5), and **BUSH ARNETT** (age 3). They lived 18 miles north of Glasgow until sometime after 1880 when they moved to Hart County, Kentucky. They were buried in the Horse Cave Cemetery, Hart County, KY. [Ref: *Kentucky Cemetery Records*, Volume I, p. 202, compiled by the Kentucky Society DAR, 1960]. In the *1880 Census of Barren County, Kentucky*, **SAMUEL ARNETT** (age 56, farmer) was head of the household in Cave City Magisterial District #2 with wife **MARY B. ARNETT** (age 49, housekeeper) and children Bush (age 22), Leona (age 19), Lillian (age 15), Lena (age 13), and Samuel (age 11) also listed as living with them.

23111. **THEODORE (THEE.) ARNETT** (Sept. 21, 1855 - 1932) attended Green River College and later became manager of his father's farm. They raised stock and cultivated grain and tobacco. He married **KATE H. MOSELEY** (1855-1918), daughter of **JOHN R. and NANCY MOSELEY** of Barren County on October 29, 1878. Kate H. was a member of the Christian Church, and Thee was a member of the Society of K. of H., Horse Cave Lodge No. 784. When he got older, Thee gave the old Short family grandfather clock (made in 1806 by Billie Savage) to his younger brother, **ROBERT SAMUEL ARNETT**, of Tennessee, some time prior to 1909. The *1860 Census of Barren County, KY*, gave his full name as **THEODORE ARNETT** and the 1880 census listed **THEO ARNETT** in Cave City Magisterial District #2. "Thee Arnett" was buried in the Horse Cave Cemetery, Hart County, Kentucky. [Ref: *Kentucky Cemetery Records*, and *South Central Kentucky Historical and Genealogical Soc. Quarterly*, Vol. 5].

231111. **HARRY M. ARNETT** (born 1879).

231112. **FRED B. ARNETT.**

231113. **CHARLES F. ARNETT** lived in Alabama, and possessed the old Short family clock made in 1806. After his death the clock went to his son, Prof. **THOMAS (TOMMY) NELSON ARNETT.**

2311131. **THOMAS NELSON ARNETT,** who moved to California, later became a Professor at the Univ. of Honolulu in Hawaii. "Tommy" had possession of the old Short family grandfather clock made in Kentucky in 1806 (by **BILLIE SAVAGE.** Its cherry case was subsequently made by **JAMES MILLER**). **THOMAS NELSON ARNETT** died in August of 1973. "This is as far as I can go with the story of the famous old Barren County clock." [Ref: Article by **MRS. CHARLES W. PEERS, JR.,** of Fern Creek, Kentucky, a grand niece of **MRS. LEONA ARNETT MURRAY** in 1975 (as published in the *South Central Kentucky Historical Quarterly*. Vol. 3, No. 3, October, 1975, page 11.) She also mentioned these relatives: **MISS MAUDE JORDAN,** dau. of **AMELIA (PAMELIA) PEDIGO JORDAN,** the first business-woman in Glasgow, KY (and sister of **MARY BLAKE PEDIGO ARNETT**), and **MRS. KATHERINE ARNETT GARVIN** who had deceased some time before 1975].

23112. **JAMES BUSH ARNETT** (September 18, 1857-1939). Bush died in Tacoma, Washington.

23113. **LEONA A. ARNETT** (1860-1917) married **SAMUEL A. MURRAY** (1859-1932) and owned the old Short family grandfather clock (made in 1806 by **BILLIE SAVAGE**). After her death the clock was given to her brother **THEE. ARNETT.** Leona and Samuel were buried in Horse Cave Cemetery in Hart County, Kentucky. [Ref: *Kentucky Cemetery Records*, Vol. I, p. 202, and *South Central Kentucky Historical and Genealogical Soc. Quarterly*, Vol. 5]. **MASSEY ARNETT VICK** (1891-1917) is also buried next to them in Horse Cave Cem.

23114. **LILLIAN ARNETT** (July 9, 1864 - Sept. 9, 1932) married **T. J. TAPSCOTT** (Aug. 9, 1861 - October 7, 1907). They lived in Hart County, Kentucky, and were buried in Horse Cave Cemetery. [Ref: *Kentucky Cemetery Records*, Volume I, page 202].

23115. **LENA RIVERS ARNETT** (September 3, 1869-September 7, 1954) married to **GEORGE ROBERT BIGGS**. The *1880 Census of Barren County* gave her age as 13, and brother Samuel's age was given as 11 [errors].

231151. **ARNETT BIGGS**.

2311511. ---- **BIGGS** married **CHARLES W. PEERS, JR.** and resided in Fern Creek, KY.

23116. **ROBERT SAMUEL ARNETT** lived in Mitchelville, Tennessee, and had possession of the old Short family grandfather clock (made in 1806 by **BILLIE SAVAGE**). When Samuel got older he gave it to nephew **CHARLES ARNETT** (son of **THEE. ARNETT**). [An error in the *1880 Census of Barren County, Kentucky*, gave his age as 11, but he was probably closer to age 9].

2312. **FLEMING DAVID ARNETT** (1826-1854) married **ELIZABETH ALLEN** (born 1829, Kentucky) on October 17, 1847, in Barren County.

23121. **ANN ELIZA ARNETT** (born 1849).

2313. **JAMES H. ARNETT** (1829 -   ), cabinetmaker.

2314. **WILLIAM B. ARNETT** (March 6, 1834 - March 11, 1907) was buried in the Arnett Cemetery with his mother and several other family members. In the *1860 Census of Barren County, Kentucky* **WILLIAM ARNETT** (age 27) lived with his mother in District No. 1. His occupation was "Dr." In the *1870 Census of Barren County, Kentucky* **WILLIAM ARNETT** was a farmer, age 35, and was living in the household his his mother Eliza.

2315. **ELIZABETH ELENOR "LIZZIE" ARNETT** (March 27, 1839 - February 14, 1916) was buried near **ELIZA ARNETT** in the Mayfield Cemetery. She was living at her mother's home in the *1860*

Census of Barren County, and never married. In the 1870 census her age was given as 45.

2316. **THEODORE F. ARNETT** (November 28, 1842 - November 4, 1851) was buried near his father in the Mayfield Cemetery in Barren County.

2317. **ANN ELIZA ARNETT** (Sept. 21, 1845 - Oct. 18, 1917) married **HARRISON RITCHIE WILLIAMS**, a son of **JAMES T. WILLIAMS and JANE D. COMER**, who were residents of Cumberland County, KY. "**ANNIE L. WILLIAMS**" was buried next to **ELIZA ARNETT** in the Arnett Cemetery in Barren Co. In the *1870 Census of Barren County, Kentucky* **ELIZA WILLIAMS** (age 24) and **ARTHUR WILLIAMS** (age 1) lived with her mother **ELIZA ARNETT**.

23171. **EARL ARTHUR WILLIAMS** (1869, KY - 1959, Mississippi) married to **LECTA CARTER**, who was born May 30, 1877, a daughter **HENRY CALHOUN CARTER** and wife **JULIA HOLLINGSWORTH**, of Monroe County, KY. In the *1920 Census of Barren County, Kentucky*, they lived in Temple Hill District No. 3, where he was a farmer.

231711. **HELEN E. WILLIAMS** (born July 4, 1905, in Glasgow, KY), moved with her parents in 1920 to Mississippi. She married to **W. A. BISHOP** and they lived in Cleveland, Tennessee in 1976. Helen had Fleming Short's arm chair, which was brought from Scotland, and also his silver tablespoon initialed "F.E.S." [Ref: *South Central Kentucky Historical Quarterly*, Vol. 3, No. 4, January, 1976, p. 27].

231712. **CARTER H. WILLIAMS** (b. 1909).

231713. **JOSEPH L. WILLIAMS** (b. 1915).

23172. **MAUD H. WILLIAMS** (October 26, 1870- August 3, 1871) was buried in Arnett Cemetery next to **WILLIAM B. ARNETT**.

2318. **AMANDA ARNETT** married **M. McMILLIAN** [?].

232. **AGNESS PERMELIA SHORT**, daughter of **FLEMMING SHORT** and

ELIZABETH CRENSHAW, married **THOMAS J. CRENSHAW**, with **BENJAMIN MILLS CRENSHAW** as surety, in Barren County, Kentucky, on January 6, 1825. Her second husband was **HENRY G. WADE**, whom she (**PAMELIA AGNESS CRENSHAW**) had married on December 26, 1827, and her third husband was **ROBERT PARRISH**, and she (**AGNES PAMELEA WADE**) wrote her own consent to marry, which she did on November 17, 1835. She had died by 1849 when her husband Robert then married to her sister, **TABITHA WALLER**, on June 9, 1849. **THOMAS J. CRENSHAW** was probably buried in the Old Short Cemetery near Old Mt. Tabor Church Cemetery in Barren County, with others whose stones have worn smooth with age. **BENJAMIN CRENSHAW and TABITHA CRENSHAW** were buried there as were these Wade children: **ANN ELIZA THOMPSON WADE** (died November 28, 1898) and **HARRIET H. WADE** (Oct. 14, 1830 - Sept. 23, 1848). [Ref: *Barren County Cem.*].

2321. **ELIZABETH FRANCES CRENSHAW** (November 10, 1825 - November 24, 1864), daughter of **THOMAS J. CRENSHAW and AGNESS PERMELIA SHORT**, married **ALONZER (ALONZO) WHITNEY** on April 15, 1839, in Barren County, KY. [Ref: *Barren County Marriage Licenses*, page 277]. From the *1850, 1870, and 1880 Censuses of Barren County, Ky*: **ALFONZUS (ALFHONZO) WHITNEY** (born 1817, farmer) and **ELIZABETH F. WHITNEY** (born 1825, KY).

23211. **JOSEPHINE C. WHITNEY** (born 1841, Kentucky).

23212. **MARY CATHERINE WHITNEY** (April 19, 1847 - July 7, 1931, in Lexington, KY) married to **JOHN T. GARDNER** (1832-1888). They are buried in the Bell Cemetery near Old Bell's Tavern, Park City, KY. [Ref: *Barren Co. Cemeteries*, Volume II, page 113].

23213. **MARTHA BELLE WHITNEY** (born February, 1850, Kentucky). Bell Whitney was "keeping house" for her father in 1870.

23214. **DANIEL WHITNEY** (December 9, 1852 - Mar. 26, 1888). Buried in Whitney Cem. at Cave City.

23215. **JOSEPH WHITNEY** (born 1855, Kentucky).

23216. **ELIZABETH (LIZZIE) P. WHITNEY** (born 1857, Kentucky). Betty Whitney was living with her father in 1870.

23127. **CHARLIE H. WHITNEY** (December 12, 1859, Kentucky - November 16, 1864?).

23218. **ANDREW McC. WHITNEY** (born 1864, Kentucky).

2322. **FANNY WADE**, daughter of **HENRY G. WADE and AGNESS PERMELIA SHORT**, apparently married a Short since she was referred to as **FANNY WADE SHORT**, daughter of **HENRY G. WADE** and the granddaughter of **FLEMMING SHORT** as named in the 1856 will of **FLEMMING SHORT**.

2323. **FLEMMING PARRISH** (1837 -), son of **ROBERT PARRISH and AGNESS PERMELIA SHORT**.

2324. **PERMELIA PARRISH** (1840 -), daughter of **ROBERT PARRISH and AGNESS PERMELIA SHORT**.

2325. **MARY MILDRED PARRISH** (1842 -), daughter of **ROBERT PARRISH and AGNESS PERMELIA SHORT**.

233. **TABITHA J. SHORT** (1814 -), dau. of **FLEMMING SHORT** and **ELIZABETH CRENSHAW**, married twice: (1) **RICHARD WALLER** by license dated February 21, 1843; and, (2) **ROBERT PARRISH** on June 9, 1849 (his first wife was **AGNES PERMELIA SHORT**, Tabitha's sister). [See Agnes and Thomas Crenshaw above]. **ROBERT and TABITHA PARRISH** had possession of the Short family grandfather clock made in 1806 (by **BILLIE SAVAGE**) until 1878 when it was purchased by **SAMUEL P. S. ARNETT. ROBERT PARRISH** was born in 1810 in Virginia according to the *1860 Census of Barren County, Kentucky*, in District #2, and *1870 Census of Barren County, Kentucky*, Glasgow Precinct. His occupation was listed as wagoner. The *1900 Census of Barren County, Kentucky*, District No. 1, states that **TABITHA PARRISH** (age 75) was born in June, 1814, in Kentucky. She was the head of household and living with her was a son **CHARLES PARRISH** (age 42), born July, 1857. It also stated she had 7 children (only 4 still living) and her occupation was "mid wife." She and Charles could both read and write English, and he was a "day laborer." **ROBERT PARRISH** died testate in Barren County and his will was probated November 19, 1894, naming his wife Tabitha.

2331. **DAVIDELLA WALLER** (born 1840). She was a daughter of **ROBERT PARRISH and TABITHA J. CRENSHAW**, who married in 1843, but the *1850 Census of Barren County* gave Davidella's age as 10 (born 1840). The 1856 will of **FLEMMING SHORT** named **DAVIDELLA WALLER** as one of his granddaughters.

2332. **ELLEN (HELEN) WALLER** (born 1844). In the *1860 Census of Barren County*, **ELLEN WALLER** was 16. In the *1870 Census of Barren County, Kentucky*, a **HELEN READ** (age 25) was listed in the house of **ROBERT PARRISH**, with **ANN ELLEN READ** (age 6) and **VIRGIL READ** (age 1), probably her children.

2333. **ELIZABETH WALLER** (born 1847/8). She lived at the home of her parents in 1870.

2334. **JONAS PARRISH** (born 1850).

2335. **HARRIET PARRISH** (born 1852).

2336. **CHARLES (CHARLEY) PARRISH** (born July, 1856).

2337. **ALICE PARRISH** (born 1859/60).

2338. **WILLIE PARRISH** (born 1864).

234. **ELIZABETH SHORT** (born 1819), daughter of **FLEMMING SHORT** and **ELIZABETH CRENSHAW**, was married to **HERNDON DAVIDSON** on February 2, 1835, by Z. Quesenberry in Barren County. In the *1850 Census of Barren County*, Herndon was age 37. In the 1856 will of Flemming Short, **ELIZABETH DAVIDSON** is mentioned as deceased and Flemming named her husband **HERNDON DAVIDSON** and their four children in said will.

2341. **THOMAS WESTERFIELD DAVIDSON** (born 1842).

2342. **GEORGE WASHINGTON DAVIDSON** (born 1846).

2343. **LEWIS DAVIDSON**.

2344. **ELIZABETH DAVIDSON**.

24. **HON. BENJAMIN MILLS CRENSHAW** (1801 - May 15, 1857), a son of **BENJAMIN CRENSHAW** and wife **TABITHA ----**, was a very prominent citizen of Barren County, Kentucky. He was admitted to the bar as an attorney at law in 1822. [Ref: *The Times of Long Ago*, by Franklin Gorin (1876), page 58]. He served in the House of Representatives, 1840-1842, and was a member of the Kentucky Legislature, 1844-1848. **B. MILLS CRENSHAW** was a Presidential Elector from Barren County in 1845. He was one of the leading attorneys of the bar at Glasgow from 1830 to 1850, serving as Barren County Judge, 1847-1851. A resident of Glasgow, he was Judge of the Court of Appeals from 1851 until his death on May 15, 1857. [Ref: *Ibid.*, pp. 48, 54, 58, 114, 137]. In the *1850 Census of Barren County* he was shown as age 49 (born Kentucky) with Nancy P. Crenshaw (age 46), Hellen Crenshaw (age 20), Ann Crenshaw (age 9), Kate Crenshaw (age 4), all born in Kentucky, and one Porter Edmunds (tailor), age 16. [Ref: *1850 Census of Barren County, KY*, in Household No. 1425]. His occupation was listed as "Judge," and his property value was $4,000 in 1850. He also served as a Commissioner of Barren County Schools from 1841 to 1848. [Ref: *Barren County Heritage*, by Goode, et al.,

(1980), pp. 201, 286, 287]. In the *1860 Census of Barren County* **NANCY P. CRENSHAW** (age 56) was head of house in District No. 1, with **HENRY C. CRENSHAW** (age 31), **HELEN CRENSHAW** (age 29), **ANN M. CRENSHAW** (age 18), and **KATE CRENSHAW** (age 13) listed also.

BENJAMIN MILLS CRENSHAW married **NANCY P. MUNFORD**, who was born on April 4, 1804, and died on May 23, 1879. They are buried in the Old Munford Cemetery in Glasgow, Kentucky. The following information has been taken from an article entitled "Historic Cemetery Restored," *The South Central Kentucky Historical and Genealogical Society Quarterly*, Volume 9, No. 1, March, 1981, page 20: "In the heart of Glasgow, at the intersection of East Front and Franklin Streets, the historic Munford-Crenshaw Cemetery has been beautifully restored by the family of **MR. AND MRS. PHILIP L. GILDRED**, of San Diego, California. Here many of Glasgow's pioneer civic leaders are buried, including Mrs. Gildred's great-great-uncle **W. E. MUNFORD**, business leader who literally held the keys of the city when he steered Glasgow thru the deadly cholera epidemic brought into the town in 1853 by a circus. **BENJAMIN MILLS CRENSHAW**, her great-great-grandfather, is buried there. He was a notable member of the Kentucky Court of Appeals from 1851 until his death in 1857, while he was serving as Chief Justice. His influence was dominant in civic, industrial, religious, and cultural progress of pioneer Glasgow, Ky. As an exponent of the English language, the historians ranked him with Horace Greeley, and George D. Prentiss, and the noted Kentucky Clays, Marshalls, and Breckinridges. His wife was the sister of **W. E. MUNFORD**, both being children of **RICHARD J. MUNFORD**, the founder of Munfordville, Kentucky, linking the interests of Hart and Hardin Counties to this cemetery. On May 9th [1981] the DAR culminated their 50th anniversary in Glasgow with an impressive public dedication of this cemetery at which the Gildred Family formally presented the plot to the town with the [Edmund Rogers Chapter] DAR as sponsors."

BENJAMIN MILLS CRENSHAW was also surety for the marriage of **BENJAMIN R. CRENSHAW, JR.** in 1845 and **BENJAMIN R. CRENSHAW** in 1846 (possibly the same man). It certainly appears that they were related, but records not available to substantiate it. See the information under "*Unidentified Crenshaws*," q.v.

241. **ARABELLA E. CRENSHAW** married to **JOHN GORIN ROGERS** on November 22, 1841. [Ref: *Barren County Marriage Records*, page 226). In the *Census of Barren County in 1850*, **JOHN G. ROGERS** was listed as head of house (age 31, lawyer), and **ARABELLE C. ROGERS** (age 24), with Henry Rogers (age 2) and Julia Rogers (age 3 months). A daughter, Arabella E. Rogers, was born in 1845 and died 1846. [Ref: *Barren County, Kentucky, Cemeteries*, Vol. I, page 229]. A deed

in Barren County, mistakenly abstracted as May 5, 1849, named the heirs of **BENJAMIN MILLS CRENSHAW** and among them was **JOHN G. ROGERS** and wife **A. E. ROGERS**, of Chicago, IL.

2411. **ARABELLA E. ROGERS** (1845-1846).

2412. **HENRY ROGERS** (born 1848).

2413. **JULIA ROGERS** (born 1850).

242. **LITTLEBERRY P. CRENSHAW** (1823 -), son of **BENJAMIN MILLS CRENSHAW and NANCY P. MUNFORD**, was a Barren County attorney and married **EDMONIA H. (MARTIN) STARR**, daughter of **HUDSON MARTIN**, on February 15, 1846, with the consent of her father. She had been married previously and had a daughter, **AUGUSTA STARR**, born 1844. **LITTLEBERRY P. CRENSHAW** served in the House of Representatives in 1848 and was the editor and proprietor of *The Kentucky Reveille* newspaper in 1849-1850. He also attempted the publication of an agricultural periodical in 1851, "but it did not reach its third number." [Ref: *The Times of Long Ago*, by Franklin Gorin (1876), pages 48, 73, 74, 114]. He was listed in the *1850 Census of Barren County* as a lawyer, age 27, born in Kentucky (Household No. 1322). In the files of *The Glasgow Journal*, 1855-1857, was a list of the business and professional men of Glasgow, Kentucky, and included among them was **L. P. CRENSHAW** who was listed as a preacher. [Ref: *South Central Kentucky Historical & Genealogical Society Quarterly*, Volume 9, No. 2, June, 1981, pages 56-57].

2421. **AMANDA C. CRENSHAW** (born 1846).

2422. **WILLIAM G. CRENSHAW** (born 1848).

243. **HENRY C. CRENSHAW** (January 18, 1825 - February 3, 1901), son of **BENJAMIN MILLS CRENSHAW and NANCY P. MUNFORD**, was listed in the *1850 Census of Barren County, Kentucky*, in the household of **JAMES L. CRUTCHER** (age 34) and **MARY E. CRUTCHER** (age 26), and "salesman" was his occupation. Henry was buried next to his mother in Munford-Crenshaw Cemetery in Glasgow, Kentucky. He died testate in Barren County (will written October 18, 1898, probated in 1901), naming **SUSAN CRENSHAW** (wife of his brother **A. CRENSHAW**) and children, and sisters **HELEN CRENSHAW and KATE CRENSHAW**. [Ref: *Barren County Wills 5:362*]. **H. C. CRENSHAW** was also a postmaster in Glasgow some time prior to 1876 [Ref: Franklin Gorin's *The Times of Long Ago*, p. 65]. **HENRY AND ALEXANDER CRENSHAW** taught at Urania College in Glasgow, Kentucky, between 1858 and 1874. [Ref: *Barren County Heritage*, by Cecil Goode, et al. (1980), p. 186]. In the *1860 Census of Barren County, KY*, **HENRY C. CRENSHAW** (age 31) was living at home with his mother and sisters. His occupation: "Merchant." In the *1880 Census of Barren County, Kentucky*,

HENRY C. CRENSHAW (age 53) was head of the household and lived in the eastern half of the Glasgow District with his sisters **HELEN CRENSHAW** (age 48, keeping house) and **KATE CRENSHAW** (age 26, helping keep house). The census stated they and their mother were born in Kentucky, and their father in Virginia.

244. **HELEN (HELLEN) CRENSHAW**, a daughter of **BENJAMIN MILLS CRENSHAW and NANCY P. MUNFORD**, was born in 1830 according to the *1850 Barren County Census*, but her tombstone in Glasgow Municipal Cemetery gave her year of birth as 1828, and the year of death of 1917. Helen was buried next to **ALEXANDER CRENSHAW** (1831 - 1909), her brother. From an article entitled "The Early Sunday Schools in Barren County" in *South Central Kentucky Historical and Genealogical Society Quarterly* (Vol. 9, No. 1, March, 1981 p. 26), we find that about 1850 there was a Sunday School that met regularly at the old Christian Church. **MISS HELEN CRENSHAW** was a teacher. Her father, **B. MILLS CRENSHAW**, afterwards Judge of the Court of Appeals, attended a Sunday School there and in the absence of the preacher often conducted services. She was never married and died testate in Barren County (will written in December, 1908, and probated on June 21, 1917), naming her sister **KATE CRENSHAW**, brother **ALEX CRENSHAW**, and nieces **BETTIE CRENSHAW and HELEN LEWIS**. [Ref: *Barren Co. Will Book 6:367*]. In the *1860 Census of Barren County, Kentucky*, **HELEN CRENSHAW** (age 29) was living at home with mother **NANCY P. CRENSHAW** (age 56). Her occupation was music teacher. Henry, Ann, and Kate lived with them. In *1910 Census of Barren County, Kentucky*, **HELEN CRENSHAW** (age 81) lived on Cleveland Avenue in Glasgow, Kentucky, and her sister **KATE CRENSHAW** (age 60) lived with her. They lived on their "own income."

245. **ALEXANDER CRENSHAW** (1831-1912), son of **BENJAMIN MILLS CRENSHAW and NANCY P. MUNFORD**, was a distinguished citizen who was born in Barren County, Kentucky and was admitted to the bar as an attorney. In the *1860 Census of Barren County* "**ALL CRENSHAW**" (age 27) lived in the household of Mary M. Helm (age 47) and family. He subsequently became County Attorney, 1866-1869, at a yearly wage of $300. [Ref: *The Times of Long Ago*, by Gorin (1876), pp. 57, 58, 142]. His death record states he "died on March 5, 1912, of pneumonia, age 80, son of **B. MILLS CRENSHAW**, of Virginia [sic] and ---- Munford; retired lawyer; buried in Glasgow Cemetery." [Ref: *Traces*, Vol. 12, No. 2, Summer, 1984] However, his tombstone indicates his year of birth is 1831, and the year of death is 1909. His wife **SUSAN ----** (1843-1918) is buried next to him. [Ref: Eva Coe Peden's *Barren County, Kentucky Cemeteries*, Volume I (1976), page 192]. **HENRY and ALEXANDER CRENSHAW** taught at Urania College in Glasgow, KY, some time between 1858 and 1874. [Ref: *Barren County Heritage*, by Goode, et al. (1980), p. 186]. It appears from his sisters' wills that he had two daughters, Bettie Crenshaw and Helen (Modie) Crenshaw. In 1910 **ALEXANDER CRENSHAW** (age 78) and **SUE**

CRENSHAW (age 66) lived in Glasgow, Kentucky, in the house of their daughter and son-in-law, **HELEN and GEORGE R. LEWIS**. Alex and Sue had been married 46 years. Also, **CRENSHAW & DICKEY** was a law office in Glasgow, Kentucky, in 1866 and they probably were connected to this particular Alexander Crenshaw family. [Ref: *Traces*, Volume 13, No. 2 (Summer, 1985), page 47].

2451. **BETTIE CRENSHAW** (1877-   ). In 1910 she lived with her sister's family, and was unemployed. [See comment under **KATE CRENSHAW** (#246) below].

2452. **HELEN CRENSHAW** (1883-   ) married **GEORGE R. LEWIS** (born 1877) in 1903. They lived on Maple Driveway in Glasgow, Kentucky in the *1910 Census of Barren County*. George was a bank cashier. Helen was born in Florida. She had 2 children, but only 1 living.

24521. ---- **LEWIS** (born & died between 1903-1910).

24522. **BETTIE G. LEWIS** (born 1906, Glasgow, KY).

246. **ANNE M. CRENSHAW** (1841-   ), dau. of **BENJAMIN MILLS CRENSHAW** and **NANCY P. MUNFORD**, lived with her mother in the *1860 Census of Barren County, Kentucky*, but was not with her in 1870. She appears to have married **WILLIAM P. OTTER**, of Louisville, KY.

247. **KATE CRENSHAW** (1846-1931), daughter of **BENJAMIN MILLS CRENSHAW** and **NANCY P. MUNFORD**, died testate in Barren County, Kentucky. She wrote her will on November 11, 1920, and it was probated on July 19, 1931. She named only her niece, **BETTIE CRENSHAW.** [Ref: *Barren County, Ky., Will Book 8:55*]. In 1860 and 1870 Kate lived with her mother in District #1. In 1920 she was listed in the census as a single resident on Maple Driveway in Glasgow, Kentucky. Her given age was 72, born in Kentucky.

CATHERINE CRENSHAW (1844-1933)
ELIZABETH CRENSHAW (1875-1962)

Buried in Glasgow Municipal Cemetery, Glasgow, Kentucky. [Note: Could this actually be **KATE CRENSHAW**, daughter of Benjamin Mills Crenshaw, and her niece **BETTIE CRENSHAW?**]

[Note: It should be pointed out that somewhere in the above family of Crenshaws the line of BENJAMIN R. CRENSHAW fits in, but where is not known. As shown in the "Unidentified Crenshaws" section of this book, BENJAMIN R. CRENSHAW, JR, married LOUISA BROWNING in 1845 in Barren County, Kentucky. His surety was BENJAMIN MILLS CRENSHAW. In 1846, just a year later, BENJAMIN R. CRENSHAW married NANCY KING.]

CHAPTER THREE

SOME AFRICAN-AMERICAN CRENSHAWS IN SOUTH CENTRAL KENTUCKY

As one might well expect, not all Crenshaws were caucasian. In the "times of long ago" when slavery was practiced, most black people only had a first name. When they became free, many chose a new name while others took the name of their former masters. The Crenshaw's slaves were no different. As a result, today we find a number of their descendants in the records of Kentucky. The genealogy of the Crenshaws would not be complete without including this information, but it is really a project for the descendants to compile. Perhaps this brief summary might get someone started on it. Those listed below do have familial connections to Barren and Metcalfe Counties. They all begin with the number "3" to differentiate them from the "1" for John Crenshaw's family and "2" for Benjamin Crenshaw's, but they are not presented in a true genealogical format. The reason is simply because they do not all descend from one common ancestor.

31. **GLOSTER CRENSHAW** (black, born 1785, Virginia) was listed in the *1850 Census of Barren County* as living alone (age 65, farmer). In the *1860 Census of Barren County*, **GLOSSY CRENSHAW** (age 70, born Virginia), **LUCY CRENSHAW** (age 67, born North Carolina) and **JANE CRENSHAW** (age 22, born Kentucky), lived in District No. 2. In the *1870 Census of Barren County*, **JANE CRENSHAW** (age 30) was a domestic servant in the house of Mike H. Dickerson in Glasgow Precinct. Listed with her was **JAMES CRENSHAW** (age 11, black).

32. **WINNIE H. CRENSHAW** (mulatto, born 1787, Virginia) was listed in *1870 Census of Metcalfe County, Kentucky*, in the household of Ezekial Crenshaw, and was probably his mother or mother-in-law.

321. **EZEKIAL CRENSHAW** (mulatto, born 1811, Virginia), was head of the household in the *1870 Census of Metcalfe County* with a wife **TEMPLE CRENSHAW** (born 1824) and the following children, all "working on the farm" and born in Kentucky. **EZEKIEL CRENSHAW** (age 60) was head of house in the *1880 Census of Metcalfe County* in the Lafayette Magisterial District, with his wife **TEMPEY CRENSHAW** (age 57) and sons **WILLIAM D. CRENSHAW** (age 34), **JOHN E. CRENSHAW** (age 16), **CHARLEY CRENSHAW** (age 13). All but William were farmers. In the *1900 Census of Metcalfe County*, **EZEKIEL CRENSHAW** (born 1808), was head of house in the Antioch District with wife **TEMPY CRENSHAW** (born March, 1823) and family. Ezekiel and Tempy had 14 children, with 13 still living.

3211. **WILLIAM D. CRENSHAW** (born 1846, mulatto, "idiotic" in the 1870 census, but "unemployed" in the 1880 census).

3212. **PAUL CRENSHAW** (born 1851, mulatto, farm laborer). In the *1880 Metcalfe County Census*, **PAUL CRENSHAW** (age 25) was head of household in Lafayette Magisterial District with his wife **ELIZA CRENSHAW** (age 23). Occupation: Farmer. In the 1900 Census **PAUL CRENSHAW** (born September, 1853) is head of household in Antioch District, with his wife **ELIZA CRENSHAW** (born February, 1856) and their children. The census taker labeled them black rather than mulatto. In the 1910 census they lived in the Knob Lick Precinct. Paul was age 62 and Eliza was age 58. The census stated they had 12 children, with 8 still living. Also listed were **BULU L. and FRANCES E. HATCHER**, both age 8 years, so they were apparently twins. Relation: granddaughters. In the *1920 Census of Metcalfe County*, ELIZA CRENSHAW (age 58?), widow, was head of household in Sulphur Well District #2, with her daughter Ann and 2 grandchildren. She was born in Kentucky. Her occupation was wash woman.

32121. **SARAH F. CRENSHAW** (born 1873/4, mulatto).

32122. **WILLIE B. CRENSHAW** (born 1875/6, mulatto).

32123. **EDLONIA CRENSHAW** (born 1877, mulatto).

32124. **CHARLES B. CRENSHAW** (born Feb., 1879, black).

32125. **BROWNEY L. CRENSHAW** (daughter, born June, 1886).

32126. **JOHN E. CRENSHAW** (born February, 1889, black) was head of household in the *1910 Census of Barren County, KY*, in Hiseville District 4, with his wife **ESTER ----** (born 1892, KY).

32127. **ANNIE M. CRENSHAW** (born March, 1891, black). Still living at home with her parents in 1910. She married ---- **WHITE** and had two children by 1920, at which time they lived with her mother.

321271. **RUTH WHITE** (born 1917, black).

321272. **THOMAS WHITE** (born 1919, black).

32128. **CORA L. CRENSHAW** (born March, 1893, black).

32129. **JAMES L. CRENSHAW** (born September 1896, black). The 1910 census gave the name **JAMES M. CRENSHAW.**

3213. **EMILY CRENSHAW** (born 1854, mulatto, farm worker).

3214. **ELIZABETH CRENSHAW** (b. 1856, mulatto, farm worker).

3215. **JOSEPHINE CRENSHAW** (b. 1858, mulatto, farm worker).

3216. **ALLEN CRENSHAW** (born May, 1859, mulatto, farm worker). He lived in Antioch District, Metcalfe County, in 1900. In the 1910 Census, in Knob Lick Precinct, Allen lived with his sister EMILY WOOD and her husband THOMAS WOOD. In the *1920 Census of Metcalfe County, KY*, in Sulphur Well District No. 2, **ALLEN CRENSHAW** (age 60, black) was living alone and the census indicated he was a widower.

3217. **MILAM CRENSHAW** (born 1862, mulatto, farm worker). In 1880 "**MILAM CRENSHAW**" (age 18) worked on the farm of THOMAS FREEMAN in Metcalfe County's Lafayette District. In 1900 "**MILUM CRENSHAW**" (born June 1861) lived at the home of his parents in Metcalfe Co.'s Antioch District. In the 1910 Census, Knob Lick Precinct, **MILAM CRENSHAW** (age 48) was head of house, with wife **ALBERTA CRENSHAW** (age 26). Milam and Alberta had been married five years. He was head of household in the *1920 Census of Metcalfe County* in Sulphur Well District #2, with wife **ALBERTA CRENSHAW** (b. 1885). He apparently was married before. **MILAM CRENSHAW** was buried in the old Crenshaw (Slave) Cemetery at Knob Lick, Metcalfe County, Kentucky, with **ALBERTA CRENSHAW** and infant **RONALD SHARON CRENSHAW** (no tombstones). Other African-Americans buried here were as follows: [Ref: *Metcalfe Co. Cemeteries*, Vol. I, p. 71]

Emlie Wood (died April 21, 1916)
John Henry Wood (September 2, 1890 - June 29, 1913)
Elmer V. Edwards (April 3, 1894 - March 21, 1921)
Nannie Essie Stockton (April 23, 1908 - June 29, 1909)
Nannie Stockton (1868-1935)
Lee T. Mitchell (December 2, 1889 - November 22, 1962)
Private, Company D, U. S. Army, World War I
Sarah F. Mitchell (1871-1959)
James A. Johnson (April 15, 1886 - September 22, 1953)
George, Cindy and Bud Johnson (no tombstones as of 1983)
Harriett Shirley (January 1, 1826 - February 3, 1908).

Children of MILAM CRENSHAW:

32171. **JAMES R. CRENSHAW** (born December, 1883, black).

32172. **ARTHUR B. CRENSHAW** (born November, 1895, black).

32173. **HALLEY B. CRENSHAW** (born February, 1897, black).

32174. **CLARENCE F. CRENSHAW** (1906-1963, black) was buried in the Clarence Crenshaw Cemetery near Knob Lick in Metcalfe County, Kentucky and a marker is also there for **NAVARRON CRENSHAW** (1966-). Others buried there: [Ref: *Metcalfe County Cemeteries*, Volume I, page 71].

Viola Martin (1913-1971)
Geraldine Kirkpatrick (1931-1978)

Alice Whiteside (1908-1968)
Emily P. Sidden (1877-1960)

32175. **CONRAD E. CRENSHAW** (1909 - August, 1982), of Knob Lick, Rt. 1, Metcalfe County, died at the T. J. Sampson Community Hospital in Glasgow, Kentucky, after an extended illness. He was buried in the Siddon Family Cemetery in Metcalfe County, after services at the Old Blue Spring Baptist Church. He had three sisters: Mrs. Lou Ann Jones and Mrs. Viola Jones of Knob Lick, Kentucky and Mrs. Lucy Gatewood, of Indiana. He also had 15 children, 29 grandchildren (only Lamont Crenshaw was named) and 6 great-grandchildren. His children were named as follows in his obituary in *The Glasgow Republican* on August 5, 1982, plus the information about the marriage of Raymond Crenshaw is from *The Glasgow Republican* dated October 4, 1984 (a very long article with the bride's photograph and many named relatives).

321751. **WINFORD (WINFRED) CRENSHAW**, of Knob Lick, Kentucky.

3217511. **RAYMOND EARL CRENSHAW** married August 11, 1984, **PAULA ROSETTA STOCKTON**, daughter of Paul Stockton of Glasgow, Kentucky, at Hopewell Baptist Church. Many relatives attended the wedding, including Mrs. **Velma Crenshaw** (grandmother), **Ricky Crenshaw** (the brother of the groom), Mr. and Mrs. **Winfred Crenshaw** (groom's parents), **Jasper Crenshaw** (of Louisville), Mr. and Mrs. **Valgo Crenshaw** (of Chicago), Mr. and Mrs. **Glen Crenshaw** (of Indianapolis), Mr. and Mrs. **Allie L. Crenshaw** (of Louisville), and many others with surnames of Twyman, Boles, Parrish, Stockton, Fishback, Maupin, Bryant, Allen, Garnett and Allen. [Ed. Note: I would venture to say that Luska Twyman, former Mayor of Glasgow, was related to this family. See the entries below for Luther and Burle Crenshaw. Judging by the names listed in their obituaries, it appears that they were also related to this family].

3217512. **RICKY CRENSHAW**, brother of Raymond E. Crenshaw.

LUTHER R. CRENSHAW (1931 - October, 1981) died in Lexington, age 50, at Central Baptist Hospital. Formerly of Glasgow, he lived in Lexington for the past 14 years. Surviving him were:

wife, **DOLLY M. CRENSHAW**, of Lexington
mother, MRS. BEATRICE MAUPIN, of Glasgow
stepfather, JOHN MAUPIN, of Glasgow
brother, **OLIVER L. CRENSHAW**, of Glasgow
brother, **WILLIAM THOMAS CRENSHAW**, of Glasgow
brother, ALLEN MAUPIN, of Louisville
sister, MRS. ZORA STOCKTON, of Glasgow
sister, MRS. JOHNETTA BOLES, of Glasgow

"and several other relatives" (not named). Funeral by Watts Funeral Home, with the burial in Oddfellow Cemetery, Glasgow, Kentucky. (Ref: *The Glasgow Republican*). Services were held at the Hopewell Baptist Church. (Luther was a mechanic for the Harlin Motor Company in Glasgow, KY, 1959.) [Ref: *1959 Glasgow, Kentucky, City Directory*, p. 33].

Children of **CONRAD E. CRENSHAW** (1909-1982), continued:

32175-2. **GLEN CRENSHAW**, of Indiana, married ----.

32175-3. **ROGER CRENSHAW**, of Indiana.

32175-4. **WENDELL CRENSHAW**, of Indiana.

32175-5. **LLOYD CRENSHAW**, of Illinois.

32175-6. **DEWEY CRENSHAW**, of Illinois.

32175-7. **JASPER CRENSHAW**, of Indiana.

32175-8. **NIVEN CRENSHAW** (Sergeant), Fort Campbell, Kentucky.

32175-9. **McQUINN CRENSHAW** (at home), Knob Lick, Kentucky.

3217510. **MARY ALICE CRENSHAW**, married ---- CLARK, of Indiana.

3217511. **YVONNE CRENSHAW**, married ---- COATES, of Indiana.

3217512. **ZOLA CRENSHAW**, married ---- DRIVER, of Indiana.

3217513. **ROZETTA CRENSHAW**, married ---- SEARS, of Cave City.

3217514. **JANICE CRENSHAW**, of Glasgow, Kentucky.

3217515. **GLORIA CRENSHAW**, of Glasgow, Kentucky.

32176. **LOU A. CRENSHAW** (born 1912, black)

32177. **VIOLA CRENSHAW** (born 1915, black)

32178. **LUCY D. CRENSHAW** (born 1917, black)

3218. **JOHN ELZY CRENSHAW** (born Sept., 1863, mulatto), son of **EZEKIEL CRENSHAW**, lived in Barren County, Kentucky, in District #4, in 1900. John married **CARRIE ----** (born in February, 1873) in 1888 or 1889. His occupation: Farmer. The *1910 Census of Metcalfe County, Kentucky*, enumerated **JACK E. CRENSHAW** (age 46, black), wife **CARRIE CRENSHAW** (age 36) and six children, all born in Kentucky.

32181. **BIRDIE CRENSHAW** (daughter, born September, 1889).

32182. **WILLIE G. CRENSHAW** (son, born March, 1891/3).

32183. **JOHN K. CRENSHAW** (born January, 1895). Not listed at home in the 1910 census.

32184. **BERNICE B. CRENSHAW** (born March, 1897).

32185. **NORA M. CRENSHAW** (born March, 1900).

32186. **LOUCILE CRENSHAW** (born 1902).

32187. **GEORGE E. CRENSHAW** (born 1904).

32188. **GOTHE [?] CRENSHAW** (son, born 1907).

3219. **CHARLES B. (CHARLEY) CRENSHAW** (born Aug., 1866, mulatto) was head of house in the *1900 Census of Metcalfe County* in the Antioch District, with his wife FLORA M. CRENSHAW (born July, 1868) and family, all born in Kentucky. He was head of house in the *1910 Census of Metcalfe County* in Knob Lick Precinct, with wife Flora and family. He was head of house in the *1920 Census of Metcalfe County* in Sulphur Well District #2. His age was 53 and listed with him were his wife Flora (age 51) and children.

32191. **THOMAS B. CRENSHAW** (October 18, 1889 - June 5, 1952). Buried in the Twyman Cemetery in Metcalfe County, KY.

32192. **OTTO S. CRENSHAW** (born May, 1892, black).

32193. **JESSIE F. CRENSHAW** (born February, 1895, black). In *1920 Census of Metcalfe County, KY*, he was head of the household in Sulphur Well District #2, with his wife **ELVIE CRENSHAW** (born 1899) and daughter Aline.

321931. **ALINE CRENSHAW** (born 1917, black).

32194. **BURLE HERBERT CRENSHAW** (Mar., 1897 - Feb. 8, 1985) died only two days after his wife VIRGIE in Knob Lick, Metcalfe County, Kentucky. She was 82 years old. Her obituary listed the following survivors: husband, **BURLE HERBERT CRENSHAW**, of Knob Lick, KY and 6 sons, 1 daughter, 23 grandchildren, and 14 great-grandchildren, plus a sister **LOLA V. BEARD** and her two brothers, **ROY and ELMER RICHARDSON.** Funeral arrangements by the Watts Funeral Home. (*Glasgow Republican*). **AVIOUS CRENSHAW** was named administrator of their estates on February 28, 1985. [Ref: *Metcalfe County Will Book 5:403*].

321941. **R. T. CRENSHAW** (son), of Louisville, KY.

321942. **ALLIE CRENSHAW** (son), of Louisville, KY.

321943. **LOUIS CRENSHAW**, of Louisville, KY.

321944. **LENWOOD CRENSHAW**, of Louisville, KY.

321945. **THEODORE CRENSHAW**, of Minneapolis, MN.

321946. **AVIOUS CRENSHAW** (son), of Knob Lick, KY.

321947. **DOROTHY CRENSHAW BREWER**, of Knob Lick, KY.

32195. **ROBERT E. CRENSHAW** (born August, 1899).

32196. **ROY A. CRENSHAW** (born 1902).

32197. **VELMA M. CRENSHAW** (born 1906).

32198. **ORSILLA CRENSHAW** (daughter, born 1909).

33. **CAROLINE CRENSHAW and ARCHIE ----** (blacks, born in Virginia).

331. **SAMUEL WILEY CRENSHAW** (1824-1911, black) drowned May 22, 1911, age 87, and was buried at Blue Spring Creek Cem. [Ref: *Traces*, Volume 12, No. 2, Summer, 1984, page 48]. His death record states he was a black man and the son of **ARCHIE ---- and CAROLINE CRENSHAW**, both born in Virginia. The *1870 Census of Metcalfe County* gives his wife's name as **BERNICY CRENSHAW**, age 38, and Samuel Crenshaw's age, was given as 43, thus born in 1827. In the *1880 Census of Metcalfe County*, **SAMUEL W. CRENSHAW** (age 48) was the head of house in Lafayette Magisterial District, with his wife **VENICY CRENSHAW** (age 47), son **ELI B. CRENSHAW** (age 19), son **SAMMY CRENSHAW** (age 10), daughter **EMILY CRAINE** (age 21), granddaughter **MARY M. CRAINE** (age 3), and grandson **SAMMY T. CRAINE** (age 8 months). In the *1900 Census of Metcalfe County, Kentucky*, **SAMUEL W. CRENSHAW** (born in February, 1834) was the head of the household with his wife **BERNICY CRENSHAW** (born March, 1837) in District #2 with his grandchildren **MARY M. CRAIN and SAMUEL T. CRAIN.** It appears that Bernicy had 11 children, 7 still living. In the *1910 Census of Metcalfe County, KY*, in Knob Lick Precinct, **SAMUEL W. CRENSHAW** (age 76) was head of house and wife **VERNICY CRENSHAW** (age 74) lived with him. They had been married 59 years and had 12 children; however, only 1 was still living in 1910, according to the census.

3311. **CAROLINE R. CRENSHAW** (born 1853, black).

3312. **EMILY F. CRENSHAW** (born 1857, black, farm worker). In the *1880 Census of Metcalfe County, Kentucky*, **EMILY CRAINE** (age 21, daughter of **SAMUEL CRENSHAW**, was living at his home with her two children. The census enumerated her occupation as "unoccupied."

33121. **MARY M. CRAINE** (born February, 1877).

33122. **SAMUEL T. CRAINE** (born October, 1879).

3313. **DELIA W. CRENSHAW** (born 1859, black, farm worker).

3314. **ELI B. CRENSHAW** (born 1861, black, farm worker). In the *1880 Census of Barren County*, **ELY CRENSHAW** (age 20) was a farm hand on John Roundtree's farm in Hiseville area; yet, **ELI B. CRENSHAW** (age 19) was a farmhand living at home with his parents [?].

3315. **ROBERT A. CRENSHAW** (born 1867, black).

3316. **SAMUEL W. CRENSHAW** (born September, 1869, black). Sammy lived at home in 1880 and worked on the farm.

332. **POLLY A. CRENSHAW** (black) was listed in 1870 in the house of **SAMUEL WILEY CRENSHAW** (born 1824) and her age was 42, so she was born 1828. It is not clear whether she was his sister or sister-in-law, and a child was listed with her.

3321. **JOHN W. CRENSHAW** (born 1866, black).

34. **GEORGE CRENSHAW** (black, born 1808, Virginia) was listed in the *1870 Census of Metcalfe County, Kentucky*, as head of household and a farm laborer, with wife **MARIA CRENSHAW** (born 1812). She might have been the "negro girl Maria" that John Crenshaw left to his son Anderson Crenshaw in his 1818 will. The children of George Crenshaw and Maria Crenshaw were all born in Kentucky.

341. **AMANDA CRENSHAW** (born 1833, black, laundress).

3411. **EUGENE CRENSHAW** (born August, 1853, black, farmer) is head of household in the *1900 Census of Metcalfe County, KY*, in District #2, with his wife **SALLY J. CRENSHAW** (born Feb., 1854), both born in Kentucky. They had 5 children, of whom 4 were living in 1900. The census also stated they were married 25 years. In 1910 **SALLIE CRENSHAW** lived with her son George and stated she had 5 children with 4 still living.

34111. ---- **CRENSHAW** (born circa 1876).

34112. ---- **CRENSHAW** (born circa 1878).

34113. **WILLIAM H. CRENSHAW** (born November, 1880).

34114. **KATIE F. CRENSHAW** (born April, 1883).

34115. **GEORGE H. CRENSHAW** (born December, 1886) married **HATTIE L. ----** (b. 1886) and lived in Hiseville District No. 4, Barren County, Kentucky, in 1910. Occupation: Farmer. The census also stated they had been married 4 years (noting the oldest child was age 6). In 1920 she was a widow with six children.

341151. **NETTIE B. CRENSHAW** (b. 1904, black).

341152. **GEORGE H. CRENSHAW** (b. 1906, black).

341153. **JAMES A. CRENSHAW** (b. 1908, black).

341154. **GENIE M. CRENSHAW** (b. 1910, black).

341155. **SALLIE F. CRENSHAW** (b. 1912, black).

341156. **HATTIE L. CRENSHAW** (b. 1914, black).

3412. **JOHN MORGAN CRENSHAW** (born 1862/3, mulatto). In 1880, **one MORGAN CRENSHAW** was a farm hand for Mrs. P. Summers in Hiseville, Barren County, KY.

3413. **WILLIAM CRENSHAW** (born 1864/5, mulatto). In 1880, one **BILL CRENSHAW** was a farm hand for Mrs. P. Summers in Hiseville, Barren County, KY.

342. **LAURA B. CRENSHAW** (born 1847, black, laundress).

343. **JOSHUA CRENSHAW** (born 1849, black, farm laborer).

35. **SAMUEL CRENSHAW** (black, born 1846, Kentucky) was listed in the *1870 Census of Metcalfe County* in the household of Andrew J. Greggs (black, born in 1834). Samuel's wife was **AMERICA ----** (born 1850) and the census record indicated they had married in February, 1870. It is most probable that her maiden name was America Greggs and they were living with her brother, Andrew J. Greggs. In the *1880 Census of Metcalfe County*, **SAMMY CRENSHAW** (age 26) was head of household, with wife America (age 30) and niece **MARY CRENSHAW** (age 8), as well as their four children as listed below, and lived in the Lafayette Magisterial District.

351. **FRANCIS CRENSHAW** (born 1871, black).

352. **CHARLEY F. CRENSHAW** (born 1874, black). **CHARLES CRENSHAW** (age 37) was head of the household in the *1910 Census of*

Metcalfe County, KY, in Knob Lick Precinct, with his wife **NORA E. CRENSHAW** (age 26), and son **STANLEY R. CRENSHAW**. (The censustaker erroneously indicated they were white.)

3521. **STANLEY R. CRENSHAW** (born 1909, black).

353. **DORA L. CRENSHAW** (born 1877, black).

354. **MARY B. CRENSHAW** (born 1879, black).

36. **MARY CRENSHAW** (1820-1910), a black woman of Glasgow, Kentucky, died Apr. 13, 1910. [Ref: *Traces*, Vol. 12, No. 1, 1984, p. 24].

37. **LOUISA CRENSHAW** (black, born 1856, Kentucky) was listed in the *1870 Census of Metcalfe County* as a farm worker living in the household of Archibald Pennick (born 1803), a black farmer.

38. **JESSIE E. CRENSHAW** (February 8, 1895 - October 28, 1963) was buried in the Jessie Crenshaw-Blue Spring Cemetery in Metcalfe County, Kentucky, with wife **ELVIE CRENSHAW** (September 17, 1898-still living in 1983). This cemetery is about 3.5 miles west of Knob Lick, near Blue Spring Church. Other blacks buried there follows: [Ref: *Metcalfe County Cemeteries*, Volume I, page 68]

Luella Roberts (1854-1903)
Alton G. Carr (June 27, 1918 - June 28, 1968)
James O. Brewer (January 24, 1913 - February 7, 1974)
    Private in the U. S. Army, World War II
John W. Barrix (April 19, 1895 - August 23, 1974)
    Private in the U. S. Army
Tom Barrix (1906-1976)
Walter Barrix (1912-1974)
J. W. and M. L. Barrix (on same stone)
Belle and Oral Barrix (no tombstones as of 1983)
MRS. ---- CRENSHAW, wife of **O. C. CRENSHAW** (no tombstone)
Welby Stockton, son of Mary (Jun 27, 1915 - Jan 21, 1916)
Susan Stockton, wife of Rheuben Stockton
    (December 25, 1828 - January 12, 1906).

In the *1920 Census of Metcalfe County, Kentucky*, there was a **JESSIE F. CRENSHAW** (age 23, black) listed as head of household in Sulphur Well District #2, with wife **ELVIE CRENSHAW** (age 21) and daughter **ALINE CRENSHAW** (age 2 years and 4 months). This census was enumerated on January 29, 1920.

39. **OTTO CRENSHAW** (May 4, 1892 - alive in 1983) and **EMMER CRENSHAW** (September 11, 1897 - December 8, 1948) are buried in Metcalfe County, Kentucky in the Summer Shade Black Cemetery. There are many other people buried here and these are the only Crenshaws as of 1983. [Ref: *Metcalfe County Cemeteries*, Vol. I, p. 153]

310. **ROBIN W. CRENSHAW** wrote his will on September 19, 1918, and it

was probated on December 25, 1922, naming his wife **SEMERAINCE CRENSHAW** [Ref: *Metcalfe County, Kentucky, Will Book 1:481*]. In the *1920 Census of Metcalfe County*, **ROBIN W. CRENSHAW** (age 69) was head of house in Sulphur Well District #2, with his wife, **MAMIE CRENSHAW** (age 69). Thus, they were both born in 1851. In the *1880 Census of Metcalfe County* **ROBIN CRENSHAW** (age 30) was head of household in Lafayette Magisterial District, with wife **SUMARIMINS CRENSHAW** (age 30) and children listed as "mulatto."

3101. **CATHERINE CRENSHAW** (born 1868, mulatto).

3102. **HENRY CRENSHAW** (born 1871, mulatto).

311. **HOWARD W. CRENSHAW** (age 49) was head of household in the *1910 Census of Metcalfe County* in the Knob Lick Precinct, with his wife **FANNIE CRENSHAW** (age 48) and a daughter **MARY L. CRENSHAW** (age 26). Howard (age 59) was head of household in the *1920 Census of Metcalfe County, Kentucky*, with his wife **FANNY** (age 53), and daughter **LIZZIE** (age 34). They lived next to **ROBIN W. CRENSHAW** and family, and also **CHARLIE B. CRENSHAW** and family, plus there were several black Stockton families as neighbors.

3111. **MARY L. (LIZZIE) CRENSHAW** (born 1885, black).

312. **SALLIE CRENSHAW** (age 16) was listed as a black cook in the household of John H. Harlin in Glasgow, Kentucky, in 1920. [Ref: *1920 Census of Barren County, Kentucky*].

313. **JOHN E. CRENSHAW** (age 56) was a black farmer and the head of household in the *1920 Census of Barren County, Kentucky*, in Hiseville District #4. No wife listed; only these children:

3131. **BERNICE CRENSHAW** (born 1898)
married **JOHN E. WILSON** (born 1888).

31311. **CARRIE B. WILSON** (born Sept., 1918).

3132. **GEORGE E. CRENSHAW** (born 1905).

3133. **GOREE CRENSHAW** (son, born 1907).

3134. **ELVIS M. CRENSHAW** (son, born 1911).

314. **KATHLEEN CRENSHAW** (born 1904, black) was listed in the house of **SIMON ESTES** (born 1844, black) as his granddaughter. [Ref: *1920 Census of Barren County, Kentucky*, Hiseville Dist. #4].

315. **WILLIAM M. CRENSHAW** (born July, 1856, black) was listed as head of household in the *1900 Census of Barren County, KY*, with his mother **KESIAH CRENSHAW** (born January, 1820, in KY) and a boarder named **LAURA GRACEN** (born September, 1876, KY).

Kesiah had 9 children and all were living. William was listed as head of household in the *1910 Census of Barren County, KY*, and his age is given as 63, and living with him were boarders **LAURA GRAYSON** (age 35) and **STELLA GRAYSON** (age 6). William was a widower in the *1920 Census of Barren County, KY*, Cave City District #6, with adopted daughter **LAURA GRAYSON** (born 1876).

316. **ED CRENSHAW** (born 1820, black, farm hand) was listed as head of the household in the *1870 Census of Barren County, KY*, in Glasgow Precinct, with **MARY CRENSHAW** (age 35, keeping house), **WILLIE CRENSHAW** (age 10), and **EDDIE CRENSHAW** (age 1 year).

317. **ROBERT CRENSHAW** (born 1857, black) was listed as a farm hand working in the household of JAMES RATCLIFF in the *1870 Census of Barren County, Kentucky*, in the Hiseville Precinct. In the *1910 Census of Barren County*, **ROBERT CRENSHAW** (age 53 or 63?) lived in Glasgow, Kentucky with wife **EASTER CRENSHAW** (age 49) and ADA GARDNER (age 12) who was listed as "adopted daughter." His occupation was "laborer in tobacco factory." They had been married 5 years, but no children. All were born in Kentucky.

318. **MALINDA CRENSHAW** (born 1810, black) was listed as head of the household in the *1880 Census of Barren County, KY*. She was born in Kentucky and her parents were born in Virginia. With her in 1880 were HELEN WILCOX (daughter, age 35) and SMITH WILCOX (grandson, age 9). They lived in the town of Glasgow.

319. **HENRY CRENSHAW** (born 1819, black) was listed as head of the household in the *1880 Census of Barren County, KY*, with his wife **MATILDA CRENSHAW** (born 1820) in the town of Glasgow.

320. **ROBERT CRENSHAW** (born 1845, black) was listed as head of the household in the *1880 Census of Barren County, KY*, with his wife **ELIZA CRENSHAW** (age 35), cousin JANE PARRISH (age 18), and **LEWIS CRENSHAW** (age 69) and wife **EVA CRENSHAW** (age 75), living with them. **ROBERT CRENSHAW** and family lived in the eastern half of the Glasgow District. He was a blacksmith. In the 1870 Census of Barren County, **ROBERT CRENSHAW** (age 28) was a blacksmith in the town of Glasgow, and living with him were **ELIZA CRENSHAW** (age 23) and **JOSEPH CRENSHAW** (age 10).

321. **LUCY CRENSHAW** (born 1800, black) lived in the household of Benjamin Combs [?] in the *1880 Census of Barren County, KY*, in the eastern half of the Glasgow Precinct. The census also indicated Lucy Crenshaw and her parents were born in Virginia.

322. **MARY CRENSHAW** (born 1831, black) was listed as head of the household in the *1880 Census of Barren County, KY*, with her daughter **MARY CRENSHAW** (age 10), daughter **HELEN CRENSHAW** (age 8), and son **JOHN CRENSHAW** (age 5). They lived in the "east of the Glasgow Precinct, west of pike, Magisterial District 9."

323. H. **CRENSHAW** (born 1860, black) was a farm hand on the farm of J. F. SUMMERS in the Hiseville area of Barren County in 1880.

324. **STEVEN CRENSHAW** (born 1818, black) was a farm hand on the farm of **HENRY A. CRENSHAW** in Hiseville District, Kentucky, in 1880.

325. G. **CRENSHAW** (born 1850, mulatto) was listed as head of house in the *1880 Census of Barren County, KY,* with wife **SARAH J. CRENSHAW** (age 24, black) and son ---- **CRENSHAW** [name blank], who was born in October, 1879. All were born in Kentucky.

326. **EDMON CRENSHAW** (born April, 1819, black) was listed as head of house in the *1900 Census of Barren County, KY,* District No. 1, with wife **MANDY CRENSHAW** (born February, 1871) and their son, **CLARANCE CRENSHAW** (born January, 1890). Edmon and Mandy had been married 12 years, and had 6 children, but only 1 living.

327. **RUSSEL CRENSHAW** (born 1884, black) was listed as head of house in the *1910 Census of Barren County, KY,* Hiseville District 4, with his wife **EMMA CRENSHAW** (b. 1882, black), married 5 years and they had two children. **RUSSEL CRENSHAW** was a farm laborer.

3271. **CLARA B. CRENSHAW** (born 1906, black).

3272. **WILLIAM L. CRENSHAW** (born 1907, black).

328. **WILLIAM H. CRENSHAW** (born 1830, black) was head of household in the *1910 Census of Metcalfe County, KY,* in the Knob Lick Precinct, with wife **ROSIE L. CRENSHAW** (age 43 or 63, unclear) and their 2 children. William and Rosie were married 8 years.

3281. **BERTIE L. CRENSHAW** (born 1902, black).

3282. **WILLIE O. CRENSHAW** (born 1905, black).

329. **EDNA L. CRENSHAW** (born 1877, black) was head of household in the *1910 Census of Metcalfe County, KY,* and lived next to the family of **PAUL CRENSHAW** (age 62). Living with Edna were her son **CLARENCE B. CRENSHAW** (age 11), son **WILLIAM R. CRENSHAW** (age 9), and daughter **RUTH A. CRENSHAW** (age 2), in Knob Lick.

330. **MINERVA CRENSHAW** (born 1820, black) was in the household of ALLEN WADE (age 24) and his wife TISHIA WADE (age 26) in the *1880 Census of Barren County, Kentucky*. She was mother-in-law to Allen Wade, so his wife's maiden name was **TISHIA CRENSHAW**. Their children were JAMES WADE (age 6) and ED P. WADE (age 2).

331. **OLIVER CRENSHAW** (born 1820, black, carpenter) was head of the household in the *1870 Census of Barren County, Kentucky*, with wife **TILDA CRENSHAW** (born 1822). Listed with them were PHIL BYBEE (born 1846) and FANNIE BYBEE (born 1847) [a daughter?].

CHAPTER FOUR

UNIDENTIFIED CRENSHAWS IN SOUTH CENTRAL KENTUCKY

AMOS CRENSHAW (Reverend) and **ALMA TOOMES** (married November 1, 1931) "of Lindseyville, Kentucky, celebrated their 50th anniversary in 1981. He has been a Baptist minister in Edmonson County and environs for 41 years, lately at Sweeden Baptist Church. She is a retired school teacher." [Ref: *Glasgow Republican*, 1981].

BENJAMIN R. CRENSHAW JR. married **LOUISA BROWNING**, daughter of William Browning on May 24, 1845. Surety was BENJA. MILLS CRENSHAW [Ref: *Barren County Marriage Licenses*, page 55].

BENJAMIN R. CRENSHAW married **NANCY KING**, daughter of John and Elizabeth King, on March 26, 1846. She married secondly to Benjamin R. Lively [Ref: *Barren County Marriage Licenses*, page 55, and *Traces*, Volume 18, No. 1 (1990), page 20].

C. C. **CRENSHAW** was a Deputy Clerk of Barren County Court in 1865. [Ref: *SCKH&GS Quarterly*, Vol. 6, No. 1 (April, 1978), p. 14].

CORRINNE CRENSHAW, of Glasgow, Kentucky, married in 1871 to **JOSEPH N. McCORMACK, M.D.** (born November 9, 1847, Nelson County, KY) who practiced medicine in Bowling Green, 1875. [Ref: *Kentucky Gene. & Biog.*, Vol. II, p. 187]. One son, **ARTHUR T. McCORMACK**.

EARL CRENSHAW wrote his will on March 10, 1983, and it was probated in Barren County on February 26, 1985. He named the following: **PARKER RITTER**'s children, **PHILLIP CRENSHAW**'s children, **FLOYD CRENSHAW**'s children, plus **GERTIE GERALDS**, **AMOS CRENSHAW**, and **MEARL ELLIS**. [Ref: *Barren County, Kentucky, Will Book 15:784*].

ELIZA CRENSHAW married **SAMUEL C. FRANKLIN** on March 4, 1834. [Ref: M. Reneau's *Barren County Marriage Licenses*, page 94].

EUGENE A. CRENSHAW and wife **LULA B.** lived at 419 Grandview Avenue, Glasgow, Kentucky in 1959; employed by Western KY Gas Company.

GARLAND CRENSHAW was one of eleven distillers in Barren County, KY around 1876 [Ref: F. Gorin's *The Times of Long Ago*, page 75].

GEORGE ANN CRENSHAW (formerly STRANGE) wrote her will on April 26, 1904 and it was probated on June 6, 1906 in Barren County. She named her husband **ROBERT CRENSHAW** and niece **LIZZIE DOTY** (now 13 and an orphan). [Ref: *Barren County, KY, Will Book 6:58*].

JAMES W. CRENSHAW (February 8, 1855 - August 18, 1931) was buried in the Houk Cemetery, Metcalfe County, Kentucky, next to his wife **FRANCES CRENSHAW** (July 13, 1863 - March 1, 1940). Their son, **AMOS LOCKARD CRENSHAW** (March 16, 1891 - June 7, 1970), was never married. He died at the Sunrise Manor Nursing Home in Hodgenville, Larue County, Kentucky. Causes of death were myocardial failure, arteriosclerotic cardiovascular disease, and recent CVA (cardiovascular accident). The informant was **MRS. R. C. NICHOLS**, Route 5, Hodgenville, Kentucky, and the death was registered by **MILDRED N. BIRD**. The funeral director was **JAMES I. WINN, JR.**, of Horse Cave, Kentucky, with burial in the Houk Cemetery in Metcalfe County, Kentucky. Amos was white, and by occupation a farmer. His parents were **JAMES W. CRENSHAW and FRANCIS [FRANCES] CRENSHAW**. [Ref: *Commonwealth of Kentucky Death Certificate No. 116-70-20260*]. Even though **JAMES W. CRENSHAW** (1855-1931) was buried in Metcalfe County, Kentucky, a search by the Kentucky Department for Health Services for his death certificate was unsuccessful, noting that they searched all Kentucky counties from 1911 to 1986, and adding that a certificate may not have been filed by the funeral director or the death could have occurred in another state. He was also not found in the censuses of Barren County and Metcalfe County, Kentucky, from 1860 through 1920, which indicates he was living in another county, most likely Hart.

MARY CRENSHAW (white female, age 1 month) died suddenly in Barren County, Kentucky, in July, 1860. [Ref: Barren County Federal Mortality Schedule, published in *Kentucky Pioneer Genealogy and Records*, Volume I, No. 2, April, 1979, page 13].

ROBERT CRENSHAW - see "George Ann Crenshaw" (d. 1906, Barren Co.)

W. M. CRENSHAW wrote his will on January 26, 1963 (probated on January 3, 1966), in Barren County, Kentucky. He named his wife **BERNICE CRENSHAW**, but only mentioned his children (no names were given). [Ref: *Barren County, KY, Will Book 12:2*].

WILL CRENSHAW (born 1889, black) was a hired farm worker for Robert Barbour in 1910 in the Goodnight Precinct of Barren County, KY. [Ref: *1910 Census of Barren County, Kentucky*].

WILLIAM T. CRENSHAW and wife **ESTHER** resided in Glasgow, Kentucky in 1959, where he was employed as a driver for Leech & Davie Co.

CHAPTER FIVE

PEARL EUGENIA CRENSHAW PEDEN'S SCRAPBOOK
BARREN COUNTY, KENTUCKY, 1913-1944

Pearl Eugenia Crenshaw (1892-1976) was the youngest child of **Henry Anderson Crenshaw and Martha Alice Embree**, of Metcalfe County, KY. She kept a scrapbook of newspaper clippings which contain a wealth of information on family, friends and acquaintances. Many of these old clippings are not dated and the relationships, if any, are not explained. The clippings appear to have been collected between 1913 and 1944, which would be from the year of her marriage to **William Henry "Will" Peden** (1891-1944) until the year he died. "Will" and Pearl Peden lived in Barren County and the clippings were primarily from the local newspaper *The Glasgow Times*. The information gleaned from these clippings was presented here in hopes of preserving at least a part of our family history as it pertains to the Crenshaws, Pedens, and other families, all of whom resided in the communities located around Glasgow, KY. I also did some additional research to identify some of the dates in these clippings and that information appears in brackets as [**My Note**], abstracted by **Henry C. Peden, Jr.**

<u>ADAMS</u>: "We wish to thank the neighbors, relatives and friends for their kindnesses and help shown to us in the death of our little girl, **BETTIE JANE ADAMS**, and especially do we thank DR. BOTTS, DR. ACTON, and UNCLE BLEFORD UNDERWOOD." MR. and MRS. LAWRENCE ADAMS.

<u>AKERS-SMITH MARRIAGE ANNOUNCEMENT</u>: **MR. FRED SMITH and MRS. BESSIE AKERS** were married in West Virginia on July 14th. MR. SMITH is a son of MR. and MRS. C. R. SMITH, of Coral Hill, and he has been making his home in West Virginia for several years where he has prospered. MRS. BESSIE AKERS SMITH is from West Virginia.

<u>ALEXANDER DEATH NOTICE</u>: Death came to **MR. OLIVER W. ALEXANDER** at his home at Hiseville on Monday. He was 84 years old on January 14th, and in early manhood moved from Cumberland County and located at Hiseville where he was an extensive farmer, stock, and tobacco dealer until ill health forced his retirement from active life several months ago and he had been confined to his bed. Fifty-nine years ago on March 15th he married to MISS ANNA BUSH, who survives him with these 11 children: MRS. VERNA WHITE, of Hiseville; MRS. JIM CRENSHAW, of Temple Hill; ARTHUR ALEXANDER, of Coral Hill; MRS. WALFORD OLSON, of Whittier, Calif.; WILL ALEXANDER, of Fullerton, Calif.; MRS. ALYNE BOYD of Bowling Green; MRS. RALPH RICHARDSON, of Bowling Green; JOE B. ALEXANDER, of Hiseville; MRS. HAROLD STILES, of Gary, Indiana; CHARLIE ALEXANDER, of Coral Hill; and HENRY CLAY ALEXANDER of Hiseville; also, 44 grandchildren and 22 great-grand-children. He was a member of the Methodist Church and a leader in his community. Services were conducted at the Hiseville Methodist Church by REV. S. A. MATTHEWS assisted by REV. KIRBY SMITH, with burial in Hiseville Cemetery. (The obituary ended with this oddly

worded sentence: MRS. B. B. NORRIS, MRS. HAZEL SMITH, MRS. WOODROW PARROT and MRS. JAMES MATTHEWS, and ROBERT daughters and grandsons of deceased.) [**Note:** OLIVER WOLCOTT ALEXANDER died April 20, 1942].

ALEXANDER DEATH NOTICE: **MRS. FLOYD CHITWOOD ALEXANDER**, 38, wife of MR. CHARLIE ALEXANDER, of Coral Hill, died suddenly at 3 o'clock, Monday afternoon, from a heart ailment. One of the best known women of her section her death was a shock to the family and her friends. She had been suffering severe heart attacks for the past week and then was stricken seriously ill. Daughter of the late ALEX CHITWOOD and IDA MORGAN, she was a native of this county, and besides her husband is survived by 6 children: MRS. ROLLIN UNDERWOOD, NORMA LEE ALEXANDER, CAROLINE ALEXANDER, CHARLES ALEXANDER, HENRY CRENSHAW ALEXANDER and RAY WALKER ALEXANDER. She had no brothers or sisters. Funeral services were held at the Coral Hill Church by REV. W. E. CHURCH, of Bowling Green, and REV. WARREN DUNAGAN, of Cave City, and burial was in the Hiseville Cem. [**My Note:** She died in 1944].

ALEXANDER DEATH NOTICE: "Mrs. Charles Alexander Succumbed Monday." The many friends of the **CHARLIE ALEXANDER** family of the Coral Hill section were shocked Monday afternoon when news of the unexpected passing of MRS. ALEXANDER spread, as if by magic, throughout Barren County. MRS. ALEXANDER has not been in the best of health for some weeks, but the gravity of the situation was not suspicioned until Sunday when she was stricken quite seriously. MRS. ALEXANDER before her marriage was MISS FLOYD CHITWOOD, the only daughter of the late ALEX and IDA MORGAN CHITWOOD, and was a native of this county. She is survived by a husband and children, viz., MRS. ROLLIN UNDERWOOD, now living at Camp Polk, Louisiana, RAY WALKER ALEXANDER, NORMA LEE ALEXANDER, CAROLINE ALEXANDER, CHARLES ALEXANDER and HENRY CRENSHAW ALEXANDER, all living at home. Services were conducted yesterday afternoon at the Coral Hill Church by REV. WALTER E. CHURCH and REV. WARREN DUNAGAN, with burial in Hiseville Cemetery afterwards. [**My Note:** FLOYD CHITWOOD ALEXANDER was born in 1903; died in 1944].

ALEXANDER-NORRIS MARRIAGE ANNOUNCEMENT: **MISS ANNA GLAYDE ALEXANDER**, daughter of MR. and MRS. A.B. ALEXANDER of Hiseville, Kentucky, and **MR. BERNICE NORRIS** [sic] were married June 6th in Jeffersonville, Indiana, the REV. E. C. McKINNEY officiating. She is a niece of MR. HASKELL MILLER, formerly of this place, and he is one of the Norris Brothers who have played an important part in the business interests of the town for a number of years.

ALEXANDER-UNDERWOOD MARRIAGE ANNOUNCEMENT: **MISS DORIS ALEXANDER**, daughter of MR. and MRS. CHARLIE ALEXANDER of Coral Hill, and **MR. ROLLIN D. UNDERWOOD**, son of MR. and MRS. FLEM C. UNDERWOOD of this city, were married Monday evening, March 10th, at 9 o'clock, at the Baptist parsonage in Bowling Green, with the REV. R. T. SKINNER officiating. They were accompanied by MISS MARJORIE DOUGHERTY, MISS HELEN REECE, and MR. FAY SMITH. MRS. ALEXANDER is a 1941 graduate of Glasgow High School, and MR. ALEXANDER is a 1940 graduate. He currently works for the Civil Service at Fort Knox.

ALLEN-JACKMAN MARRIAGE ANNOUNCEMENT: **MISS ANNIE MAE ALLEN**, of Glasgow, and **MR. N. M. JACKMAN**, of Cave City, were married in Bowling Green, Kentucky, on October 12, 1929.

ALLEN-JACKMAN MARRIAGE ANNOUNCEMENT: **MR. N. M. JACKMAN and MISS ANNIE MAY ALLEN** were married in Bowling Green, October 12th. The groom is a farmer and a son of MR. E. J. JACKMAN. The bride is a teacher and a daughter of MR. J. C. ALLEN.

ALLEN-PEMBERTON MARRIAGE ANNOUNCEMENT: **MISS MARY FRANCES ALLEN**, of Glasgow, and **MR. TERRY PEMBERTON**, only son of MR. and MRS. L. W. PEMBERTON, were married in Scottsville on Wednesday. They were accompanied by MR. CHARLES STRADER and MISS MARTHA JEAN COPPAGE, of Glasgow. They will reside at her parents' home for the present.

ALLEN-TUCKER MARRIAGE ANNOUNCEMENT: **MR. DEPP E. ALLEN and MRS. GARY TUCKER** were married on October 8th at Morgantown. MR. ALLEN is a nephew of the late MISS NETTIE DEPP, of Glasgow. He is a farmer in Missouri. MRS. TUCKER is a daughter of MR. and MRS. H. H. HUNTSMAN, of this city, and her former husband died several years ago while they resided in St. Louis. She is bookkeeper for the H. A. McElroy Company, of Bowling Green. MR. ALLEN was reared in Barren County.

AMOS-MOULDER MARRIAGE ANNOUNCEMENT: **MISS MARY F. AMOS**, of Cave City, and **MR. H. E. MOULDER**, of Dallas, Texas, were married June 13th, ----, in Louisville. They will make their home in Dallas.

ANDERSON DEATH NOTICE: **MRS. CASSIE F. ANDERSON**, who departed this world, Sunday, February 17, 1935, at the age of 80 years, 5 months, and 1 day. (Included a poem written by a niece, CHRISTINE ARNOLD).

BAGBY DEATH NOTICE: **THOMAS C. BAGBY** died at the Community Hospital Monday night at the age of 59 years after a month's illness from a combination of diseases. He was a son of the late CHARLES R. BAGBY who died fifty years ago. His mother died only a year or two ago. He is survived by two brothers, EUGENE BAGBY and JAMES BAGBY, both of Coral Hill. He made his home with his brother James. For the past 30 years TOM BAGBY has been identified with the insurance firm of Dickinson & Trigg, now Thomas Dickinson & Son. He was a member of the Christian Church at Coral Hill, and the Masonic fraternity. Funeral services were held at the home of DR. HOWARD, after which the remains were taken to the home of his brother at Coral Hill. Burial was in the family cemetery near the home of CHARLEY SMITH.

BAGBY DEATH NOTICE: "Former Barren Countian Dies in Metcalfe Co." Funeral services for **MR. W. S. BAGBY**, age 79, well known resident of the Wisdom section in Metcalfe County, were held Sunday morning with REV. BARTON and REV. PEDIGO of Edmonton in charge. Burial was in the family cemetery near his home. He was born and reared in the Hiseville community of this [Barren] county and moved to Metcalfe County some 35 years ago. He was a devout member of the Christian Church at Pleasant Hill. He is survived by his wife, MRS. LOU DEPP

BAGBY, to whom he had been wedded for 55 years. He is also survived by these children: MRS. J. R. RAY, of Edmonton; MRS. B. W. DOWNING, of Fountain Run; MRS. LUTHER WORD, of Summer Shade; MRS. JEWELL BRYANT, of Bowling Green; MR. JOHN BAGBY, of Hiseville; MR. ADOLPH BAGBY, of Edmonton; MR. J. Y. BAGBY, of Casper, Wyoming; MR. WILLIE BAGBY, of Wichita Falls, Texas; and 22 grandchildren. The following brothers and sisters survive him: MR. RODDY BAGBY and MR. LUTHER BAGBY, of Coral Hill; MR. CHARLES BAGBY, of Cincinnati, Ohio; MRS. J. W. DEPP, of Sapulpa, Oklahoma; and MRS. ANNIE BURRIS, Hiseville. [**My Note:** W. S. BAGBY died on November 14, 1935, and was buried in the Bagby-Slemmons-Munday Cemetery in Metcalfe County, Kentucky].

BAGBY DEATH NOTICE: **CHARLES MORGAN BAGBY** died in Gary, Indiana, Monday the 28th, and the remains will be brought here today for burial. MR. BAGBY died under an operation for ruptured appendix, at the age of 30 years. He is survived by his wife, who was a native of Gary, and one child. His parents, MR. and MRS. EUGENE BAGBY, of Coral Hill, also survive, two brothers, WALKER BAGBY, of Glasgow, and TED BAGBY, of Coral Hill, and one half-sister, MRS. ELLU BALE, of Canmer. MR. BAGBY was born and reared in the Coral Hill country.

BAGBY DEATH NOTICE: **MR. EDWARD L. BAGBY**, 71 years of age, died at his home at Hiseville Tuesday, after a long and lingering illness. He is survived by his wife, MRS. IRENE BAGBY, one daughter, MRS. EMMA WILLIAMS, and three sons, MR. ARTHUR BAGBY, of Beckton, MR. ROE BAGBY, of Gary, Indiana and MR. ELVIN BAGBY, of Hiseville. He also leaves two sisters, MRS. JENNIE DEPP, and MRS. ANNIE BURRIS, both of Hiseville; and, four brothers, MR. W. S. BAGBY, of Wisdom, MR. LUTHER BAGBY, of Houston, TX, MR. CHARLEY BAGBY, of Redding, Ohio, and MR. RODDY BAGBY, of Coral Hill. The funeral services were conducted by REV. OMER in the Christian Church in Hiseville, of which the deceased was a member, after which the remains were interred in the Hiseville Cemetery.

BAGBY DEATH NOTICE: "Mrs. Lou Bagby Buried Today." **MRS. LOU HANSON DEPP BAGBY** died at the home of her son, JOHN BAGBY, at Hiseville Tuesday afternoon, at age of 85. Her husband, WILLIE S. BAGBY, died seven years ago. Surviving are three sons and three daughters: MRS. B. W. DOWNING, of Scottsville; MRS. LUTHER WORD, of Summer Shade; MRS. J. E. (GERTRUDE) BRYANT, of Bowling Green; JOE BAGBY, of Casper, Wyoming; ADOLPH BAGBY, of Wisdom; and, JOHN BAGBY of Hiseville. Funeral services were conducted at the home of ADOLPH BAGBY at Wisdom, by ELDER ALLEN PHY. Burial in the Bagby cemetery.

BAGBY DEATH NOTICE: "Mrs. Irene Owen Bagby Dies At Coral Hill Today. Widow Of Late Edward L. Bagby Succumbs At Home of Son." **MRS. IRENE OWEN BAGBY**, 73, widow of the late EDWARD L. BAGBY, died at the home of her son MR. ELVIN BAGBY, in the Hiseville-Coral Hill section today at 8 a.m. She was a member of the Hiseville Christian Church. She is survived by one brother, MR. G. M. OWEN, of Glasgow, one sister, MISS JOSIE OWEN of Glasgow, and the following children: MRS. EMMA WILLIAMS, of Horse Cave; ELVIN BAGBY, of Beckton; and ROE

BAGBY, of Gary, Indiana. Funeral services will be conducted by the REV. C. C. OMAR at the Hiseville Christian Church on Wednesday at 2 p.m. Burial will be in the Hiseville Cemetery. [**My Note:** IRENE BAGBY died October 12, 1937. EDWARD BAGBY died November 19, 1930].

BAGBY DEATH NOTICE: **MRS. MARY MARIA BAGBY**, 83 years of age, died at the home of her son MR. JIM BAGBY near Coral Hill last Friday. She was the widow of the late MR. CHARLEY BAGBY, who died 48 years ago. Surviving children are MR. TOM BAGBY, MR. GENE BAGBY, and MR. JIM BAGBY, all living in Coral Hill. Before marriage she was MISS MARY MARIA WATKINS and is survived by two brothers and a half-sister: MR. W. M. WATKINS, the coroner of the county, ROBERT WATKINS, and MISS BETTIE WATKINS, all of Coral Hill. She was a member of the Christian Church, and spent her entire life near Coral Hill, KY.

BAILEY-NUCKOLS MARRIAGE ANNOUNCEMENT: **MISS ETHEL BAILEY**, of Temple Hill, and **MR. JESSE D. NUCKOLS**, married in Jeffersonville, Indiana.

BAIRD DEATH NOTICE: "Judge Virgil H. Baird Buried Today." Headed by his devoted compatriot and staunch friend GOVERNOR ALBERT CHANDLER ...and other prominent state officials...a vast throng of friends and associate overflowed the First Christian Church to pay their last respects to the late **VIRGIL H. BAIRD** [a very long obituary followed]. JUDGE BAIRD was in his 77th year and is survived by his wife, MRS. KATHERINE SHIRLEY BAIRD, and a sister, MRS. ADA (J. T.) VINCENT, of Beaver Dam. Three nephews also survive: VIRGIL VINCENT, of Owensboro; CLAY VINCENT, of Hartford; and, CHARLES VINCENT, of Beaver Dam. Burial was in Glasgow Cemetery under the auspices of the Masonic Lodge. He was also a member of the Knights of Pythias.

BAIRD-BOND MARRIAGE ANNOUNCEMENT: **MISS MARY BAIRD**, daughter of MRS. EUGENE BAIRD, of near Goodnight, and **MR. OSCAR BOND** were married at the home of her sister, MRS. WILLIAM CHAMBLISS, JR., in Anderson, MO, Tuesday the 14th. MR. BOND is president of the Bond Brothers Creosoting Company of Louisville.

BARBOUR DEATH NOTICE: **MISS PEARL BARBOUR**, daughter of MR. and MRS. W. L. BARBOUR, died at her home here last Wednesday. Death was caused by spinal meningitis after an illness of only a few days. MISS BARBOUR was in her 22nd year, a very lovely and estimable young lady. She had been a member of the Methodist Church for several years. Surviving are her two sisters and parents: MRS. ADDIE SHARP, MRS. G. C. HARLOW, and MR. and MRS. W. L. BARBOUR. Burial in Glasgow Cemetery, February 27th, ---- [no date given].

BARBOUR DEATH NOTICE: "Death Of Mrs. Sarah Barbour At Goodnight." **MRS. SARAH BARBOUR** died at her home at Goodnight at an early hour Monday morning of a complication of diseases at the age of 83, lacking 5 days. Surviving are four children: MISS BEULAH BARBOUR, and MR. RUFUS BARBOUR, at home; MRS. L. U. CORNELIUS, of Seattle, Washington; and Lt. Commander HERBERT L. BARBOUR, of San Diego, CA. Five grandchildren also survive. MRS. BARBOUR was a member of the

Baptist Church, where funeral services were held by REV. SELVES, MR. W. P. COOMBS, and REV. IRVIN GREEN. Interment was at Goodnight.

BARBOUR SURPRISE BIRTHDAY DINNER: One of the most enjoyable affairs of the season was the birthday dinner given **MRS. SALLIE BARBOUR** at her home near Goodnight, KY, September 20th, in honor of her 80th birthday. Thanks was offered by MR. VIRGIL BAIRD; a beautiful cake was baked by MRS. EUGENE BAIRD; real nice talks were given by MR. VIRGIL BAIRD and MR. WILL COOMBS; MRS. RUFUS BARBOUR and daughter SARABETH sang a song. Those present were: MRS. EUGENE BAIRD, MABLE PARKER, MR. and MRS. MOTE PEDEN, MISS MABLE PEDEN, MRS. TAYLOR REDFORD, MISS FLORENCE REDFORD, MRS. HENRY REDFORD, MRS. LUTHER PARRISH, MR. and MRS. MASSEY OWENS, MR. and MRS. ELLA PARRISH and family, MR. and MRS. G. F. QUIGLEY, MR. HASKELL QUIGLEY, MR. and MRS. W. R. JACKMAN and family, MRS. MILLS PARRISH and two sons, MR. and MRS. WILLIAM HARLOW and family, MR. and MRS. WILL CHURCH, MRS. RALPH RICHARDSON and family, MISS PATTIE SUMMERS, MISS ANITA STEEN, MR. and MRS. O. W. ALEXANDER, MR. and MRS. JOHN BAGBY, MRS. L. H. SUMMERS and granddaughter MISS LOUISA PARRISH, MR. CHARLIE REDFORD, MR. and MRS. H. B. RICHARDSON and family, MRS. ANNIE PARRISH, MISS BETTIE ROGERS, MISS ROHOMETTA ROGERS, MISS MARY WHITE, MR. H. J. WHITE, MRS. BELLE PARRISH, MR. and MRS. H. N. PARRISH, MISSES MARY AND PAULINE PARRISH, MISS LURA TURNER, MRS. ANNIE MILLER, MRS. MARY ROSS, MRS. H. N. FISHBACK, MRS. BALUS FISHBACK, REV. W. O. KERSEY, MR. and MRS. CHARLIE DICKEY and daughter, MR. and MRS. JACK BOYD, MR. and MRS. WILL FARRIS, MR. and MRS. J. P. BOYD, JR., VIRGINIA and JAMES BOYD, MRS. MARY SMITH, MR. and MRS. VIRGIL BAIRD, MR. and MRS. WILL COOMBS, MR. and MRS. ISH CHRISTMAS, MRS. E. Y. FERGUSON, MR. and MRS. J. D. GRADY, MRS. G. W. WALTON and son ROGERS WALTON, of Munfordville, MRS. CHARLES WEAVER, MR. and MRS. HERBERT BARBOUR and daughter, of Louisville, MR. SLAYTON BOLES, MR. and MRS. RUFUS BARBOUR and MISS BEULAH BARBOUR, and MISS SARABETH BARBOUR.

BARBOUR-DICKEY MARRIAGE ANNOUNCEMENT: **MISS LOIS BARBOUR**, daughter of MR. and MRS. RUFUS R. BARBOUR, of Goodnight, and **MR. JOHN EDWARD DICKEY**, son of REV. and MRS. C. K. DICKEY, of Louisville, married at the groom's home on May 28 by the groom's father. MRS. DICKEY's mother, MRS. R. R. BARBOUR, and her sister, MISS SARABETH BARBOUR, witnessed the marriage.

BERRY-LAWRENCE MARRIAGE ANNOUNCEMENT: **MISS RUBY BERRY**, daughter of MR. and MRS. HARRY BERRY, on Leslie Avenue in Glasgow, and **CLYDE T. LAWRENCE**, a Tennessee boy who was reared in Morrison, Tenn., and came to Glasgow 3 years ago to work for the Kentucky Utilities Co., were married at the home of REV. R.F. GRIDER on Cherry Street.

BIGGERSTAFF-ALLEN MARRIAGE ANNOUNCEMENT: **MATTIE BLAINE BIGGERSTAFF** of Warren County, and **MR. ROGER ALLEN**, merchant at Dugantown, were married a few days ago and are now at home in Dugantown. MRS. ALLEN has been head nurse at the local hospital [in Glasgow] for awhile.

<u>BLACK DEATH NOTICE</u>: **MR. JOSEPH T. BLACK**, an 80 year old veteran of the Spanish American War, died Sunday at the Veterans Hospital in Murfreesboro, Tennessee, after a few days illness. He had been in declining health for the past several years. He was a native of Glasgow, the son of the late JOSEPH TAYLOR BLACK and SARAH BARLOW. He was employed in Louisville for about 42 years before retiring and returning here to make his home with his brother, the late MR. JAMES BLACK. He was the last survivor of his immediate family and was descended from two of Barren County's earliest pioneer families on both his maternal and paternal lines. His nearest relatives are: two sisters, MRS. JOE LEWIS GOODMAN, of this city; MRS. AUBREY RINGLING, of White Sulphur Springs, Montana; four nephews, MALCOLM BLACK, U.S. Army, stationed in Kansas City, Missouri; VERNON BLACK, of Cumberland Falls, KY; JERRY T. BLACK, of Lexington, KY; and, HORACE BLACK, U.S. Army, now overseas. The funeral services were held at the cemetery yesterday morning, conducted by REV. K. H. McCORKLE, of the Christian Church.

<u>BLANKENSHIP-RENFRO MARRIAGE ANNOUNCEMENT</u>: Announcement has been made of marriage of **MISS GEORGIA BLANKENSHIP** to **MR. BILLIE RENFRO**, of Gary, Indiana, formerly of this place, in Crown Point, Indiana, on February 28. MRS. RENFRO had been visiting MR. and MRS. JAMES PETTY in Louisville 2 weeks before the wedding.

<u>BLEDSOE-SMITH MARRIAGE ANNOUNCEMENT</u>: **MISS JULIA BLEDSOE**, daughter of MR. and MRS. C. D. BLEDSOE, of Hiseville, and **MR. CARL SMITH**, son of MR. and MRS. R. LUTHER SMITH, of Bearwallow, have announced their marriage in Louisville last Sunday, March 31st. They were accompanied by MISS DOROTHY VINCENT and MR. J. T. WINLOCK.

<u>BOONE-BAKER MARRIAGE ANNOUNCEMENT</u>: **MISS AGNES BOONE**, daughter of MR. and MRS. JOHN BOONE of this city, and **MR. JAMES K. BAKER**, son of MR. and MRS. PAUL BAKER, formerly of this city, were married in Louisville last Saturday. They will make their home in Louisville.

<u>BOWLES DEATH NOTICE</u>: **MISS LIZZIE EVALINE BOWLES** died at the home of her parents, MR. and MRS. H. H. BOWLES, in the Owl Spring section, a few days ago. Death was caused by pneumonia. She was in her 21st year, and is survived by five brothers and two sisters, viz. HARRY BOWLES, GEORGE BOWLES, WESLEY BOWLES, WILLIAM BOWLES, CLIFFORD BOWLES, MRS. RUFUS TURNER, of Hiseville, and MRS. ROY THRUMB, of Morgantown, West Va. She was a niece of MISS LIZZIE WORTHINGTON, of this place. Funeral services were conducted by REV. DUNCAN, of the Baptist Church, of which she was a member, and interment was in the Hiseville Cemetery. [**My Note:** EVALINE BOWLES died March 28, 1922].

<u>BOYD-PARRISH MARRIAGE ANNOUNCEMENT</u>: **MISS IDA BERNICE BOYD**, daughter of MR. ALBERT BOYD, of this city, and **MR. ROY AUBREY PARRISH**, a son of MR. and MRS. ELA PARRISH, of Goodnight, were married last Friday in New Liberty by REV. WALTER O. KERSEY, former pastor of the Hiseville Baptist Church. MR. BOYD is a farmer and MRS. BOYD is a

graduate of the Business University, Bowling Green. They will be residing in their new home eight miles north of Glasgow.

BROADY DEATH NOTICE: **MILLS BROADY**, age 78, father of W. H. BROADY, the well-known Hardyville banker, died at his home at Canmer, KY, Monday morning. Interment was at Goodnight. [**My Note:** H. M. BROADY died on February 2, 1931].

BRYANT DEATH NOTICE: "Death Of Mrs. Lula D. Bryant At Horse Cave." **MRS. LULA DICKEY BRYANT**, 55, died at her home in Horse Cave, Monday morning, following only a few days illness of pneumonia. She is survived by four children--MRS. TOM MORAN, DR. FRANK BRYANT, NEWMAN BRYANT, and JOHN BRYANT, all of Horse Cave. [**My Note:** Written on the newspaper clipping in pencil is the date "January 6, 1930."]

BRYANT-FOASD MARRIAGE ANNOUNCEMENT: **MRS. LOUISE BRYANT and MR. JACK FOASD**, of Gary, Indiana, married in Crown Point, Indiana, on Friday afternoon. They will reside in Gary for and then move to Chicago. MRS. FOASD will be remembered as MISS LOUISE RENFRO, of Glasgow.

BURKMAN DEATH NOTICE: "Aunt Maggie Burkman, Age 106 Years, Is Dead" [**My Note:** This article included a photograph and was very long, so only part of it that is genealogically significant was abstracted]. **MRS. MAGGIE TRENT BURKMAN**, beloved resident of Metcalfe County and believed to be the oldest woman in Kentucky, died at her home near Sulphur Well Sunday morning at 3 o'clock following a week's illness of complications. "Aunt Maggie," as she was affectionately known, was 106 years, 11 months, and 28 days old and would have celebrated her 107th birthday on February 28th. She was born in 1835 near the present post office in Sulphur Well, KY. Her birthplace was then in Green County, but the spot later became Metcalfe County when the political subdivision was formed in 1860. Small, thin, and slightly stooped, the white-haired little lady had lived through the terms of 23 presidents of the United States. Her parents died when she was very young, and, in her own words, she practically "reared herself." She was brought up in the homes of neighbors and shortly before the War Between the States she went to Louisville to seek employment. She found work with realtor J. C. MEDDIS, and family. She married MR. JOHN BURKMAN, a Swedish painter, in 1886 and he died shortly after the turn of the century. Following his death she returned home to Metcalfe County and purchased a home 8 miles from Edmonton on the Greensburg Road and has lived there ever since. Her brother, JOE TRENT, fought in the Civil War. Maggie has only two distant relatives living--two great nephews. The funeral services at Pink Ridge on Monday were conducted by the REV. CLAUD SQUIRES.

BURNS-FINLEY MARRIAGE ANNOUNCEMENT: **MISS WYNNIE [?] BURNS**, daughter of MR. J. H. BURNS, of Paris, TN, and **MR. ALBERT B. FINLEY, JR.**, son of MRS. ALBERT B. FINLEY, SR., of Louisville, were married on Thanksgiving Day at the home of her father on Head Street, with the REV. E. G. HAMLETT officiating. MR. and MRS. J. C. BURNS, of Atlanta, GA, were guests at the wedding.

<u>BURRIS DEATH NOTICE</u>: **MR. OTHO BURRIS**, 60 years old, died at his home on the Edmonton Road Tuesday morning at 6:30 o'clock of paralysis. He was stricken with paralysis two years ago, since which he has been in a serious condition. He is survived by his wife, who was MISS ANNIE BAGBY, of Hiseville, and four children: MRS. MITT RICHARDSON, of Hardyville; MRS. HEZZIE HILL, MR. HOWARD BURRIS, and MR. RODDY BURRIS, of this county. Two brothers also survived: MR. BART BURRIS, of St. Louis, and MR. WILL BURRIS, of Morrison, Illinois. Also three sisters: MRS. GEORGE LYON, of Tulden, Illinois; MRS. LAUGH LIVELY, of Sparta, Illinois; and... [the third sister was not named in the article]. MR. BURRIS was a devout member of the Christian Church and funeral services were held in Hiseville by REV. J. L. PIERCY on Wednesday afternoon.

<u>BUTTON-NICKELS MARRIAGE ANNOUNCEMENT</u>: **MISS ALYNE BUTTON**, daughter of MR. and MRS. TOM BUTTON, and **MR. LOUIE NICKELS**, a prosperous farmer of the Coral Hill section, were married in Louisville on Wednesday of last week. They will make their home in Coral Hill.

<u>CALDWELL DEATH NOTICE</u>: **MISS MARIA CALDWELL**, one of the most beloved and finest women the county ever knew, died at her home here last Thursday night. Death followed an illness of only a few days as a result of a fall a week before. Surviving are the following brother and sister: MR. ROBERT CALDWELL, of Memphis, Tennessee, and MRS. PHILIP CALDWELL, of Waco, Texas. Nieces were MRS. BEN T. ROGERS, of Glasgow, and MRS. L. L. WELLS, of Cave City. Services were at the home Saturday, with REV. T. H. ALDERSON, of the Christian Church in charge. Burial was in the cemetery here. MISS MARIA CALDWELL was a daughter of the late SHIP CALDWELL and AMERICA GARNETT, of the Rich Grove section. For many years she conducted a boarding house in Glasgow, KY. [**My Note:** MARIA D. CALDWELL died in 1934, age 80].

<u>CALLAHAN DEATH NOTICE: "Friends Shocked At Sudden Death Of Mr. E. L. Callahan. Ill Only A Few Moments Before The End Came."</u> One of Glasgow's most popular business men passed away in the death of MR. **EUGIE LEE CALLAHAN**, who died last Saturday morning at two o'clock from acute indigestion, after an illness of only a few minutes. The night watchman, MR. HENRY JONES, saw the light come on in the house from across the square and walked over to see what was the matter. He passed away almost instantly, just as MR. and MRS. PATE WALKUP entered the door. MR. CALLAHAN was born and reared in Hiseville, a son of the late MR. JOHN CALLAHAN, and his wife who survives. MR. and MRS. CALLAHAN moved to Oklahoma 20 years ago with their family except "Democrat" who remained behind a year and then followed the family there. A year later he returned to Hiseville where he lived until 1914 and then he came to Glasgow and engaged in the barber business, first with MR. FOSTER and MR. SETTLE, and later on his own account. At the time of his death he was the proprietor of the O.K. Barber Shop and lived in the apartment above. His father died about a year ago, but his mother is living in Tuttle, Oklahoma. His two brothers, MR. WILLIAM CALLAHAN and MR. AVERY CALLAHAN, and his four sisters, PEARL, BEULAH, DORA, and MARY, all live in Oklahoma.

In October, 1916, he was married to MISS RUTH WINN, a daughter of REV. and MRS. JOHN WINN, who survive. It is said when a boy he was asked if he was a Republican or a Democrat he would answer "I am a Democrat" and so he was always after called "Democrat" and few knew him by any other name. He was a member of the Baptists Church of Hiseville, of the Knights of Pythias, the Modern Woodmen, and had taken the first degree in Masonry. He was also president of the Barren County Fish and Game Commission, and president of the local Chapter Izaak Walton League of America. Funeral services were held at the residence Monday afternoon by REV. J. A. EASLEY, assisted by REV. J. L. PIERCY, with the burial in the cemetery at Horse Cave.

CAREY DEATH NOTICE: **MRS. WILLIE CAREY,** died on March 13, 1927. Poem was written "In Memory of Dear Mother," by VERA ELIZABETH LOHDEN.

CASSITY-HARLIN MARRIAGE ANNOUNCEMENT: **MISS LUCILLE CASSITY,** of Stamping Ground, Kentucky, and **MR. SEWELL C. HARLIN,** of Glasgow, will be married at Stamping Ground Christian Church, Jan. 5th ---.

CHAMBERS DEATH NOTICE: "We take this method to sincerely thank our friends and neighbors for their kindness during the illness and death of our dear wife and mother. May God's richest blessings rest upon you." **J. C. CHAMBERS, THOMAS B. CHAMBERS, CURTIS C. CHAMBERS.**

CHANEY DEATH NOTICE: "William Chaney Killed When Struck By Truck." **WILLIAM CHANEY,** age 26, a tenant on the farm of MOTE PEDEN, near Goodnight, was fatally injured Saturday afternoon about 1 o'clock when he was struck by a lumber truck driven by JIM LIVESAY on the Jackson Highway, two miles north of Glasgow, near the BEN MYERS property. MR. CHANEY was reared at Three Springs Creek in Metcalfe County. Together with his family he moved to the Goodnight section some six years ago, where he has been a tenant ever since, having been on the farm of MR. MOTE PEDEN for two years. He is survived by his wife MRS. PAULINE CHANEY, one small daughter GERALDINE CHANEY, and four brothers: WELDON, LUTHER, and GORDON CHANEY, of Goodnight, and FLOYD CHANEY, of C.C.C. Camp No. 3 at Mammoth Cave. Two sisters also survive: MRS. VERA EUDY, of near Glasgow, and RUBY CHANEY, of Goodnight. Burial was in the Houck Cemetery in Metcalfe County. [**My Note:** WILLIAM CHANEY was struck and killed on September 21, 1935].

CHENAULT DEATH NOTICE: **MRS. LUCY CHENAULT** died Monday at the home of her daughter, MRS. ED WINN, in Nashville, Tenn. She was the widow of the late REV. JAMES CHENAULT who died at Hays, several years ago. She is survived by two daughters, MRS. WINN, at whose home she died, and MRS. WILL DEPP, of Smiths Grove. MRS. CHENAULT was MISS LUCY PEDEN before her marriage, and was born and reared in the Boyds Creek section, a few miles from Glasgow where she married MR. CHENAULT and where they lived for many years. Later they moved to Hays, near Smiths Grove where MR. CHENAULT had died. Lucy was the last of her generation to pass away, and was a member of the Baptist Church. Services were held in Nashville and the burial was in Glasgow Cemetery. [**My Note:** LUCY PEDEN CHENAULT died in 1929].

CHITWOOD DEATH NOTICE: "Death Of Mr. J. W. Chitwood, Age 81" **JOHN W. CHITWOOD**, 81, and former resident of this county, dropped dead at his blacksmith shop at Star Mills, Hardin County, at nine o'clock Monday morning. MR. CHARLES CHITWOOD, this county, was a brother, and MRS. MOSS SPEAR, also of Barren County, was a sister. Funeral and burial was at Stone Church, near MR. CHITWOOD's home.

CHITWOOD DEATH NOTICE: **MR. R. A. CHITWOOD**, known to his host of friends as ALEX CHITWOOD, died at his home at Coral Hill, of heart trouble from which he had been a sufferer for a year or two. Her is survived by his wife, who was MISS IDA LOVE, and one daughter, MRS. CHARLES ALEXANDER, of Coral Hill. His surviving brother and sisters are MR. MORGAN CHITWOOD, of Beckton, MR. JOHN CHITWOOD of Glendale, MR. CHARLES CHITWOOD and MR. HENRY CHITWOOD, who live in the West, and MRS. TOM SPEAR, of Beckton. MR. R. A. CHITWOOD was a life long citizen of the Coral Hill country, and for most of his life was a blacksmith. He was a member of the Christian Church, and stood high in the esti-mation of the people as a fine citizen and gentleman. He was above 60 years of age and his passing is widely mourned. Services were conducted at the Christian Church in Coral Hill by Elder ROY H. BISER, of this place, and after which burial was in the cemetery at MR. C. R. SMITH's. [**Note:** ROBERT ALEXANDER CHITWOOD died April 12, 1924. His wife IDA M. CHITWOOD died Oct. 3, 1925].

CHURCH DEATH NOTICE: "Harrison Church Instantly Killed. Shot Six Times By Brother-In-Law When He Enters His Home Near Sulphur Lick, In Monroe County, In Effort To Win Back Estranged Wife." **HARRISON CHURCH**, 38, son of W. T. CHURCH, of Goodnight, was shot and killed at Sulphur Lick, Monroe County, Sunday afternoon. HOWARD HAYS, a brother-in-law of Church, did the killing, Church was shot 6 times and died instantly. The shooting was at the home of HARMON HAYS, with whom JACK HAYS made his home, and the father of MRS. CHURCH. HOWARD HAYS, together with his brother Jack, surrendered to the Sheriff of Monroe County at Tompkinsville on Monday. HARRISON CHURCH had become estranged from his wife who had returned to her home at Sulphur Lick, sought reconciliation. Together with ELLIS CHURCH, HUEY PEDIGO, CHES BRAGG, and "COL" BUNCH, he drove to the Hays home to bring his wife back home. Leaving his companions seated in the car, MR. CHURCH entered the home. As the door closed behind him pistol firing was heard. ELLIS CHURCH rushed to the door but stopped when he learned his brother was dead. He returned to Temple Hill and then notified officers at Tompkinsville. Just what happened behind the closed door is not known. HARRISON CHURCH is survived by his mother and father, MR. and MRS. W. T. CHURCH, one sister, MRS. G. C. LONG, his wife ---- and three children, and the following brothers: WALTER CHURCH, HOMER CHURCH, and ELLIS CHURCH, all of Goodnight. He was a member of the Salem Baptist Church, and funeral services were held at the home by REV. HALE, with interment in the cemetery at this place. [**My Note:** HARRISON F. CHURCH died on November 11, 1928, and was buried in Glasgow Municipal Cemetery].

CHURCH DEATH NOTICE: "Death Of Mr. W. T. Church At Goodnight."

MR. W. T. CHURCH, age 74, one of the leading citizens of North Barren County, died at his home at Goodnight Monday morning, at ten o'clock. Death followed a short illness of pneumonia. Surviving are his wife and the following children: MESSRS. ELLIS, WALTER, HOMER and CHARLIE CHURCH, all of this county. The following brothers and sisters also survive: MR. ED CHURCH, MR. JIM CHURCH, MR. CHARLES CHURCH, and MR. HORACE CHURCH, all of this county; MRS. CLARENCE PRITCHARD, of Jeffersonville, Indiana; MRS. LAURA DENISON, of this county; MRS. MATT UNDERWOOD, of Bowling Green; and, MRS. BEINTY GARRISON, of this place. He was a member of the Baptist Church. The funeral was held at the home on Wednesday, and burial was in the cemetery here. [**My Note:** WILLIAM T. CHURCH died February 20, 1933].

CLARK DEATH NOTICE: "Suicide, Blows End Lives, Porter Clark, Mrs. Clark. Was Former Resident Of This County And Well-Known In Coral Hill Section; Family Trouble Said To Be Cause Of Tragedy." **PORTER CLARK**, while on a visit in Barren County Christmas, made a call on *The Times* office. He appeared in good health and spirits and remarked that he would like to move back to this country to again be with his old home friends. Although a coroner's jury returned a murder and suicide verdict, finding that PORTER CLARK, 49, beat his wife, MRS. BETTY CLARK, 47, to death, and then took his own life by hanging, an air of mystery was cast over the case when officers of Hoopston, Illinois, the Clark's home, failed to locate a death weapon, and testimony of a physician showed the husband had been dead longer than the wife. MR. and MRS. CLARK, former residents of the Coral Hill section, and parents of eight children, moved to Hoopston two years ago. Theory is advanced that threat of the wife to seek divorce from Mr. Clark upon his return from Kentucky as reason for the slaying and suicide. SAMMY CLARK, age 16, found his mother's body in the house. Officers located the body of Mr. Clark in a shed near the house. He was a son of the late M. H. "DOC" CLARK, the Coral Hill miller, and was born and reared in that section. He was here Christmas on a visit with his brother MR. ARTHUR CLARK, and MRS. RODDY BAGBY, both of Coral Hill. MRS. CLARK, a daughter of the late JIM PARKER, is survived by these brothers and sisters: MR. WILLIAM PARKER, of Goodnight, MRS. ANNE WHEELER, of Hiseville, CARLOS PARKER and MRS. GENE WALKUP, of Coral Hill and JAMES PARKER of Indiana. Both are buried in Hoopston, Ill.

COLE-ROGERS MARRIAGE ANNOUNCEMENT: **MR. J. B. ROGERS**, of this place, the well known farmer and former liveryman, was married to **MRS. MARGARET COLE**, of Louisville, a few days ago, the ceremony being solemnized in Jeffersonville, Indiana. They are making their home here [in Barren County, Kentucky], where MR. J. B. ROGERS is looking after his extensive farming operations. [No date given].

COLEMAN DEATH NOTICE: **MR. A. J. COLEMAN**, 71, well known farmer of the Rocky Hill section die at his home there Saturday afternoon at 5 o'clock, after an illness of 18 months, of a complication of diseases. For many years MR. A. J. COLEMAN was a resident of the

Hiseville section, but moved to the Rocky Hill section some 20 years ago. He was a member of the Beaver Creek Baptist Church. He is survived by his wife, MRS. DORA COLEMAN, three sons, LUCIAN COLEMAN and WILLIAM COLEMAN, at home, and ERNEST COLEMAN, of Akron, Ohio; one daughter, MRS. C. M. PEDEN, of Glasgow; a sister, MRS. MARY KINSLOW, of Haywood; and a brother, G. L. COLEMAN, who resides in Oregon. Funeral service was conducted at the home Tuesday, 11 a.m., by REV. T. C. ELLIS, and burial in the Hiseville Cemetery. [**My Note:** ALEXANDER J. COLEMAN died in 1938].

COLEMAN-PEDEN MARRIAGE ANNOUNCEMENT: **HAZEL COLEMAN,** the daughter of MR. and MRS. A. J. COLEMAN, of Route 1, and **MR. M. C. PEDEN,** of Glasgow, were married in Bowling Green on Wednesday, November 18th, at the Presbyterian Church at that place, with the REV. GEORGE W. CHEEK solemnizing. [**My Note:** Written in pencil is year "1932".]

COOMBS DEATH NOTICE: **MRS. ALLIE COOMBS,** mother of our own MR. W. P. COOMBS, died at her home in Cave City, on Monday morning at 12:15, aged 80 years, after a lingering illness. She was the widow of the late DR. H. W. COOMBS, who died 12 years ago. She was a native of the northern section of the county, where she spent her entire life, most of the time at Goodnight, KY, where the doctor practiced his profession. She is survived by two children, W. P. COOMBS, of this place, and MRS. ANNIE PARRISH, of Cave City. Before her marriage she was MISS ALLIE PARRISH and is survived by one sister, MRS. SALLIE BARBOUR, of Goodnight. MRS. COOMBS was a devout member of the Christian Church. Funeral services held in the Christian Church in Cave City, Tuesday, by ELDER L. C. REESE, her pastor, assisted by ELDER T. H. ALDERSON, after which she was laid to rest beside her late husband in the family burying ground at Goodnight.

CRAWFORD DEATH NOTICE: "Death Of Young Lady Shock To Community." **MISS DOVIE MAY CRAWFORD** of Hiseville died at the Infirmary here Sunday from blood poisoning. She was the daughter of MR. and MRS. J. E. CRAWFORD, merchant of Hiseville. She was to have graduated from Hiseville High School last night, and it is said she was to have been married very soon. Under these circumstances her death is exceedingly sad, much more so than the average death. MISS CRAWFORD is survived by her parents, 2 sisters, MISS NELL CRAWFORD and MISS CHRISTINE CRAWFORD, and one brother, MASTER BERLIN CRAWFORD. MISS CRAWFORD contracted appendicitis several days ago, but being deeply engrossed in her studies neglected to call a physician until the appendix ruptured, and she did not arrive at the hospital until a successful operation was impossible, and the next day she passed away. The funeral services were conducted at the Baptist Church in Hiseville by REV. EASLEY of this place. Owing to the fact that she was valedictorian of the class, all commencement exercises of the Hiseville School were abandoned. [**My Note:** She died May 11, 1924].

CRAWFORD-ROSS MARRIAGE ANNOUNCEMENT: **MISS NELL CRAWFORD,** with the Hartford Insurance Company, and the daughter of ED CRAWFORD, of

Hiseville, and MR. JOHN ROSS, of North Barren, son of LESLIE ROSS, were married last Sunday in Louisville.

CRAWFORD-STEEN AND BLEDSOE-SMITH DOUBLE MARRIAGE ANNOUNCEMENT: The double wedding of **MISS VERA C. CRAWFORD**, daughter of MRS. BETTY CRAWFORD, of Hiseville, and **MR. J. PARRISH STEEN**, son of MRS. J. T. STEEN, of near Hiseville, and MISS ANNIE LEE BLEDSOE, daughter of MR. and MRS. CHARLES BLEDSOE, of Hiseville, and MR. ROBERT SMITH, son of MR. and MRS. BENNETT SMITH, of Hiseville, took place in the Christian Church in Celina, Tennessee, on August 9th, ----.

CRENSHAW DEATH NOTICE: "Mr. H. T. Crenshaw Is Called By Death. Was 59 Years Of Age, And Spanish-American War Veteran; Burial Today." **MR. H. T. CRENSHAW**, age 59 years, died on Tuesday morning at 5:30 o'clock, following a long illness of heart trouble. Surviving are his wife and two children, JOE CRENSHAW and ELIZABETH CRENSHAW, and the following brothers: MR. R. F. CRENSHAW, MR. J. C. CRENSHAW, and MR. HARRY CRENSHAW, all of this county; and, MR. A. C. CRENSHAW, of Smithfield, Texas. One sister, MISS MILDRED CRENSHAW of Coral Hill, also survives. Funeral is this afternoon at 2:30 at Coral Hill, in charge of REV. ALDERSON of the Christian Church, with burial in the home burying ground. MR. CRENSHAW was a splendid man, fine neighbor and devoted, loyal friend. He was a veteran of the Spanish-American War, and spent thirteen years [sic] in the Philippines.

CRENSHAW DEATH NOTICE: "Heart Trouble Fatal To Mr. H. T. Crenshaw After Long Illness. Third Member Of Family To Die Within Past Two Months." The long-looked for came to **MR. H. T. CRENSHAW**, the Coral Hill merchant, on Tuesday morning, when death relieved him of his suffering from heart disease and complications, at the age of 59 years. He is survived by his wife, who was MISS MINNIE MAYFIELD, and two children, MISS ELIZABETH CRENSHAW and MR. JOE CRENSHAW. It will be remembered that MR. CRENSHAW was not able to attend the double funeral of his brother and sister MR. BEN CRENSHAW and MRS. ROGER ALLEN, which occurred April 12th. [**My Note:** The rest of this obituary is partially torn off, but the names of his brothers and sisters can be gleaned from the above mentioned obituaries of his brother MR. BEN CRENSHAW and his sister MRS. ROGER (NANNIE) ALLEN. However, there was also another obituary about him which follows].

CRENSHAW DEATH NOTICE: **MR. WALLER CRENSHAW** died of heart trouble at his home at Goodnight, Monday morning. He leaves his wife, who was a MISS VANZANT, and two daughters, EUGENIA and MODIE CRENSHAW. He also leaves two brothers, MR. NEWT CRENSHAW of Goodnight and MR. ELMORE CRENSHAW of Hiseville and two sisters, MRS. MALISSA THOMAS and MRS. LUCY SHIRLEY, of Hiseville. WALLER CRENSHAW was born and grew up in the Hiseville section and has been a merchant most of his business life, for many years at Seymour and the latter years at Hiseville. He was a good merchant and quite popular with many friends. Burial was in Hiseville Cemetery. [**My Note:** Died in 1930].

CRENSHAW-ALLEN DEATH NOTICE: "Sister-Brother Die 36 Hours Apart."

<u>SISTER</u>: **MRS. NANNIE ALLEN**, 45 years of age, died at her home, the Old Crenshaw home near Coral Hill, very suddenly on Monday, of pneumonia. She was a native of the section in which she died, and in which she spent her entire life. Before her marriage she was MISS NANNIE CRENSHAW, daughter of the late MR. and MRS. RICHARD CRENSHAW. She is survived by her husband and six children, ranging in age from 19 down to 2 years: RICHARD ALLEN, MARY FRANCES ALLEN, CECIL ALLEN, RUBY ALLEN, JAMES HOWARD ALLEN, and MARGARET ALLEN. Her surviving brothers and sister are HENRY THOMPSON CRENSHAW and RICHARD CRENSHAW, of Coral Hill, BEN M. CRENSHAW, of Hiseville, JAMES G. CRENSHAW, near Temple Hill, A. C. CRENSHAW, of Smithville, Texas, HARRY CRENSHAW, of Bruce, and MISS MIT CRENSHAW, of Coral Hill. MRS. ALLEN was a member of the Christian Church. The remains were interred in the family burying ground near Coral Hill, after funeral services conducted by ELDER T. H. ALDERSON, of this place. [**My Note**: Another obituary stated MRS. ROGER ALLEN was in her 46th year and her brothers were: RICHARD and TOM CRENSHAW, both of Coral Hill; JAMES CRENSHAW, of Temple Hill; ALEX CRENSHAW, of Smithfield, TX; and, HENRY CRENSHAW, near Bruce. They omitted BEN M. CRENSHAW, and stated her youngest child was 19 months old. [See "BROTHER"]. **<u>BROTHER</u>**: Friends and relatives have not recovered from the shock of **MRS. ROGER ALLEN**'s death before they were informed of the death of MR. BEN CRENSHAW, which occurred Tuesday night, at his home between Hiseville and Bearwallow, pneumonia causing his death. He was never informed that his sister was dead. He leaves his wife, who was MISS EMMA PALMORE, a sister of PROF. R. A. PALMORE and MRS. OREN DEPP of this place, DR. E.E. PALMORE of Horse Cave, and others well known. He also leaves two children, MARY CRENSHAW, 9 years of age, and WILLIAM CRENSHAW, age 7. The brothers and sisters of MRS. ALLEN also apply to MR. CRENSHAW. He, too, was a consecrated member of the Christian Church, and he was among the best citizens of his community. His death is certainly a hard blow to his family and friends, who are numbered by his acquaintances. The remains of MR. CRENSHAW were brought to the Allen home, and the two coffins laid side by side, while ELDER T. H. ALDERSON, of this place, pronounced the funeral services, after which the burial took place at the same time in the Crenshaw burying ground near Coral Hill. [See "SISTER"] **<u>A SAD COINCIDENCE</u>**: It is a sad coincidence the older brother, **MR. RICHARD CRENSHAW**, who lives in the Allen home, is ill with a deep cold, and, **MR. THOMAS CRENSHAW**, another brother, is confined to his bed with heart trouble, and neither of these were able to attend the burial of their brother [Ben] and sister [Nannie].

<u>CRENSHAW-HOLLOWAY MARRIAGE ANNOUNCEMENT</u>: **MISS RUTH CRENSHAW**, the daughter of MR. and MRS. J. G. CRENSHAW, and **MR. PAUL HOLLOWAY**, of Gary, Indiana, were married last Saturday at the home of MRS. HENRY REYNOLDS in Cave City. In attendance were MR. and MRS. GLEN ROPP. MISS RUTH CRENSHAW has been a successful teacher in the local city school. They will be residing in Gary, Indiana.

<u>CRENSHAW-PEDEN MARRIAGE ANNOUNCEMENT</u>: **MR. WILLIE PEDEN**, of Coral Hill, and **MISS PEARL CRENSHAW**, of near Antioch, Metcalfe County,

KY, were married in Nashville, TN last Friday. The groom is the son of MR. MOTE PEDEN and the bride is a daughter of the late MR. HENRY CRENSHAW. They are popular and excellent young people, and their many friends will wish them all the happiness in their marriage. [**My Note**: Their marriage took place on December 29, 1913].

CRENSHAW-REYNOLDS MARRIAGE ANNOUNCEMENT: **MISS BERNICE CRENSHAW**, daughter of MR. and MRS. J. G. CRENSHAW, of Temple Hill, and **MR. ELLIS REYNOLDS**, a salesman of Cave City, were married in Louisville on last Saturday [no date given], where they will make their home.

CRENSHAW-TRAVIS MARRIAGE ANNOUNCEMENT: **MISS BERNICE CRENSHAW**, the daughter of MR. and MRS. JAMES G. CRENSHAW of near Temple Hill, KY, and **TERRELL TRAVIS**, son of MR. and MRS. J. E. TRAVIS, merchant at Temple Hill, married Saturday [no date given] at Gallatin, TN.

CRENSHAW-VANSANT-PEDEN VISITATION: **MISS FRANCES VANSANT**, from Jeffersonville, Indiana, has returned home after a visit with her sister, **MRS. WALLER CRENSHAW**, and MISS **MABEL PEDEN**.

CRENSHAW IN SCHOOL PICTURE: "1925 Graduating Class Is Largest in G.H.S. History" -- MARCHALL WATKINS, ALROY BOYD, **HENRY CRENSHAW**, LOUIS WOOLSEY, ROBERT OLIVER, SAM FRANKLIN, MARGRET PEDIGO, MARY PEDIGO, MARY C. NUCKOLS, DERA RICHARDSON, ELLIE WILLIAMSON, DELVA FRAZIER, GLADYS ADWELL, AMY McQUOWN, GRACE BEEBE, **RUTH CRENSHAW**, MARY McFARLAND, R. D. RIDLEY, R. A. PALMORE, MARY BRIDGEWATER, ANNIE McFARLAND, ESTHER MINICK, ELIZABETH HATCHER, HELEN COOMBS, DOROTHY JONES, LAURA JEAN DRANE, CLARINE DOSSEY, DICKEY WILKINSON, and PROFESSOR H. M. STICKLES. [**My Note:** The photo was too faded to reproduce. "G.H.S." most likely stood for "Gamaliel High School"].

CROCKETT-SMITH MARRIAGE ANNOUNCEMENT: **MISS HELEN CROCKETT**, of Frankfort, KY, and **MR. BASIL SMITH, JR.**, the eldest son of MR. and MRS. ED. H. SMITH, were married last week in Lexington. He was reared here [in Barren COunty], but will be living in Frankfort.

CUNNINGHAM-YATES MARRIAGE ANNOUNCEMENT: **MR. HENRY YATES and MISS MADALENE CUNNINGHAM**, of Horse Cave, were married in Bowling Green on Thursday by DR. A. B. HOUZE, of the Christian Church [no date].

DAVIS DEATH NOTICE: **CHARLES OTHO DAVIS**, little son of MR. and MRS. CHARLES DAVIS, age 2 years and 5 months, died ---- [no date].

DAVIS DEATH NOTICE: "One Of Barren County's Oldest Citizens." **MR. JOHN MILTON DAVIS** died at his home near Goodnight, Wednesday of last week, lacking until next month of being 89 years of age. He was a native of Barren, in fact he was born and lived all his life in the neighborhood in which he died. His wife is dead, but he is survived by the following children: MR. GERSHON DAVIS and MISS NELL DAVIS, at home; MR. E. M. DAVIS, of Louisville; CLEVINGER DAVIS, of Colfax, Illinois; MRS. WILL DAVIS, of Portsmouth, Ohio; MRS. TOM PRITCHARD and MRS. Willis GADBERRY, of Hiseville. MR. DAVIS was a quiet, law-abiding citizen, who had many friends. The burial was in the Baird burying ground near his home.

DAVIS DEATH NOTICE: "Two Weeks Illness Fatal To Ernest Curd Davis." Following a two weeks' illness, **MR. ERNEST CURD DAVIS** passed away at home in Cave City, Sunday morning at 6:15 o'clock. MR. DAVIS was president of the H. Y. Davis Bank, his election to that position following the death of his brother, MR. SAM B. DAVIS, who died on Feb. 26th. MR. DAVIS was 52 years old and had lived his entire life in Cave City, a consistent member of the Cave City Baptist Church where funeral services were held Monday afternoon by REV. W. M. BURNS, assisted by REV. C. C. OMER of the Christian Church. He is survived by his wife, MRS. LIZZIE FORD DAVIS, and two sons, CECIL and MURRELL DAVIS; his mother, MRS. H. Y. DAVIS, SR.; one sister, MRS. CHESTER SHAW; two brothers, MR. H. Y. DAVIS, JR., president of the Davis Banking Company of Upton, and MR. ARCHIE DAVIS, recently elected vice-president of the Liberty National Bank and Trust Co., of Louisville. [**My Note:** He died in 1935; buried in Cave City Cem.]

DEPP-MANSFIELD MEMORIAM: Twice within the last few months I have had to read of the death of dear little people I have learned to love almost as tenderly as if they were my own little niece and nephew. First was the death of my dear little cousin **MARGARET DEPP** and then last week my sweet little cousin **ROBERT THOMAS MANSFIELD,** who died March 23rd and was buried March 25th. He was born December 16, 1915, and while Robert was always a delicate looking child, he seemed well. [**My Note:** It included a poem written by ORA ETHEL].

DEWEESE DEATH NOTICE: "Mrs. DeWeese To Be Buried Friday." **MRS. VIRGIL D. DEWEESE,** one of Barren County's best beloved women, died at her son's home in the Bearwallow section this afternoon, having been ill since February with pneumonia and complications incident to age. She was 82 years old the 20th of the month, and was born and reared in the Goodnight section. In early womanhood she was married to VIRGIL D. DEWEESE and they lived beyond Lecta on the Edmonton Road for many years and reared their family. Following MR. DEWEESE's death a number of years ago, the old house, which was a landmark, was burned and a new house was erected on their farm. Before her marriage she was ROBERTA BROADY and is the last of her generation to pass on. Five children survive: MRS. MILTON (BESS) COE, of Orlando, Florida; MRS. ADA SMITH, of Munfordville; HALL DEWEESE, of Bearwallow; JESSE DEWEESE, and OTTO DEWEESE, of Lecta. [**My Note:** This obituary is partially torn, but it appears that she had another child who had died a number of years ago and the family lives in Glasgow. Also, she had 8 grandchildren, and was a devout member of the Christian Church. She was buried beside her husband].

DICKINSON DEATH NOTICE: "T. P. Dickinson Death, November 27. Died In Louisville Following Heart Attack. Was One Of Glasgow's Best Known And Most Beloved Citizens. The Funeral Here Last Saturday." Funeral rites for **THOMAS P. DICKINSON,** well known banker of this city, were held at the home Saturday afternoon at two. REV. W. E.

THOMAS, of Nashville, was in charge of the service. Interment was in the cemetery here. Surviving him are his wife, MRS. HADEE TRIGG DICKINSON, of this city; a son, Lieutenant Commander HAIDEN TRIGG DICKINSON, of Newport News, VA (who was prevented from attending the funeral because of confinement in the hospital); a daughter, MRS. J. W. BETHEL, of Louisville; his mother, MRS. MARY DICKINSON, of Paris, TN; and two sisters, MRS. J. W. LOVING, of Edgewood, TX, and MRS. WILLIAM ELLIS, of Paris, TN. MR. DICKINSON was president of the Trigg National Bank. [**My Note:** This obituary is longer and cites his many civic accomplishments. His tombstone in Glasgow has spelled his name THOMAS PAGE DICKERSON (died November 27, 1930)].

DODD-BUTTON MARRIAGE ANNOUNCEMENT: **MISS PEARL DODD**, daughter of MRS. J. A. DODD, of Haywood, and MR. **ELBERT BUTTON**, son of MR. and MRS. J. H. BUTTON, of near Lucas, were married in Louisville Saturday at the Courtland Hotel, by REV. CREE. MISS PEARL PRITCHARD and MR. LEO GREER were in attendance.

DOYLE-BETHEL MARRIAGE ANNOUNCEMENT: **MISS LUCILLE DOYLE**, popular young lady of Glasgow, married **MR. JOE LEWIS BETHEL**, a young business man of this place, in Bowling Green last Sunday, the REV. DR. GROSS of the Baptist Church officiating.

DRANE-McQUOWN MARRIAGE ANNOUNCEMENT: **MISS WILLIE FRANCES DRANE**, daughter of MR. and MRS. M. L. DRANE, of Glasgow, and **MR. GEORGE McQUOWN**, the son of MRS. LULA McQUOWN, were married in Jeffersonville, Indiana, on January 24th. Accompanying them were MISS TOMMIE HINDMAN and MR. JOHN L. THOMAS. Sgt. McQuown is a caretaker at the 123rd "Cavary Barns" [sic] in Glasgow, and they are making their home with MRS. McQUOWN on North Race Street.

DUFF DEATH NOTICE: "Death of Mr. Henry W. Duff Here Sunday Morning" **MR. HENRY DUFF**, in his 71st year, died at his home on North Jackson Way Sunday morning at 1 o'clock. Death was caused by heart trouble. Surviving are his widow, one sister, MRS. LIZZIE JONES, of Coral Hill, and one brother, MR. ELMORE DUFF, of Glendale. Funeral was at the residence Tuesday at 10 o'clock, with DR. J. A. GAINES, of the Baptist Church in charge. Interment was in the Glasgow Cemetery. [**My Note:** HENRY WALTON DUFF died on January 13, 1935].

EDWARDS-SMITH MARRIAGE ANNOUNCEMENT: **MISS VIRGIE KATE EDWARDS**, of Hiseville, and **REV. KIRBY SMITH**, of Livingston, Tenn., were married last week in Jackson, Tenn. They have many friends in Barren County and surrounding counties. They will reside in Livingston, Tenn.

EDWARDS-WATKINS MARRIAGE ANNOUNCEMENT: **MISS BLANCHE EDWARDS**, the daughter of MRS. E. S. EDWARDS, and MR. J. F. WATKINS, son of **MR. R. G. WATKINS**, both of Hiseville, were married in Scottsville on September 27, 1930.

ELLIOTT-MILLER MARRIAGE ANNOUNCEMENT: **MISS MAUDE ELLIOTT**, a teacher and the daughter of MR. and MRS. CURD ELLIOTT, of near Temple Hill, and **MR. SAM MILLER**, son of MRS. SARAH MILLER, of Freedom, but now of Detroit, were married in Cincinnati, Ohio, last Saturday. A dinner was prepared by MRS. MILLER's sister, MRS. INMAN WOODS, of Detroit. The couple will be living in Detroit.

ELLIS DEATH NOTICE: "Death Of Mrs. George Ellis Feb. 12. Taught In Schools Of County 47 Years. Burial In The Cemetery Here On Tuesday" **MRS. GEORGE W. ELLIS**, age 74, one of the most beloved and respected women of Barren County, died at her home two miles south of Glasgow on Sunday morning, after an illness of several months. MRS. ELLIS was a teacher in the schools of Barren County for 47 years, and was a member of the Baptist Church. Surviving are her husband, GEORGE W. ELLIS, and three sons: MR. EARL ELLIS, of Ocala, Florida, and MR. CECIL ELLIS and MR. FLOYD ELLIS, of this place. Two brothers and two sisters also survive: DR. O. P. NUCKOLS, of Pineville, J. R. NUCKOLS, MRS. CORA OWENS, and MISS LELIA NUCKOLS, of Goodnight. Funeral services were held at the Baptist Church Tuesday morning, by REV. T. F. GRIDER, with burial in the cemetery at this place.

ELMORE DEATH NOTICE: "Little Girl Dies." Sunday evening at 7:25 o'clock, the death angel entered the home of MR. and MRS. CURTIS ELMORE and brought to an end the early career of their youngest child, **EVA NELL ELMORE**. She was 8 years and 4 months of age. Besides her father and mother she leaves two little sisters, CHRISTINE ELMORE and MARGARET ELMORE, also a host of other near relatives and many friends. Heart trouble was responsible for he death. She had been sick for about four months and grew weaker and weaker. She was only 8 years old, but ready to take her place in the 6th grade next term. Funeral services were held Monday at Lick Branch, conducted by REV. J. L. FURKIN, pastor of Lick Branch Church. She was tenderly laid to rest in the Lick Branch Cemetery. [Poem written by her teacher, MARY L. SPENCER, was included here].

EVANS-CHERRY MARRIAGE ANNOUNCEMENT: **MISS MAGGIE EVANS**, a sister of MR. ----[page torn] EVANS, formerly of Tompkinsville, and MR. HI--- [page torn] CHERRY, were married in Moss, Tennessee, last November.

EVANS-GIESECKE MARRIAGE ANNOUNCEMENT: **MISS SHIRLEY EVANS**, a daughter of MR. and MRS. R. E. EVANS, of this place, and **MR. WILLIAM GIESECKE** of Anderson, Missouri, were married in Neosho, Missouri, last Sunday. They will reside in Anderson, MO.

EVERETT DEATH NOTICE: **BEN EVERETT** died on January 24, 1932. Poem was written "in memory of our dear father" by MRS. CHRIS LEWIS.

FAKES-PRICE MARRIAGE ANNOUNCEMENT: **MISS RELMA FAKES**, of Fulton, Missouri, and **MR. FRANK C. PRICE**, son of MR. and MRS. JOHN PRICE, of this place, were married last week in Dreslen, Tennessee.

FARRIS-VELUZAT MARRIAGE ANNOUNCEMENT: Announcement of the marriage of **MISS WILLIE JOE FARRIS**, daughter of MR. & MRS. HENRY G. FARRIS, of the Cave City section, to **MR. EUGENE W. VELUZAT, JR.**, son of MR. EUGENE VELUZAT, of Horse Cave. The marriage was September 3, 1927.

FISHBACK DEATH NOTICE: Funeral services for **MR. JAMES FISHBACK** were held at the home of his daughter, MRS. MARY WOOD, near Hiseville, Tuesday afternoon. Burial was in the Glasgow Cemetery. MR. FISHBACK was 92 years of age and was one of the best known men in Barren County. He had been in declining health for some time and has made his home with his daughter, MRS. WOOD, for several years. He is survived by 2 other children besides MRS. WOOD: son HARRY FISHBACK, of Kansas City, and MRS. ANNIE MILNER, of Palo Alto, California. MR. FISHBACK devoted most of his life to the farming industry. [**My Note:** JAMES FISHBACK died in 1935 and his wife Janie died in 1907].

FISHBACK DEATH NOTICE: "Death Of Clarence Fishback in St. Louis." **MR. CLARENCE FISHBACK**, formerly of Barren County, died at his home in St. Louis, Missouri, Wednesday night of last week at 11:30 p.m. He was 63 years of age. The remains were brought here and funeral service was conducted by the REV. T. H. ALDERSON at the Christian Church. Burial was in the Glasgow Cemetery. MR. FISHBACK was born and reared at what is now known as the Ben Myers place, one mile from Glasgow on the North Jackson Highway. He left Barren County in 1891 to make his home in Missouri. A number of years ago he married MISS ALLIE WOOD of Illinois. Besides his wife, he is survived by his father MR. JAMES FISHBACK, of Hiseville; two sisters, MRS. MARY WOOD, of Hiseville; and MRS. ANNIE MILNER of Palo Alto, California; and, one brother, MR. HARRY FISHBACK, of Kansas City, Missouri.

FORBIS DEATH NOTICE: **MR. W. M. FORBIS**, age 62, died suddenly at his home Monday morning of heart failure. His death was a great shock to everyone, as he had been in his usual good health. MR. FORBIS had planned to go to Glasgow, but complained of not feeling well, and died before a doctor could be called. No better man or citizen ever lived than MR. FORBIS. He had been a successful merchant at this place for years, and was Master of the Masonic Lodge. He was also a member of the Christian Church. He leaves a wife and one son, MR. JACK FORBIS, of this place; two daughters, MRS. CHARLES McCOY, of Kokomo, Indiana, and MRS. WILBUR KESSINGER, and two grandsons, of Louisville; one sister, MRS. ROBERT HATCHER, and two brothers, MR. WALTER FORBIS and MR. HARRY FORBIS, of this place, also mourn his loss. Funeral service was conducted by BROTHER OMAR, of Cave City, at one thirty at the Christian Church, and interment was in Hiseville Cemetery. [**My Note:** WILLIAM M. FORBIS died 1931].

FORBIS-PEMBERTON MARRIAGE ANNOUNCEMENT: The announcement has been made by MR. and MRS. W. S. GADBERRY, of Hiseville, of the marriage of their daughter, **MRS. KATIE G. FORBIS**, to **MR. G. T. PEMBERTON**, of Gary, Indiana. The marriage was done in Louisville, Kentucky on January 1st, and they will reside in Gary.

FORREST DEATH NOTICE: "Mr. U. J. Forrest Dies At Coral Hill."

MR. U. J. FORREST died at his home at Coral Hill Tuesday afternoon following two strokes, the first on February 4, the second Tuesday. He lacked until March 4th of being 76 years old. He had lived his entire life in that section. Surviving are one daughter, MISS ANNA MERLE FORREST, a commercial teacher in Glasgow High School; one sister, MISS LUTIE FORREST, of Los Angeles; five nieces and five nephews: MS. G. U. BALL, of Hodgenville, C. B. FORREST, of Wisdom, EARL FORREST, of Green County, Ky., MRS. LISSIE HENSLEY, MRS. L. H. PEDIGO, MRS. ED POLSON, MRS. J. P. OAKES, O. P. and ERNEST FORREST, and H. E. SMITH, of Knob Lick. Funeral services were conducted at the Christian Church at Coral Hill, of which he was a member, and burial was in the Johnson Cemetery.

FOSTER: "We want to sincerely thank our friends and neighbors for their kindness in the sickness and death of our dear husband and father, **B. C. FOSTER**. May God's blessings be with you all." MRS. B. C. FOSTER and daughters, MRS. J. T. SHERFEY, MRS. W. T. FOSTER, and MRS. C. H. CHENAULT.

FRANKLIN DEATH NOTICE: "Death Of Mrs. G. T. Franklin At Home Here." **MRS. GARLAND THOMAS FRANKLIN**, age 80, died at her home on Race St. Saturday night following an illness of pneumonia. Surviving are two children, MRS. C. C. HOWARD and L. G. FRANKLIN, both of Glasgow, and three brothers, JAMES SAUNDERS, of Louisville, H. S. SAUNDERS, of Hiseville, and JOHN SAUNDERS, of South Fork. MRS. FRANKLIN was a member of the Church of Christ. After funeral at the home of DR. C. C. HOWARD, Sunday afternoon, in charge of REV. WILLIS THOMAS, of Nashville, interment followed in the Glasgow Cemetery.

FRANKLIN DEATH NOTICE: **MRS. SUSAN F. FRANKLIN** died at the home of her daughter and son-in-law, DR. and MRS. C. C. HOWARD on North Race Street, Saturday, at the age of 80, of pneumonia. Surviving her are a daughter and a son, MRS. HOWARD and MR. L. G. FRANKLIN, both of this place. She also leaves three brothers, JOHN SAUNDERS, of South Fork, SHIELD SAUNDERS, of Hiseville, and JAMES SAUNDERS, of Louisville. She was the widow of the late MR. GARLAND FRANKLIN, who died about 12 years ago. MRS. FRANKLIN was born and reared at South Fork but spent most of her married near Coral Hill. She was a member of the Christian Church. The funeral services were held at the home of DR. HOWARD, by REV. WILLIE THOMAS, a relative of DR. HOWARD, and she was buried to the family cemetery near Coral Hill.

GATEWOOD DEATH NOTICE: "The Death of Mr. Charles S. Gatewood." **MR. CHARLES SCOTT GATEWOOD** died at Marine Hospital in Louisville on April 5th, of bronchial pneumonia, at the age of 68. MR. GATEWOOD was born October 15, 1860, at the old Gatewood homestead near Coral Hill. He was a son of A. J. and FANNIE W. GATEWOOD, and the brother of R. H. and J. W. GATEWOOD, and MRS. ED LONG, all deceased. He is survived by one nephew, GROVER C. LONG; four nieces, MRS. JAMES BAGBY, MRS. FRED JONES, MRS. GLENN FISHER, and MRS. FELIX E. ALLEN; and, by nine great nieces and nephews. The death of MR. GATEWOOD removes the last of the immediate members of the old Gatewood family, who were among the pioneer families of southern Kentucky.

GATEWOOD DEATH NOTICE: "The Death Of Chas. Gatewood Last Thursday." **MR. CHARLES H. GATEWOOD**, in his 67th year, died in Louisville last Thursday. He was a resident of Coral Hill, and interment was in the Gatewood burying ground near that place, after funeral services by REV. WARREN DUNAGAN. He is survived by several nieces and nephews.

GLASS-DEPP MARRIAGE ANNOUNCEMENT: **MISS OLLIE GLASS and MR. FLOYD C. DEPP** married in Bowling Green last week, with the REV. M. L. MOORE officiating. They will live in Glasgow.

GLASS-SOUTH MARRIAGE ANNOUNCEMENT: **MR. EMERSON SOUTH**, son of MR. J. C. SOUTH, of Cave City, and **MISS FERN E. GLASS**, daughter of MR. and MRS. C. E. GLASS, of this city, were married in Bowling Green last Tuesday, where they will live.

GOFF-ALEXANDER MARRIAGE ANNOUNCEMENT: **MISS GOREE GOFF**, the young daughter of MR. and MRS. J. A. GOFF, and **MR. H. C. ALEXANDER**, son of MR. and MRS. O. W. ALEXANDER, married in Cave City Saturday afternoon at the home of REV. and MRS. C. C. OMAR. They were accompanied by MISS GLADYS GOFF and CLIFTON PEDIGO.

HADDEN DEATH NOTICE: **MRS. ANNIE HADDEN**, office lady of the Overall Factory, died Monday night just before midnight of brain or spine trouble. She was taken suddenly while in the office Saturday and called for a bus to take her home. Soon after reaching home she became unconscious and never regained her mind. She gradually sank into death. She was about 53 years of age, a daughter of MRS. SALLIE MYERS of this place, who survives her. She also leaves one son, MR. BEN MYERS HADDEN, of California, and the following brother and sisters: MR. ERNEST L. MYERS, the well known planing mill man of this place, MISS HETTIE MYERS, also of this place, MRS. HARRY MORAN, of Horse Cave, MRS. HENRY K. HILL, of Louisville, and MRS. DAN HATCHER, of Fort Worth, Texas, all of whom arrived for the funeral. MRS. HADDEN was born and reared in Glasgow, and was member of the Christian Church. Funeral services were held at home on West Washington Street by BROTHER ALDERSON; burial in Glasgow Cemetery.

HALE DEATH NOTICE: "Young Lady Dies." **EMMA HALE**, the 16 year old daughter of MR. and MRS. JOHN HALE died at home here several days ago of typhoid fever, leaving her parents. two brothers, and two sisters. She was a member of the Christian Church and was a most lovable young lady. The remains were interred in the cemetery at this place after funeral services by Elder T. H. ALDERSON at the Christian Church. [**My Note:** EMMA MAE HALE died in Glasgow in 1927].

HALE DEATH NOTICE: **MR. TURNER HALE**, 75 years of age, died at the home of his son, MR. WILLIE HALE, in Warren County last Friday, following several months illness. MR. HALE formerly resided in the Coral Hill section, but for the last year had made his home in

Warren County. He was a good citizen and a member of the Coral Hill Christian Church. His wife, MRS. SARAH HALE, died about a year ago. MR. HALE is survived by two brothers, MR. TOM HALE, of Lecta, and MR. WOOD HALE, of Arkansas. Also, the following children: MRS. BOB PARRISH, of Coral Hill; MR. JOHN HALE, of Glasgow; and, MR. WILLIE HALE, at whose home he died. MRS. EULAN BRADSHAW is a niece of the deceased. The funeral services were conducted on Saturday and the remains interred in Mt. Pleasant Cemetery in Warren County, KY.

HALE DEATH NOTICE: **MRS. TURNER HALE**, 77, died at the home of her son, MR. WILLIE HALE, in Warren County, Monday. Death was caused by heart failure. MRS. HALE had only recently moved to Warren County from Coral Hill, where she had lived the greater part of her life. She is survived by her husband and the following children: MRS. BOB PARRISH, of Coral Hill; MR. JOHN HALE, of Glasgow; and, MR. WILLIE HALE, of Warren County. She was member of the Christian Church. The funeral services were held at Pleasant Hill Church in Warren County on Wednesday afternoon, with burial in the Pleasant Hill Cemetery.

HALE-ALEXANDER MARRIAGE ANNOUNCEMENT: **MISS MAYDE HALE**, well-known in Glasgow where she has frequently visited her sister MRS. EULAN BRADSHAW, and **MR. JACK ALEXANDER**, of Hiseville, were married in Jeffersonville, Indiana, last Saturday.

HALE-LOHDEN MARRIAGE ANNOUNCEMENT: **MISS MARY HALE**, daughter of MR. and MRS. JOHN HALE, of Route 1, and **MR. HENRY LOHDEN**, son of MR. and MRS. ADAM LOHDEN of Lecta, married on the stage at the tent show Friday, JUDGE V. H. JONES, presiding.

HALL DEATH NOTICE: Relatives and friends in this community were shocked to learn of the death of **MR. CHRIS HALL**, of St. Louis. MR. HALL was raised in this neighborhood where he has many friends who extends their deepest sympathy to the bereaved ones [no date].

HALL DEATH NOTICE: "Tragic Death Of J. M. Hall Shocks Friends." **MR. J. M. HALL** committed suicide at the home of his daughter, MRS. W. E. SHIRLEY in the western part of town about 2 o'clock Monday, by hanging himself in the barn. He had secured a new rope, tied it to a beam over some bales of hay, adjusted it around his neck, and stepped off. When found by his daughter his heart was still beating slowly, but before help could be obtained, he had expired. There is no apparent reason for the rash act, unless poor health caused his despondency. He was around delivering milk that morning, and went to the home of his son, MR. C. E. HALL, only a few minutes before he went to the barn. He had bought the new rope at a store that morning. He is survived by his wife and six children, C. E. HALL, O. R. HALL, and MRS. SHIRLEY, of Glasgow, CECIL B. HALL and MRS. JOHN HARLAN, of Tompkinsville, and MRS. W. W. JOHNSON, of Dover, Tennessee. MR. HALL came to Glasgow from Tompkinsville about 12 years ago. He was a member of the Christian Church. He is the last of his generation to pass away, unless it be a sister, who was last heard from in Texas. MR. HALL lacked until August 18th of being 77 years of age, and had spent practically all his life in Monroe and Barren Counties. The remains were interred in the Glasgow Cemetery Tuesday after brief services conducted by the REV. J. L. PIERCY.

HARGIS-PIELET MARRIAGE ANNOUNCEMENT: News has been received of the marriage September 12th of **MRS. ARLEE HARGIS to MR. ARDRE PIELET**, both of Scottsville, in Westmoreland, Tennessee. The bride is a sister of MR. ELWIN POYNTER, of this city, and is a former resident of Glasgow. The groom has been engaged in the oil industry in Allen County, Kentucky, and they will make their home in New York City.

HELM DEATH NOTICE: **MRS. ELIZABETH HELM**, known to her friends as MRS. BETTIE HELM, died at the home of her daughter, MRS. E. C. NICKOLS, of this place, on Saturday night, at the age of 75 years. She was the widow of the late MR. FRANK HELM, who died about six years ago. She leaves two children, MR. W. C. HELM, who lived on the home place at Dry Fork, and MRS. NICKOLS of this place, at whose home she was visiting when stricken with paralysis. Before her marriage she was MISS THOMERSON and leaves five sisters and three brothers: MRS. MORRIS FERGUSON of Oklahoma City; MRS. RACHEL FERGUSON and MRS. G. B. ELLIS, of this place; MRS. J. H. TRACY, MRS. GEORGE WOODSON, MR. W. V. THOMERSON, MR. S. D. THOMERSON, and MR. G. E. THOMERSON, all of Dry Fork. MRS. HELM was a devout member of the Christian Church and spent her entire life in Barren County. Burial was in family cemetery, after services by ELDER J. D. SMITH.

HENSLEY- SLAUGHTER MARR. ANNOUNCEMENT: **MISS RUTH HENSLEY**, of Horse Cave, and **MR. A. B. SLAUGHTER**, married in Jeffersonville, Indiana.

HILL DEATH NOTICE: **MRS. ALLIE HILL**, 73, widow of MR. --- HILL, died at the home of her ---- HEZZIE HILL, in the Bon ---- Tuesday night at 10 ---- been in declining ---- several months. [**My Note:** This notice was partially torn off and only parts were legible]. Before her marriage she was a MISS GASSOWAY. She was a devout member of the Methodist Church. She is survived by two sons, MR. ---- HILL, ---- Ayr, and MR. MA--- HILL, ----, three brothers ----, and HANS GAS----, ---- Glasgow. [The wife of J. W. HILL aforementioned].

HILL DEATH NOTICE: **MR. J. W. HILL**, known to his best friends as JOE HILL, died at his home near Oak Hill Monday morning at the age of 75 years, leaving his wife, who was MISS OLLIE GASSAWAY. He also leaves two sons, MR. HEZZIE HILL, of Oak Hill section, and MR. MARION HILL, of Glasgow Junction. MR. HILL's remaining brothers and sisters are: MRS. JIM ANDERSON and MRS. H. HAMILTON, of Louisville; MR. BILLIE HILL, of Red Cross; and, MRS. PAT HILL, of Glasgow Junction. MR. HILL was a son of MR. HEZZIE KIRK HILL who once was jailor of Barren County. Services were held at Walnut Hill Church Tuesday afternoon and the remains were laid to rest in the cemetery at that place. [**My Note:** JOE W. HILL died March 5, 1928, and ALLIE HILL died March 28, 1939. Buried in the cemetery north of Bon Ayr].

HINDMAN DEATH NOTICE: "Death Of Mrs. Maggie D. Hindman At Her Home"

MRS. MAGGIE DEPP HINDMAN, age 43, died at her home on North Race Street, in this city, on Saturday morning, following an illness of several months. She was a member of the Christian Church. She is survived by her husband, THOMAS F. HINDMAN, and six children: MARY ELIZABETH HINDMAN, WALTER HINDMAN, VIRGINIA THOMAS HINDMAN, ROBERT WOOD HINDMAN, MARGARET HINDMAN, and EUGENIA HINDMAN; her parents, MR. and MRS. ADOLPH DEPP; and two brothers, DR. HENRY DEPP, of Louisville, and MR. WALTER DEPP, of this place. Funeral services were conducted by REV. ALDERSON, with burial here. [**My Note:** MAGGIE DEPP HINDMAN died in 1931 and THOMAS FRANKLIN HINDMAN died in 1958]

HOLMES DEATH NOTICE:
"We desire to express our thanks for the kindness extended to us during the illness and death of our loved one, **VIRDA HOLMES**. To those who contributed the beautiful flowers for her last resting place. We especially want to thank DR. HOWARD and the nurses for their kindness." HELTON HOLMES and family.

HUDSON DEATH NOTICE: **MR. TOM HUDSON**, of Horse Cave, died at the home of his parents in Rocky Hill last Thursday very suddenly. He is survived by his wife MRS. ELIZABETH HUDSON, his parents, MR. and MRS. HENRY HUDSON, and brothers ROBERT HUDSON of Bowling Green, and CHARLEY HUDSON of Rocky Hill. [**My Note:** Written in pencil: "1932"].

HUMBLE DEATH NOTICE: "Mr. Terry Humble Succumbs Following A Three Year Illness. He Was Known Over Kentucky As Political Leader and Business Man." **MR. TERRY LANKFORT HUMBLE** died at his home on East Main Street Sunday morning, at an early hour, after an illness of more than three years. He was a native of Russell County, but spent most of his youth and young manhood in Pulaski County, where he became very prominent in business and political life, being an ardent Republican, and was intimate with the leaders of that party in the eastern part of the state. MR. HUMBLE lived in Tompkinsville for about 16 years, where he engaged in the lumber business and became one of the most prominent citizens of Monroe County. After coming to Monroe County he was married to MRS. LUCY GRAY, a sister of JUDGE BASIL RICHARDSON, of this place, who survives him. He is survived by a daughter by a former marriage, MRS. HERSHELL BOGGESS, of Louisville. Eleven years ago the Humbles moved to Glasgow and bought the brick residence on East Main Street, which they have since occupied. He was stepping to the front in Barren County and developing into a man of great influence and prominence, when three years ago last November he was stricken with a fatal malady, which finally removed him from this life. He is survived by several brothers who live in eastern Kentucky, the well known lumber men, McClendon Brothers of Monroe County, being nephews. MR. HUMBLE was a prominent member of the Baptist Church and the Masonic Fraternity and his death is widely mourned. Funeral services were conducted at the home Monday afternoon by REV. J. H. SWANN, of Tompkinsville, and assisted by REV. J. A. EASLEY, of the Baptist Church at this place, followed by burial in the Glasgow Cemetery under the auspice of the Masons from Tompkinsville, Bethlehem and this place. Among out of town visitors who attended the funeral, aside from Masons, were two of his brothers, HENRY HUMBLE and LEWIS HUMBLE, relatives from Somerset, KY, his daughter and son-in-law MR. and MRS. BOGGESS and family of Louisville, KY. [**My Note:** He died on April 8, 1928].

HUTCHENS DEATH NOTICE: **MR. JOHN W. HUTCHENS**, 63 years old, died at his home on East Cherry Street at 8 o'clock Tuesday evening. MR. HUTCHENS suffered a stroke of paralysis before Christmas and after several weeks he seemed to improve. On Tuesday about noon he suffered the second stroke from which he never rallied. He is survived by his wife and two brothers GEORGE HUTCHENS, of Horse Cave, and WILL HUTCHENS, of Coral Hill. He was a member of the Church of Christ and funeral services were held at the church at 2 o'clock yesterday afternoon by the REV. PHY and burial was in Coral Hill Cemetery. [**My Note:** JOHN W. HUTCHENS died February 12, 1929, and his widow, DORCAS PAGE HUTCHENS, died October 5, 1954. They are buried in the Eubank Cemetery in the Lecta area of Barren County].

HUTCHENS DEATH NOTICE: "Death of George Hutchens in Horse Cave, KY" **GEORGE HUTCHENS**, prominent former citizen of Barren County, died at his home in Horse Cave Sunday morning at 10:30 following a slight stroke of paralysis which he suffered last Saturday. He was 71 years of age. While living near Eighty-Eight he was elected to the office of magistrate several terms. He moved to Horse Cave about 20 years ago. Funeral services were held at the home at Horse Cave on Monday afternoon at 2 o'clock, the REV. T. F. GRIDER officiating. Interment was in the Horse Cave cemetery. Besides his wife, MRS. MARY DEPP HUTCHENS, formerly of the Eighty-Eight section, he is survived by three daughters, MRS. MAY DAVIS, of Marrowbone, MISS PEARL HUTCHENS, and MISS ELIZABETH HUTCHENS, both of Horse Cave. MR. GEORGE HUTCHENS was also a member of the Presbyterian Church.

JACKMAN-BERRY MARRIAGE ANNOUNCEMENT: **MISS FRANCES JACKMAN and MR. ARIE BERRY** were married last week. She has been an assistant to DR. W. A. WELDON, and he is the junior partner of Devasher & Berry.

JACKMAN-FORD MARRIAGE ANNOUNCEMENT: **MISS MABEL JACKMAN**, a daughter of MR. and MRS. E. G. JACKMAN, of this place, and **MR. HAROLD FORD**, a son of MR. and MRS. EARL FORD, of Glasgow, were married in Bowling Green, Kentucky, on March 5th ----.

JOHNSON DEATH NOTICE: "Death Of Mrs. George Johnson Sunday Night." **MRS. GEORGE W. JOHNSON**, in her 66th year, died at her home in this city Sunday night. Death was caused by influenza. Surviving are her husband MR. GEORGE W. JOHNSON, MRS. H. W. JOLLY, MRS. W. M. TOTTY, MISS HAZEL JOHNSON, MRS. GARNETT VANCE, of Cave City, MISS PEARL JOHNSON, of Mayslick, HENRY JOHNSON, of Coral Hill, T. T. JOHNSON and H. C. JOHNSON, both of Louisville. Funeral was conducted by REV. M. L. MOORE, of Franklin, and the burial was in the Glasgow Cemetery yesterday. MRS. JOHNSON was one of the most lovable and best-known ladies of the county. She was beloved by a wide circle of friends, and her devotion was intense. She was a consecrated christian, and the world is loser because of her passing. [**My Note:** CORNELIA REED JOHNSON died in 1925. GEORGE JOHNSON died in 1934].

JOHNSON DEATH NOTICE: "Miss Nell Johnson Dead." One of the saddest deaths recently in Barren County was at the home of MR. and MRS. GEORGE JOHNSON at Coral Hill when the life of their lovely young daughter, **MISS NELL JOHNSON,** passed on Saturday night. Death was due to rapid tubercular trouble developed as a result of an operation in Louisville the last week. After the operation at St. Joseph Infirmary, Louisville, she rapidly grew worse and about two weeks ago her condition became very serious and her recovery was doubtful, and she was then brought home. Everything possible with friends and loved ones to help alleviate her suffering, was done. Miss Nell was one of the most popular teachers in the county. She was pleasant, cultured, studious, and a woman of the very noblest ideals. Since early childhood she had been an active member of the Christian Church. Interment was made in the family burying ground at her home in the presence of the largest crowd that ever attended a burial in the Coral Hill country. REV. M. L. MOORE, of Franklin, conducted the exercises. Besides her father and mother, she is survived by three brothers and five sisters, viz., TOM JOHNSON, HARRY JOHNSON, CLAUD JOHNSON, PEARL JOHNSON, HAZEL JOHNSON, MAYE JOHNSON, MRS. GARNETT VANCE, and MRS. HUEY JOLLY, of this county.

JOHNSON DEATH NOTICE: "Mr. George W. Johnson Passes To His Reward." Funeral services for **MR. GEORGE W. JOHNSON,** 78, who died at the home of his son-in-law, MR. H. W. JOLLY, Tuesday morning of a heart attack, was held from the Church of Christ, conducted by REV. ALLEN PHY. He had been in declining health for some time. Surviving are seven children: MRS. H. W. JOLLY, MISS HAZEL JOHNSON, of Glasgow; H. E. JOHNSON, of Coral Hill; T. T. JOHNSON, of Louisville; MRS. GARNETT VANCE, of Cave City; MRS. GEORGE DISHER, of Mays Lick, KY; and, CLAUDE JOHNSON, of Chicago. Burial was in Glasgow Cemetery. [**My Note:** GEORGE JOHNSON died in 1934. His wife had died in 1925].

JONES DEATH NOTICE: "Community Loss Is Death Of Hon. W. H. Jones On March 24. Was Seventy-nine Years Old And Sick Only Four Days Before Death. Funeral And Burial Monday. Was Outstanding Man Of This Part Of State." **W. H. JONES** was born in Glasgow on August 14, 1854, son of the late NICHOLAS WREN JONES and MARY GLAZEBROOK. He was one of six children, only one of whom now survives, MR. LEWIS JONES, of this place. MR. W. H. JONES married on September 10, 1880 to MISS MOLLIE BELL, and at the age of 37 he was elected to the Kentucky Senate. He was postmaster at Freedom, KY, from 1884 to 1891, and in Glasgow from 1908 to 1912. In 1901 he bought *The Glasgow Republican* newspaper and was the Republican nominee for Congress in 1904. His funeral was at the Christian Church, with W. P. COOMBS delivering the address, assisted by the pastor REV. T. H. ALDERSON and REV. J. A. GAINES, pastor of the Baptist Church. Surviving are his wife, MRS. MOLLIE BELL JONES, a brother MR. LEWIS JONES, this city, and the following children: MR. W. H. JONES, JR., MRS. ANNIE McFARLAND,

and MRS. WILLIAM POTEET, of Glasgow. The interment was in Glasgow Cemetery. [**My Note:** WILLIAM HENRY JONES died on March 23, 1934, and his wife died on February 16, 1935, according to their tombstones].

JONES DEATH NOTICE: **MISS M. T. JONES** died at her home at Coral Hill, Tuesday night, in her 82nd year, after a long and lingering illness. She was born and reared in the Coral Hill country, where her brothers, JOHN JONES and FRANK JONES, engaged in the mercantile business, but both have passed away, and since their death, she has lived alone except for those who stayed with her, just to help her. "Miss T" was the last of her generation to pass on. MAID JONES, CLARENCE JONES and WILLIE JONES were her nephews. W. H. JONES and L. W. JONES, of Glasgow, were her only cousins. These five were the only living relatives of even the second generation, at least on her father's side. She was a member of the Christian Church and had been an invalid for many years. The burial will be in the family burying ground today. [**My Note:** Another obituary gave her name as MELISSA T. JONES and stated she was buried in the Munday burying ground near Owl Springs. Her tombstone inscription indicates she died on February 21, 1928].

JORDAN-NUCKOLS MARRIAGE ANNOUNCEMENT: **MR. ALLEN NUCKOLS**, son of MR. and MRS. GEORGE NUCKOLS, and **MISS ANNA LEE JORDAN**, the youngest daughter of MR. and MRS. HACKNEY JORDAN, were married in Bowling Green last Friday. They will make their home in Horse Cave, where MR. NUCKOLS works with the Ford agency.

JUMP-NUCKOLS MARRIAGE ANNOUNCEMENT: Marriage of **MR. CARLOS NUCKOLS and MISS JESSIE JUMP**, both of this place, came as a surprise to their many friends. They motored to Bowling Green where they were married in the study of REV. A. B. HOUZE. MR. NUCKOLS is the son of MR. and MRS. SID NUCKOLS, and has a farm out on the Tompkinsville Pike. MRS. NUCKOLS is the youngest daughter of the late MR. S. J. JUMP and is an excellent young lady.

KILGORE DEATH NOTICE: "The Death of Reed Kilgore - One Of Finest Men Of The City; Carried Mail On Route 3 More Than Eighteen Years." Glasgow was grievously shocked Friday to hear of the death of MR. **REED S. KILGORE** at his home here at an early hour that morning. MR. KILGORE was in his 41st year. Surviving are his wife, two children, his parents, MR. and MRS. E. Y. KILGORE, and the following brothers and sisters: REV. LEWIS KILGORE, BOLTON KILGORE, MRS. S. D. GORDON, MURRAY KILGORE, JOE KILGORE, and MRS. EVELYN BUTTMAN. The funeral was at the home here on Saturday, conducted by REV. GILLESPIE of the Presbyterian Church, assisted by REV. EASLEY, of the Baptist Church, and REV. PIERCY, of the Methodist Church. The interment was in the Glasgow Cemetery. [**My Note:** REED S. KILGORE died in 1925].

KILGORE DEATH NOTICE: "Beloved Lady Passes Away." **MRS. ANNIE ROGERS KILGORE** died at her home on West Washington St. last Friday, March 30th, at the age of 80 years, after a long and lingering illness. She was the widow of the late MR. E. Y. KILGORE, who died only 17 months ago, at a very advanced age, and who had spent his entire life in the business activities of Glasgow. MRS. KILGORE was a native of Glasgow, her father, the late DR. JOHN T. ROGERS, and his wife OLIVIA LEWIS, being prominently identified with the earlier life of Glasgow. The marriage of MR. KILGORE and MISS ANNIE ROGERS occurred May 17, 1870, and to this union nine children were born, six of whom survive. They are: REV. JOHN LEWIS KILGORE, of Stone Mountain, Georgia; MR. BOLTON G. KILGORE, of San Angelo, Texas; MRS. S. D. GORDON, of this place; MR. JOE L. KILGORE of California; MR. MURRAY KILGORE, of Princeton, West Virginia; and MRS. EVELYN BUTTMAN, of Maryville, Tennessee. MRS. KILGORE also leaves 3 sisters and 3 brothers: MR. JOE U. ROGERS, the well known financier of this place; MR. EDMUND ROGERS, of California; MR. JOHN ROGERS, of Franklin, KY; MRS. BYRD THOMPSON, MISS HATTIE ROGERS, and MRS. LOULIE RICHARDSON, widow of the late HON. J. M. RICHARDSON and mother of MR. JOE RICHARDSON, editor of *The Glasgow Times*. MRS. KILGORE was a member of the Presbyterian Church. Funeral was held Saturday, conducted by her son-in-law, MR. S. D. GORDON, assisted by REV. J. L. PIERCY, with burial in Glasgow Cemetery. [**My Note:** ANNIE E. KILGORE died in 1928 and EDWARD Y. KILGORE died in 1926].

LACY-MOODY MARRIAGE ANNOUNCEMENT: **MISS RELLA ENA LACY and MR. CECIL T. MOODY,** of Paris, Tennessee, were married June 28. MRS. MOODY has often visited MISS MABEL PEDEN here and is pleasantly remembered by all who met her. MR. MOODY is employed by L.& N. R.R. and they will make their home in Paris, TN. [**My Note:** Written in pencil: "1931"].

LAMBIRTH-RAY MARRIAGE ANNOUNCEMENT: **MISS ALMA LAMBIRTH and EUGENE B. RAY,** of Indianapolis, were married Monday morning at the home of the REV. J. L. PIERCY.

LANCASTER-PARKER MARRIAGE ANNOUNCEMENT: **MISS GLADYS LANCASTER,** the daughter of MR. and MRS. SAM LANCASTER, of Lebanon, Indiana, and **MR. ISAAC PARKER,** the son of MR. and MRS. FRANK PARKER, of Cave City, were married Friday, by the REV. W. T. CHURCH, of Goodnight.

LANDERS DEATH NOTICE: "The Death of Mrs. Sarah Landers on May 30." **MRS. SARAH LANDERS** died at her home near Coral Hill, May 30th. She was in her 79th year and had been an invalid for ten years. She was a member of the Baptist Church, and from her girlhood had been a conscientious and devoted christian. That beautiful principle of mother-love was never more beautifully exemplified than in this life. Her children were equally devoted to her, never leaving a wish of her's ungratified. The burial was at the family burying ground at Coral Hill after funeral services which were held at the residence. BROTHER DUNCAN, in an impressive manner, urged friends and bereaved ones to look upon death not as a calamity, but as a transition, a passing from the sorrows of life to the joys of eternity. Surviving her are four brothers and four sisters, viz., VIRGIL JOHNSON, GEORGE W. JOHNSON, T. F. JOHNSON, CLARENCE JOHNSON, MRS. U. J. FORREST, MRS. AMANDA EUBANK, MRS. MALISSA MAGGARD, and

MISS ELLEN JOHNSON. The surviving children are MR. TOM LANDERS, MISS MARY LANDERS, MRS. TOM BRIDGES, and MRS. SAM BROWNING.

LANDERS DEATH NOTICE: "Death Of Miss Mary Landers At Lecta Monday" **MISS MARY M. LANDERS**, age 66, died at the home of her sister, MRS. SAM BROWNING, near Lecta, early Monday. MISS LANDERS had been ill only a short while. Surviving her are two sisters and one brother MRS. SAM BROWNING, of Lecta, MRS. TIM BRIDGES, of Beech Grove, and MR. TOM LANDERS, of the Coral Hill section. Funeral was at Hickory Grove Church of Christ. Burial was in Johnson cemetery near Lecta.

LANE-TRAVIS MARRIAGE ANNOUNCEMENT: **MR. TERRELL TRAVIS**, son of MR. J. E. TRAVIS, of Temple Hill, and **MISS MAY LANE**, daughter of MR. JOHN LANE, of Tompkinsville, were married at Tompkinsville last Saturday, and will make their home at Temple Hill, Kentucky.

LEE DEATH NOTICE: "Heart Trouble Fatal To W. Scott Lee." **W. SCOTT LEE** died at the home of MR. and MRS. J. L. WRIGHT, three miles out the Coral Hill Road, Saturday night, of heart trouble, from which he had suffered occasionally for some years. MR. LEE spent Saturday in Glasgow and went home feeling as well as usual, but was taken quite ill a short time before his death. He was a native of Barren County, and spent his life here, except for a few years spent in Edmonson County, and in the State of Arkansas. He lived a bachelor until late in life when he married MRS. IDA MANSFIELD, who survives him. He leaves two sisters, MRS. MACY HAZELIP, of Louisville, and MRS. JENNIE WILLIAMS, of Arkansas. His surviving half-brothers and sisters are MR. H. G. LEE, of St. Louis, CHURCH LEE, of Wichita, Kansas, MRS. ---- JAMES of St. Louis and one sister [no name given] of Edmondson County. MR. LEE was a member of the Baptist Church and was an honorable man and citizen, quiet and industrious. The burial was in the cemetery at Poplar Log, after services conducted by REV. J. P. BROOKS. [**My Note:** WALTER SCOTT LEE died on August 30, 1924].

LESSENBERRY DEATH MEMORIAM: "Splendid Tribute To A Dear Friend." "I (MRS. C. H. CALLAHAN) am so sorry to have to report the death of one of my very dear friend, **MRS. J. D. LESSENBERRY**, which occurred on Tuesday, February 3rd, at 2:30 p.m., at the home of her daughter MRS. J. H. TURK, and MR. TURK in Hiseville, she having been brought to her daughter's home after she had become ill at her home in the country. She was 71 years, 4 months, and 26 days of age. She was a faithful member of the Baptist Church and a good, kind neighbor, a devoted wife and mother." [**My Note:** The eulogy is longer than what has been abstracted here]. She is survived by her husband MR. J. D. LESSENBERRY, and children: MRS. W. E. COOK, of Horse Cave; MRS. J. H. BILLINGS, MRS. J. H. TURK, MESSRS. LAWRENCE LESSENBERRY, ROBERT LESSENBERRY, MORRIS LESSENBERRY, and JOE LESSENBERRY, of Hiseville; DAN LESSENBERRY, of Pittsburgh; and, MRS. D. TALBOTT, of Elkins, West Virginia, all of whom were at her bedside when the end came. Her funeral was beautifully conducted at home by BROTHER GRIDER. [**My Note:** MATTIE BELL LESSENBERRY died on February 3, 1931. J. D. LESSENBERRY died in 1935. They are buried in Hiseville Cemetery].

<u>LESSENBERRY-BEARD MARR. ANNOUNCEMENT</u>: **MISS MARY AGNES LESSENBERRY**, only child of MR. and MRS. L. L. LESSENBERRY, and **MR. WAYNE BEARD**, only son of MR. and MRS. WILL BEARD, of Knob Lick, Metcalfe County, married in Louisville on December 24. They were accompanied by MR. and MRS. LLOYD GADBERRY.

<u>LOWREY DEATH NOTICE</u>: Little **EDNA LOUISE LOWREY**, oldest daughter of L. H. and VERDA LOWREY, died after an illness of one week. She is survived by her parents and one little sister, ELAINE LOWREY, and a number of close relatives. She was born February 13, 1920, and died April 30, 1924. [**My Note**: Included a long poem by "a friend"].

<u>MAGGARD DEATH NOTICE</u>: The Hiseville section lost one of its best citizens in the death of **MR. JAMES MAGGARD** on Monday, leaving his wife, who was MISS MAUD GOFF, and their four daughters: MRS. J. L. SPILLMAN, of Hiseville; MRS. TOM LANDERS, of Coral Hill; MISS BLANCH MAGGARD; and, MISS ZOYE MAGGARD. MR. MAGGARD was an elder in the Christian Church in Hiseville, with burial in the Hiseville Cemetery following the funeral services by ELDER T. T. ALDERSON.

<u>MANSFIELD DEATH NOTICE: "Mrs. Ida Mansfield Dies in California."</u> Relatives have been notified of the death of **MRS. IDA MANSFIELD**, which occurred at her home in Los Angeles, California, on Monday, January 12th, at 11 p.m. She was eighty odd years of age. Born in Cumberland County, MRS. MANSFIELD was a daughter of the late MILTON R. and MARY JANE WILLIAMS, who moved to this county when she was quite young. She was married to MR. J. T. MANSFIELD of the Ritter Mill section. He preceded her to the grave a number of years ago. About 15 years ago MRS. MANSFIELD went to California to join her sons who were living in that state. She and MR. and MRS. MORRIS MANSFIELD were living in Los Angeles since the death of her son, MILTON MANSFIELD. MRS. MANSFIELD was a devout member of the Baptist Church. Her body was taken to Fresno, California, for burial beside her late son MILTON MANSFIELD. Beside her son MORRIS MANSFIELD, she is survived by one sister, MRS. ELLEN SANDERS, of this city, and one brother, MR. M. R. WILLIAMS, of Prospect, Kentucky.

<u>MANSFIELD DEATH NOTICE</u>: **MR. MILTON MANSFIELD** died at his home in Fresno, California, on November 14th, very suddenly, of heart trouble. Surviving him are his wife and two children, his mother, MRS. IDA MANSFIELD, who lives in the same town, and two brothers, MORRIS MANSFIELD and JOE MANSFIELD, both of California. MR. MILTON MANSFIELD was born in Glasgow where his father was a blacksmith as was he. The family moved to California many years ago. Burial was in Fresno Cemetery. MRS. ELLEN SANDERS (of Glasgow, KY) is an aunt.

<u>MARTIN-BAGBY MARRIAGE ANNOUNCEMENT</u>: **MR. MURRAY BAGBY**, youngest son of MR. and MRS. EUGENE BAGBY, of Coral Hill, and **MISS MAUD MARTIN**, daughter of MR. WILLIAM MARTIN, of Tompkinsville, have announced their marriage in Moss, Tennessee, on April [May?] 27th. They were accompanied by MR. OSCAR PAGE, of this place [Glasgow, Kentucky].

McCOY DEATH NOTICE: C. C. **McCOY**, "a year ago today June 21, our hearts were saddened by the death of daddy." [no date given].

McFARLAND-MERCER MARRIAGE ANNOUNCEMENT: **MISS ANNE McFARLAND**, of the City Schools, daughter of MR. & MRS. U. G. McFARLAND, of Lexington, married **MR. FORREST MERCER**, of the Anchorage City Schools, at the home of her sister, MRS. LEO PAGE, last Saturday, with REV. J. A. GAINES officiating. Originally from Glasgow, MISS McFARLAND was a University of Kentucky honor student.

McQUOWN DEATH NOTICE: **RICHARD MEREDITH McQUOWN** known to his friends as "DICK" McQUOWN, died at his residence near Dugantown, Saturday morning, of heart trouble. MR. McQUOWN shocked millet hay Thursday and sat up reading till near eleven o'clock that night. He then retired, seemingly in good health, and about three in the morning his family heard him groaning, and in a very short time he had expired. However, his friends have known for a year that his heart was badly affected, and his sudden demise was not altogether a surprise. He was 65 years of age, a native of Glasgow, being a son of the late MR. BURR McQUOWN, one of the best citizens of the town. He is survived by his wife, who was MISS LULA McFERRAN, and the following children: MISS MARY McQUOWN, MISS PHOEBE McQUOWN, MISS AMY McQUOWN, and MISS ADY McQUOWN, MR. LESLIE McQUOWN, and MR. GEORGE McQUOWN, all living here except Leslie who is married and has been living in Danville, Illinois. He came in for the burial, and may remain here. MR. McQUOWN is survived by three brothers, MR. LESLIE McQUOWN, of Montecello, California, MR. AL W. McQUOWN, of Washington, D.C., and MR. BURR McQUOWN, of Bowling Green. The brother LESLIE McQUOWN has not been here for 38 years, and none of the family have seen him during this time. A letter from him was received Saturday, telling that he was coming Christmas. RICHARD McQUOWN was a member of the Christian Church and was an excellent citizen. Funeral services were held at the residence on Sunday afternoon by Elder R. H. BISER and the burial followed in Glasgow Cemetery. [**My Note:** RICHARD MEREDITH McQUOWN died in 1925].

McQUOWN DEATH NOTICE: "Death Of Mrs. Lula McFerran McQuown Sunday." **MRS. LULA McFERRAN McQUOWN**, age 64, died at her home on North Race Street Sunday morning at 11 o'clock, following a few hours illness. Although she had been in declining health a number of years, her death was not expected. MRS. McQUOWN, the widow of RICHARD McQUOWN, whose death occurred eight years ago, was a daughter of the late SAMUEL McFERRAN and PHOEBE HODGEN, one of the first families of Barren County. Surviving are the following children: MISSES MARY, PHOEBE, AMY, and MR. GEORGE McQUOWN, all of this city, MRS. GILBERT LEE, of Owensboro, and MR. LESLIE McQUOWN, of Danville, Illinois. Sisters, MRS. NELLIE SATLEY, of Louisville, and MRS. ROSA McGEE, of Cunningham, KY, also survive. MRS. LULA McQUOWN was a member of the First Christian Church where funeral services were held on Tuesday morning by REV. T. H. ALDERSON, with interment in Glasgow Cemetery.

<u>McQUOWN-LEE MARRIAGE ANNOUNCEMENT</u>: **MISS ADAH McQUOWN**, daughter of MRS. R. M. McQUOWN, of Glasgow, married **GILBERT LEE** in Elizabethtown last Friday. MR. LEE holds a position with the Neely-Ewing Motor Company here.

<u>MILLER MILITARY NOTICE</u>: **DR. T. F. MILLER**, who has been stationed at Camp Meade, Maryland, several months ago, has been promoted from a First Lieutenancy to a Captaincy. This is no surprise as we knew "Doc" and knew that he would soon begin to rise in rank. He will go to Camp Shelby in a few days to mobilize for a departure overseas.

<u>MINICK-BURKS AND MINICK-SMITH MARRIAGE ANNOUNCEMENTS</u>: **MISS ESTHER MINICK and MR. YANCY BURKS**, and **MISS LORELLE MINICK and MR. VERNON SMITH**, were married in Jeffersonville, Indiana, Friday. They were accompanied by MISS LAURA ELLEN MILLER, of Horse Cave, and MRS. S. S. CROWDER, of Nashville. The brides are the daughters of MR. and MRS. JODIE MINICK of this place. MR. SMITH is the son of MR. and MRS. FLOYD SMITH of Horse Cave. MR. BURKS is the son of MR. and MRS. J. N. BURKS, of Horse Cave. MRS. BURKS has been a stenographer for Davidson Bros. for several months, and MRS. SMITH has been with Leech & Davis since last fall. The double wedding came as a surprise to their friends. Both couples reside at Horse Cave, KY. [A second newspaper article presented it as follows -- MISS ESTHER MINICK, of this city, daughter of MR. and MRS. JODY MINICK, and MR. YANCY LEWIS BURKS, of Horse Cave, son of MR. J. N. BURKS, and MISS LORELLE MINICK, also a daughter of MR. and MRS. JODY MINICK, of Glasgow, and MR. VERNON SMITH, son of MR. and MRS. R. F. SMITH, of Horse Cave, were parties to a double wedding in Jeffersonville, Indiana, Thursday last week. They were accompanied by MISS LAURA ELLEN MILLER and MR. ---- CROWDER, both of Horse Cave, Kentucky].

<u>MOUSER DEATH NOTICE: "Child Meets Tragic Death."</u> A most horrible tragedy occurred on the farm of MR. PETE MOUSER, just in Barren County, near the Hart County line, at Bearwallow, Wednesday of last week when MR. MOUSER's little eight year old son, **WILLIAM MITCHELL MOUSER**, was killed and the body horribly mangled by hogs. It seems that the evening before, MR. MOUSER had driven a load of coal to the back of the coal house, but as it was raining, he did not unload that night, and the next day he went to work on the farm, still leaving the load of coal on the wagon. Wednesday afternoon the little son seems to have decided to unload the coal himself, as a large lump was on the ground and the little fellow's cap under it indicating the coal had fallen in the boy's head. An old sow and some shoats came along, and the blood attracted them and they dragged the body quite a distance over the field, as was shown by the blood stains. The boy's right hand had been eaten off, his left hand partly eaten, and one side of his face mangled. MRS. MOUSER had missed the boy, went down in the field where her husband was at work expecting to find him there, and then the search began. When he was found only a few steps away from the house, the hogs were still at work on the body. It was a heart-rending scene which met the eyes of the distracted parents. Coroner W. M. WATKINS held an

inquest and the jury brought in a verdict in accordance with the facts as above stated. "We, the jury, believe from the examination, that WILLIAM MITCHELL MOUSER came to his death by a lump of coal that he was unloading, and afterwards was torn up by hogs in the field near the house, on this the 25th day of January, 1928, in Barren County, near Bearwallow." [There were two articles on this].

MURRAY POLITICAL ANNOUNCEMENT: On the back of a photograph of **J. A. MURRAY** (dressed in his Confederate uniform) is this political ad: "Dear Friend: I am a candidate for County Clerk in the primary of August, 1913. You know whether I have given my time and money for the democratic cause for forty years past, and tried to be true and useful to the people of "Old Barren." You have been good to OLD REB and his old comrades. It is probable that this it the last time you will have an opportunity to honor an old Confederate with your vote as we are fast passing "over the river." I believe I have conducted YOUR clerk's office satisfactorily, and I make a PERSONAL APPEAL to you for your support. If elected, I promise faithful performance of my duties, and whether you nominate me or not, I will be found as ever fighting for democratic principles and the best interests of the people of Barren County. Yours truly, J. A. MURRAY."

NEWBY-DEPP MARRIAGE ANNOUNCEMENT: **MISS WILLIE NEWBY**, daughter of MR. and MRS. WILLIAM WHALEN NEWBY, announces her engagement to **MR. WALTER BAGBY DEPP**. The marriage will be early in December. [From another newspaper clipping: MISS BILLY NEWBY, whose parents live in Bellebuckle, Tennessee, and MR. WALTER DEPP, the son of MR. and MRS. A. DEPP, of the Bradford Mill section, were married at the Baptist Church yesterday morning at 10 o'clock. MRS. F. H. JACKSON, sister of the bride, was the matron of honor, and DR. H. W. DEPP, of Louisville, the brother of the groom, was best man. MRS. DEPP has been the bookkeeper for the Neely-Ewing Motor Company. They will live on their farm on Beaver Creek].

NICHOLS DEATH NOTICE: "The Cause Of Death Of Four Is A Mystery" The bodies of four persons, all members of one family, were found in the debris of their fire-swept home four miles from here at two thirty o'clock Monday afternoon. The dead are **EARL NICHOLS**, age 37; **MRS. POLLY NICHOLS**, age 33, his wife; **EARLINE NICHOLS**, 3 year old daughter; and, **WENDELL NICHOLS**, 5 month old son. Besides the two children who died in the fire, the Nichols couple had three others: OVAL NICHOLS, age 11; JOE NICHOLS, age 8; and, HARVEY NICHOLS, age 6, who were in school at the time of the tragedy. Within 100 yards of where the four Nichols lost their lives Monday *The Times* recalls the following tragic events: OWEN BROADY, October, 1920, lost his life by a tree falling on him; J. W. REEDER, in August, 1922, was killed when his auto plunged over the bridge embankment nearby; G. T. WILLIAMSON, shot himself at his barn nearby on December 1, 1926; and, about 8 years ago, SAM CRENSHAW, colored preacher, was drowned at the creek ford close by. MR. NICHOLS resided at the old REV. W. NEAL farm (later Dohoney), 4 miles from town on Edmonton Pike. Many theories have ben advanced as to how the deaths occurred. Nobody will ever know the truth. Theory is that MR. NICHOLS, in mental aberration, killed his family, fired the house, and then committed suicide is most generally expressed. Indications point to the fact that MRS. NICHOLS and the two children had tumbled from the closet in which the bodies had been jammed; that MR. NICHOLS' body was in an adjoining room. A hole in MRS. NICHOLS' head, believed to have been inflicted by a gun, was pronounced. MR. NICHOLS' body, minus the head, was found huddled over a double-barrel 12 gauge shotgun in which two discharged shotgun shells were found. MR. NICHOLS was a son of MR. H. B. NICHOLS, and MRS. NICHOLS was the daughter of MR. DICK SHIRLEY. Interment was in the cemetery here last Tuesday.

NICHOLS DEATH NOTICE: "Nat Nichols Died Sunday At Coral Hill."
NAT NICHOLS, one of Barren County's best known citizens, died at his home at Coral Hill, Sunday afternoon at the age of 86 years, after three weeks' illness. He was born at Brownsville, son of THOMAS Y. and MARY FRANCES NICHOLS, and moved to Barren County 60 years ago. He was married to CORNELIA PEDEN, daughter of HARLAN PEDEN and SALLIE WATTS, who passed away 19 years ago. [**My Note:** It was EDMUND HARLIN PEDEN who died 19 years ago, i. e., in 1914, so NAT NICHOLS died in 1933]. MR. NICHOLS went into business with his stepfather "DOC" CLARK in Nichols and Clark's Mill at Coral Hill and after retiring from the mill was a merchant for 30 years. He leaves one daughter and four sons: MRS. MORRIS (MYRTIE) KING, of Hardyville, SEAY NICHOLS, of Munfordville, LOUEY NICHOLS and WILL NICHOLS, of Coral Hill, and CARL NICHOLS, of Glasgow; also 2 half-sisters, MRS. RODDY BAGBY, of Coral Hill, and MRS. ELLA WILLIAMS, of Hoopston, Illinois; one half-brother, HINK CLARK, of California. The late TOMMY NICHOLS, at one time miller here, was his brother.

NICKOLS DEATH NOTICE: "Death Of Mrs. Nat Nickols Last Week."
MRS. CORNELIA NICKOLS, age 61 years, died at her home near Coral Hill on Tuesday of last week. Tuberculosis caused her death. Surviving are her husband and five children--MISS MYRTLE NICKOLS, LOUIE NICKOLS, CARL NICKOLS, SEAY NICKOLS, and WILL NICKOLS, all of this county; also, one brother and one sister survive -- MOTE PEDEN of Goodnight, and MRS. NAT CLAYTON, of Coral Hill. After funeral services at the residence, interment was in the Glasgow cemetery. MRS. CORNELIA NICKOLS was a splendid lady of many admirable traits of character and her passing is mourned by friends all over the county. [**My Note:** CORNELIA F. (PEDEN) NICKOLS died in 1923].

NICKOLS SURPRISE BIRTHDAY DINNER: "Nat Nickols Surprised."
On September 23rd, friends, relatives and neighbors gathered at the home of **MR. NAT NICKOLS** of Coral Hill and gave him a surprise 79th birthday dinner. About 150 persons were present, including all his children and grandchildren: MR. and MRS. CARL NICKOLS, and daughter SARAH WATTS, of Glasgow; MR. and MRS. MORRIS KING, of Hardyville; MR. and MRS. SEAY NICKOLS and son CLINT SEAY, of Munfordville; MR. and MRS. WILL NICKOLS, and children, MILDRED and MORRIS; and, MR. and MRS. LOUIE NICKOLS and children, LOUIE HALL and GEORGIE TERRY,

of Coral Hill. The table was loaded with good things to eat, the birthday cake baked and decorated by his niece MISS MABEL PEDEN. Thanks for the blessings was offered by MR. WILL WATKINS, a life long friend. Among those from a distance were MR. and MRS. EULA GATEWOOD and MR. JONES, of Central City; MRS. FELIX ALLEN and MRS. GLYN FISHER, of Bowling Green; MR. and MRS. WILL WILLIAMS, MR. and MRS. ELMER WILLIAMS, of Hoopeston, Ill.; MR. and MRS. TOM BUTTON, MRS. BERNICE NORRIS and two children, MR. and MRS. CLIFF GOFF, MR. and MRS. VEACHEL PEERS, and MRS. H. W. Jolly, of Glasgow. [**My Note:** NAT NICHOLS was born September 24, 1855, so this party was in 1934]

NICKOLS VISITATION NOTICE: **SEAY NICKOLS** was down from Camp Taylor last week visiting relatives at Coral Hill, KY. [no date given].

NORRIS-JONES MARRIAGE ANNOUNCEMENT: MR. and MRS. L. F. NORRIS announce the marriage of their daughter, **KITTIE LEE NORRIS**, to **MR. FRANK W. JONES.** The marriage ceremony was performed May 3rd, ----, at Jeffersonville, Indiana, in the study of the pastor of the Methodist Church of that city, REV. E. C. McKINNEY. MR. JONES, son of MR. and MRS. W. E. JONES, is a prominent young Glasgow attorney.

NUCKOLS BIRTH ANNOUNCEMENT: MR. and MRS. C. D. NUCKOLS announce the arrival of their daughter **BETTY JOE NUCKOLS** on October 10th, ----, 9 a.m., in Lindsay, California [this announcement was on a card].

NUCKOLS DEATH NOTICE: "Death Of Dr. O. P. Nuckols At Middlesboro." **DR. O. P. NUCKOLS**, age 73, died suddenly at the court house in Middlesboro, KY, at noon Monday. He had just concluded testifying at a trial and as he sat down dropped dead. DR. NUCKOLS was native of Barren County, having been born and reared in the neighborhood of Old Salem. Surviving are his widow and the following children: MR. NORWOOD NUCKOLS, of Middlesboro; MR. PAUL NUCKOLS, Huntington, West Virginia; MR. LEON NUCKOLS, Pineville; and, MRS. LALLA FOSTER, of the Old Salem section. Two sisters, MRS. OSCAR OWENS, and MISS LELIA NUCKOLS, and one brother, MR. JAMES NUCKOLS, of the Old Salem section, also survive. DR. NUCKOLS was a prominent physician and he formerly lived in Louisville and Nashville before finally moving to Pineville where he is buried. FLOYD ELLIS, a nephew, also attended.

NUNN DEATH NOTICE: "The Death of Mrs. R. H. Nunn at Hiseville, KY" **MRS. R. H. NUNN,** age 54 years, 9 months, and 13 days, died at her home at Hiseville, Wednesday evening, April 15th, after 11 days' illness of pneumonia and other complications. MRS. NUNN was the daughter of RICHARD SLEMMONS and MARY C. DEPP, of Edmonton. She was united in marriage in 1901 to MR. R. H. NUNN. Surviving are her husband, MR. R. H. NUNN, two sisters and two brothers, viz., MRS. A. B. MAYFIELD, of Summer Shade, MRS. J. W. BARTON, of Edmonton, MR. W. A. SLEMMONS, of Seattle, Washington, and MR. JAMES DILLON of Park, a half-brother. Funeral was conducted at the residence by the REV. DEWITT of the Hiseville Methodist Church, and REV. MERRITT of the Munfordsville Baptist Church. Interment was in the cemetery at Hiseville. [**My Note:** VIRGIE NUNN, wife of R. H. NUNN, died on April

15, 1928, and her husband, REUBEN HENRY NUNN, died August 22, 1954. Another obituary identified her as VIRGIE NUNN, wife of the banker at Hiseville, and she was MISS VIRGIE SLEMMONS before her marriage; also that her sister MRS. J. W. BARTON was the wife of the Baptist minister at Edmonton, and another sister was the wife of MR. WATT SLEMMONS, of Seattle. It also identified her two half-brothers REV. POLK DILLON, of Hopkinsville, and G. W. G. DILLON, of Columbia].

OLIVE-HIGH MARRIAGE ANNOUNCEMENT: **MISS ELSIE OLIVE**, daughter of MR. and MRS. ELTON OLIVE, of Cottage Grove, married **MR. HUBERN HIGH**, son of MR. ELZIE HIGH, of Martin, on Sunday afternoon at the home of the bride's parents. The wedding ceremony was performed by REV. W. A. LAMPKINS, of Martin, uncle of the groom. Also present were the cousins of the bride, MISS DUDLEEN and MISS BURNIDEAN OLIVE, and DOLORES OLIVE and JIMMIE JOE OLIVE.

OWENS DEATH NOTICE: **OSCAR P. OWENS** died on December 10, 1932. Poem "in loving remembrance of my dear husband," by CORA NUCKELS OWENS.

OWENS DEATH NOTICE: **MRS. ELLA FIELDS OWENS** died at the home of her son CHARLIE OWENS, of Coral Hill, Saturday at the age of 84 years, after an illness incident to advanced age. She was the widow of TOM OWENS, who died five years ago. MRS. OWENS had lived in the Coral Hill section all her life and was a member of the Christian Church. Three sons, all of Coral Hill, survived: CHARLIE, BOB and WALTER OWENS. She leaves six grandchildren. Services were conducted by ELDER HARDY WOODWARD, with burial in the Fields burying ground.

OWENS DEATH NOTICE: "Mrs. Walter Owens Dies At Coral Hill." **MRS. WALTER OWENS** died at her home at Coral Hill, Tuesday morning. Before her marriage she was MISS TRUDE PRITCHARD. She is survived by her husband and 2 children, MRS. W. T. EVERETT and MISS LOUELLA OWENS, and one grandson, W. T. EVERETT, JR. Also surviving are one sister and one brother, MRS. BETTIE MARCUM and MR. DOSS PRITCHARD, all of Coral Hill. MRS. OWENS was a member of the Church of Christ. Her entire life was spent near Coral Hill. Funeral services were conducted at the home by ELDER HARDY WOODWARD, of Bowling Green, KY, and burial was in the Fields burying ground, near the home.

OWENS-EVANS MARRIAGE ANNOUNCEMENT: **MISS CAROLYNE LOUISE OWENS and MR. CECIL EVANS** were married on January 25th, ----, the wedding having been solemnized at Jeffersonville [Indiana].

PAGE DEATH NOTICE: **MRS. LOU ANN PAGE** died at her home on Route 6 at the age of 67 years, leaving her mother, MRS. J. R. NICHOLS, who lived with her, one son MR. CLIFTON PAGE, and one brother, MR. W. E. NICHOLS, of Wisdom, KY. She was the widow of the late MR. BEN PAGE, who had died several years ago. MRS. PAGE was born and reared in the Wisdom country and was an excellent lady. The funeral was held at Dripping Spring Church near Wisdom. [**My Note:** LOU ANN PAGE died August 28, 1929, and was buried in the Nickols Cemetery].

<u>PARKER-MORGAN MARRIAGE ANNOUNCEMENT</u>: MR. WILL PARKER announces the marriage of his daughter, **MISS MABEL PARKER**, of the Goodnight section, to **MR. JOE MORGAN**. The wedding was in Jeffersonville, Indiana, February 10th, ----. MRS. MORGAN has been making her home with MRS. EUGENE BAIRD for some time. MR. MORGAN is a farmer in that neighborhood, where they will make their home.

<u>PARRISH DEATH NOTICE: "County Suffers Loss In Death Of G. Parrish."</u> Friends of **MR. GEORGE T. PARRISH**, and that means everyone who knew him, were shocked when the report became current that he had passed away at the home of his daughter, MRS. JENNIE BARLOW, on North Race Street, about 6 o'clock, Sunday afternoon. MR. PARRISH was stricken about 9 o'clock Saturday night with something like colitis and the family did not realize that he was seriously ill until a short time before the end came. MR. PARRISH was 85 years old last April. For more than a half century he took an active part in the affairs of Barren County. He served this county twelve years as County School Superintendent and four years as Sheriff [The obituary is longer on the kind of person and politician he was, i. e., fair and honest]. He was a member of the Baptist Church and an active member of the Masonic Lodge. He is survived by his two daughters, MRS. JENNIE P. BARLOW, with whom he had made his home since the death of his wife, and MRS. J. B. GARDNER, of Cave City; and his three sons, MR. W. T. PARRISH, of Louisville, DR. MACK PARRISH, pastor of Baptist Church at Greenville, and MR. NAT PARRISH, of Greenville, all of whom were in attendance at the funeral services held at the Barlow residence, by REV. JOSEPH A. GAINES, with the burial in the Glasgow Cemetery.

<u>PARRISH WEDDING ANNIVERSARY</u>: It was a happy celebration that marked the 40th wedding anniversary of **MR. and MRS. F. E. PARRISH** in the Goodnight community October 26 (last Wednesday) when 85 friends and relatives gathered in a huge feast prepared by the celebrants. Here is hoping they have at least 50 more such celebrations which will put both of them far beyond the century mark. MR. and MRS. PARRISH have two sons, CHARLES R. PARRISH and POWELL PARRISH, of Goodnight, and a daughter MRS. JAMES T. PHILPOTT, of Tompkinsville. [Photo].

<u>PARRISH-VANZANT MARRIAGE ANNOUNCEMENT</u>: **MISS WILLIE MAE PARRISH**, daughter of MR. and MRS. ELA PARRISH, of North Barren, and **MR. GARY VANZANT** were married on February 8th, ----, in Bowling Green, KY, by REV. R. T. SKINNER, pastor of the First Baptist Church. They were accompanied by MR. and MRS. ROY PARRISH.

<u>PAYNE-HALE MARRIAGE ANNOUNCEMENT</u>: **MISS WILLIE BEATRICE PAYNE**, daughter of MR. and MRS. WILLIAM THOMAS PAYNE, of Glasgow, and **MR. HENRY CLAY HALE JR.**, of Burksville, have announced their marriage and will make their home in Bowling Green, Kentucky.

<u>PEDEN DEATH NOTICE</u>: **MR. WILL PEDEN** died at his home on the Knob Road today at 12:30. Though he had been in poor health for some time, his death came suddenly, before aid could reach him. He was a farmer and was 52 years old. WILL PEDEN was known throughout the

county and was liked by everyone. He leaves two daughters and five sons: CLINT PEDEN, in the Army at Kelly Field, Texas; MRS. O. R. FROEDGE and MRS. MARY STEPHENS, of Glasgow; CLYDE PEDEN, EWELL PEDEN, HARLAN PEDEN, and CLAYTON PEDEN, of Lecta; his mother, MRS. MOTE PEDEN, of Goodnight; 2 sisters, MRS. SALLIE SMITH, of Owl Springs, and MRS. MABEL WILLIS who lives with her mother; also seven grandchildren. MR. WILL PEDEN was a member of the Hickory Grove Church of Christ near Lecta. The remains were moved to the home of his mother where funeral services will be held Sunday afternoon at 3 o'clock by REV. KIRBY SMITH and REV. WALTER CHURCH and the burial will be in Glasgow Cemetery. Pall bearers will be HADE McGUIRE, WALTER BROWNING, VANCE TAYLOR, ARTHUR ALEXANDER, WILLIE BOWLES, and ELLIS CHURCH. [**My Note:** WILLIAM HENRY "WILL" PEDEN, only son of ELMORE PEDEN, died on February 24, 1944].

PEDEN DEATH NOTICE: "Horrible Death Of William H. Peden."
MR. WILLIE H. PEDEN, of Temple Hill, met a most horrible death in the early hours last Saturday, when he committee suicide in one of the most horrible ways imaginable. Some time during Friday night he emptied two cans of oil on a stack of straw, lay down on the straw, set fire to it and was practically burned beyond recognition. His neighbors saw the fire before day Sunday, and upon investigation found the body in the fire, and his dog and the oil cans nearby. He is survived by his wife, MRS. LOU PEDEN, and 2 sisters, MRS. PORTER MILLER of Eighty-Eight, and MRS. J. M. SMITH of Tulare, California. His step-mother, MRS. SUSAN PEDEN, widow of his father, the late MR. ANDREW PEDEN, lives on an adjoining farm. MRS. ERNEST PEDEN and family, wife and children of his late brother, REV. ERNEST PEDEN, also live nearby. MR. PEDEN was about 60 years of age, and was one of the best citizens in the county. He was owner of 3 fine farms, and had much personal property, in addition to being industrious and a good money-maker. His trouble was in his kind-heartedness, and his inability to say "no" when asked for a favor. The result was that his friends--if that is what you call them--imposed on him and got him to go on their notes until he was covered with debts. Suits were brought and some personal property was advertised for sale by the sheriff on Monday morning, December 4th. This was more than he could stand, and as the strain was undermining his health, it affected his mind. His host of friends are greatly distressed at the turn of affairs and are in deep sympathy with his relatives. He was a member of the Baptist Church. His sister wired and requested that the body to be held until she could come in from California, after which the funeral was conducted at Temple Hill by REV. J. R. BRUNSON, of Bowling Green, followed by burial in the Peden burying ground nearby. [**My Note:** WILLIAM H. PEDEN died on December 2, 1933]

PEDEN DEATH NOTICE: **W. H. PEDEN** died on December 2, 1933. Poem was written "in memory of Uncle Willie" by his niece (no name given).

PEDEN DEATH NOTICE: **MR. ELMORE (MOTE) PEDEN,** well known Barren County farmer, died at his home in the Goodnight section Sunday night around 8:30 o'clock following a paralytic stroke. He was 76 years of age. A son of the late HARLAN and SARAH PEDEN, he was born and reared near Glasgow and had spent his entire life in Barren County. He was engaged in farming in the Goodnight section for the past 19 years. He was a Democrat of the old school and had been a subscriber of *The Times* for more than 50 years. He took an active part in all elections and was widely known throughout the county. He was a member of the Baptist Church. MR. ELMORE PEDEN was married to MISS JANIE ROGERS, daughter of the late MR. CHARLES ROGERS, who survives. MR. and MRS. PEDEN recently celebrated their 53rd wedding anniversary. Besides his wife, he is survived by a son, MR. WILL PEDEN; two daughters, MRS. SALLIE SMITH, of the Owl Spring section, and MISS MABEL PEDEN, at home; three half-brothers, MR. ED PEDEN and MR. LUCIAN PEDEN, of Russellville; MR. BONNIE PEDEN, of Canmer; and a half-sister, MRS. NELLIE WALTON, of Canmer; also a sister, MRS. MINNIE O'NEAL, of Wellington, Kansas. Funeral services were held Tuesday, 1 p. m., at the Peden residence in Goodnight, the REV. WALTER CHURCH in charge, with burial in the Glasgow Cemetery. [**My Note:** ELMORE "MOTE" PEDEN died on April 6, 1941. A "Card of Thanks" was also published in *The Glasgow Times* newspaper by MRS. MOTE PEDEN, MRS. NUMA SMITH, WILL PEDEN, and MABLE PEDEN].

PEDEN DEATH NOTICE: **MR. EDMUND H. PEDEN** died suddenly at his home near Canmer, last Thursday, of heart trouble. MR. PEDEN went to the spring house and was gone so long that the family became alarmed, and upon looking for him, found him dead close by the spring. MR. PEDEN was a most estimable man, a good citizen, and highly esteemed by all. He was 75 years old at the time of his death, and was a member of the Christian Church. He is survived by his wife and 7 children, 3 of whom are: MISS MINNIE PEDEN, MRS. CARL NICHOLS, of Coral Hill, and MR. MOTE PEDEN, of Coral Hill. He was interred in the Glasgow Cemetery Friday afternoon, after services conducted at the grave by MR. W. P. COOMBS and MR. BLAKEY, of Canmer, KY. [**My Note:** MR. EDMUND HARLIN PEDEN died in 1914. The article mistakenly gave his name as "EDWARD H. PEDEN." Also, the name of his son was mistakenly given as "MAPE PEDEN" when it was ELMORE "MOTE" PEDEN].

PEDEN DEATH NOTICE: "Mrs. Peden In Suicide Attempt." The funeral services for **MRS. HAZEL PEDEN**, 32, wife of MR. M. C. PEDEN, were conducted at the Glasgow Baptist Church here Saturday afternoon at 2:30 o'clock, the REV. DR. JOSEPH A. GAINES officiating. The burial was in the Glasgow Cemetery. MRS. PEDEN died at Sampson Community Hospital here Friday morning from a self-inflicted shotgun wound. She was the daughter of MRS. DORA COLEMAN of the Rocky Hill section and a member of the Baptist Church. Besides her husband and mother she is survived by an infant daughter, DORIS JEAN PEDEN, and three brothers, WILLIAM and LUCIAN COLEMAN, of Rocky Hill, and ERNEST COLEMAN, of Ohio; also, one step-daughter, MAXINE PEDEN. [**My Note:** HAZEL COLEMAN PEDEN was born on November 18, 1906, was married on November 18, 1932, and died on November 18, 1938]. Another article stated she had attempted to end her life by firing a shotgun charge into her left side. She was rushed to the hospital and regained consciousness, stating that she did not know why she committed the act. MRS. PEDEN was subject to melancholia and at times displayed a mental condition during these attacks that was not normal].

PEDEN DEATH NOTICE: **KATHLEEN PEDEN**, the two year old daughter of MR. and MRS. WILLIAM PEDEN, of near Lecta, died of measles and pneumonia last Wednesday. Burial was in Glasgow Cemetery after services by REV. ELLIOTT. The heart-broken parents have the sympathy of the entire community. [**My Note:** She died in 1920].

PEDEN DEATH NOTICE: **WILLIAM C. PEDEN**, the ten year old son of MR. C. PEDEN, died at the home of his grandfather, MR. A. E. PEDEN, on Cleveland Avenue, of pneumonia, after a brief illness. He had been an invalid all his life and his constitution was not able to resist the onslaught of flu and pneumonia. He is survived by his father and one little sister, the mother having died only a few days ago, and the little sister is very ill. The burial was in the Glasgow Cemetery beside the newly made grave of his mother. [**My Note:** His mother, Lillie, died January 2, and William died January 7, 1929].

PEDEN DEATH NOTICE: "Death, Mrs. Bettie Peden At Her Canmer Home." **MRS. BETTIE PEDEN**, former resident of the Bearwallow section, died at her home at Canmer on Monday afternoon. MRS. PEDEN was the widow of MR. HARLIN PEDEN who was a former resident of Glasgow. Surviving are one daughter, MRS. NELLIE WALTON, and three sons, ED PEDEN and BONNIE PEDEN and LUCIAN PEDEN. MR. MOTE PEDEN, of the Goodnight section, was a step-son, and MRS. MINNIE PEDEN O'NEAL, of Kansas, was a step-daughter. Funeral and burial were at Canmer on Tuesday.

PEDEN DEATH NOTICE: "Sam D. Peden Died Friday. Is Victim Of Stroke Of Paralysis At Home Of Daughter." **MR. SAMUEL D. PEDEN** died at the age of 83 at his daughter's home, MRS. L. E. POYNTER, on Columbia Avenue, Friday, following a stroke of paralysis. Funeral services were held at the Refuge Church at Eighty-Eight on Saturday by REV. W. C. CHRISTIE and T. V. HARWOOD. He was laid to rest beside his wife in the Refuge Cemetery. Four children survive him: MRS. M. H. STEVENS, of Des Moines, Iowa; MRS J. H. CHISM, Glasgow, Route 5; MR. BURL PEDEN, Glasgow, Route 5; and, MRS. L. B. POYNTER, of this place. [**My Note:** He died in 1935].

PEDEN DEATH NOTICE: "Miss Willie A. Peden Dies In Nashville." **MISS WILLIE ANN PEDEN**, 85 years old, formerly of Glasgow, died at the home of her niece, MRS. ED WINN, in Nashville Saturday. Five years ago MISS PEDEN fell and broke her hip, since which time she has been unable to walk. She had been a member of the Baptist Church since childhood. She is survived by one sister, MRS. JAMES CHENAULT, of Smiths Grove, one uncle, MR. ALONZO PEDEN, of Glasgow, together with a number of nieces and nephews. The remains were brought to Glasgow Sunday afternoon and funeral services were at the Glasgow Baptist Church by REV. JOSEPH A. GAINES, pastor, and assisted by REV. J. L. PIERCY, with burial in Glasgow Cemetery and services there by REV. MACK PARRISH. [**My Note:** She died in 1929].

PEDEN DEATH NOTICE: "Death, Mrs. Effie Farris Peden In Albany, GA" **MRS. EFFIE FARRIS PEDEN** died at the home of MRS. J. C. BARREN in Albany, Georgia, June 24th, at 2:30 a. m., following a stroke of paralysis two weeks before. The remains were taken to her home in Louisville, where funeral services were held June 26th by REV. E. F. ESTES, pastor of the 40th and Broadway Baptist Church. Interment was in the Cave Hill Cemetery. Surviving are four daughters, six grandchildren, one stepdaughter, two step grandchildren, five brothers and one sister. The children are: MRS. B. F. CHRISTY, of Smithville, Georgia; MRS. J. C. BARRON, of Albany, Georgia; MRS. E. N. DEESENDOCH, MRS. NELL LEE MILLER, and MRS. IRENE MONEYPENNY, of Louisville. The brothers and sisters are: MR. C. S. FARRIS, of Smithville, Georgia; MR. I. W. FARRIS, of Cave City; MR. J. K. FARRIS, of Cave City; MR. J. L. FARRIS, of Bowling Green; and MISS NELL FARRIS, of Cave City. MRS. EFFIE FARRIS PEDEN was reared in the Salem neighborhood, and she had many friends in Barren County.

PEDEN DEATH NOTICE: **MRS. LILLIE WHITNEY PEDEN**, wife of MR. C. PEDEN, died at their home in the Chestnut Grove country, lacking until February of being 41 years of age. She is survived by her husband, one small son, and one small daughter. Her parents, MR. and MRS. FES WHITNEY, of Lucas, also survive, as do the following brothers and sisters: MR. VOLDA WHITNEY, MR. R. S. WHITNEY, and MR. GARLAND T. WHITNEY, of Lucas, MRS. J. E. CELSOR, of Russellville, and MRS. G. G. MILLER, of Eighty-Eight. MRS. PEDEN was a member of the Baptist Church and funeral services were held in that church in Glasgow by the REV. J. H. SWANN, of Tompkinsville, with burial in the Glasgow Cemetery. [**My Note:** She died on January 2, 1929].

PEDEN DEATH NOTICE: **MR. ALONZO E. PEDEN** died at his home just outside the corporate limits of the city, on the Lower Bowling Green Road, last Thursday, very suddenly. He had been in poor health for some time, but was able to be about. He was working in his garden when he was stricken and died in a few moments. MR. PEDEN was 82 years of age, and was one of the best known and most highly respected citizens in the county. He was born and reared a few miles south of Glasgow, and spent his entire life in Barren County, except the time he was in the Confederate Army. He enlisted at the age of 14 years and was in GEN. MORGAN's army. He was one of the only 4 Confederates left in the county, and was the youngest. The 3 remaining Confederates are MR. BILL NEIGHBORS, of Etoile, MR. JOHN CLAYTON, of Beckton, and MR. SHEL MARTIN, of Cave City. MR. PEDEN is the last of his generation to pass over the River. He leaves 6 children, 11 grandchildren, and 3 great-grandchildren. The children are as follows: MRS. SHEL MARTIN and MR. MORGAN PEDEN, of Detroit, MRS. R. L. MONTGOMERY, of Paducah, MRS. CLARENCE OSBORNE, MRS. EBLEY PEDEN, and MR. C. PEDEN, of this place, and all the children were at the funeral. MR. PEDEN was twice married, first to MISS MOLLIE ADAMS, the mother of all his children, and some years after her death he was married to MISS HELEN WEBB, who survives him. MR. PEDEN was a member of the Baptist Church at South Fork, and had the confidence of all his acquaintances. Funeral services were held at the residence by his pastor, REV. HOWELL, of Scottsville, after which he was interred in the Glasgow Cemetery. [**My Note:** ALONZO ELEAZER PEDEN, son of ELEAZER PEDEN, died in 1929].

<u>PEDEN INJURY ANNOUNCEMENT: "C. M. Peden Improving."</u> **CHESTER MOTE PEDEN**, who was painfully injured while fencing on his farm near Goodnight several days ago, was in town Saturday mingling with his many friends. His hand was badly bruised from the accident and is still being carried in a sling, but it is reported to be healing satisfactorily. [**My Note:** His name was "Mote" not "Chester" Peden. The article apparently should have called him **"MISTER MOTE PEDEN"**].

<u>PEDEN REUNION--5TH ANNUAL EVENT, 1930</u>: The fifth annual reunion of the **PEDEN FAMILY** was held at the old home place in Canmer, KY, on Sunday, at the old home place of the late MR. HARLAN PEDEN. Next year's reunion will be at the home of MR. MOTE PEDEN, at Goodnight. Those in attendance were: MRS. BETTIE PEDEN, MR. and MRS. BONNIE PEDEN and son, all of Canmer; MR. and MRS. LUCIAN PEDEN and family, of Hopkinsville; MR. and MRS. K. S. PEDEN an family, of Louisville; MR. and MRS. W. H. PEDEN and family of Louisville; MR. and MRS. MOTE PEDEN and daughter, of Goodnight; MRS. HELEN PEDEN, MR. C. PEDEN and daughter, of Glasgow; MR. and MRS. G. H. BAIRD and family, of Elizabethtown; MR. and MRS. G. W. WALTON and son, of Munfordville; MRS. JOHN MILLER and children, of Louisville; MR. and MRS. J. H. STONER and son, of Louisville; MRS. GEORGIA HARDY, of Horse Cave; MR. and MRS. JOE TOMS and family, of Horse Cave; MR. and MRS. WILL NICKOLS and daughter, and NAT NICKOLS of Coral Hill; MR. and MRS. CARL NICKOLS and daughter, of Glasgow; MR. and MRS. MORRIS KING, MR. LANDRETH KING and son, and MR. J. L. KING, of Hardyville; MR. SEAY NICKOLS and son, of Munfordville; MRS. EUGENE BAIRD and grandsons, of Goodnight; MR. and MRS. W. P. OWENS and family, of Munfordville; MR. H. M. BROADY, of Canmer, and MR. W. H. BROADY, of Canmer; MR. PRICE MORAN, of Hopkinsville; MR. CHARLIE REDFORD, of Goodnight; MR. STANLEY KELLY, of Detroit; MR. JOHN REID and MR. IVAN VANCE and MR. C. W. LAWSON, all of Canmer; and "Uncle" JIM THONTON, colored, and "Aunt" LUCY THONTON, colored.

<u>PEDEN REUNION: "Reunion Of Peden Family Is Held Sunday, August 10."</u> The sixth annual reunion of the **PEDEN FAMILY** was held at the home of MR. MOTE PEDEN, August 10 [1931]. Next year's reunion will be held at MR. WILL MILLER's at Loneoak, the fourth Sunday in August [Hart County]. Those in attendance Sunday were: MR. and MRS. WILL NICKOLS and daughter, MR. and MRS. LOUIS NICKOLS and children, MR. NAT NICKOLS, of Coral Hill; MR. and MRS. L. E. POYNTER, of Glasgow; MR. and MRS. BONNIE PEDEN and son of Hardyville; MRS. EUGENE BAIRD, MR. and MRS. HENRY REDFORD, MRS. TAYLOR REDFORD, and MISS FLORENCE REDFORD, of Goodnight; MR. and MRS. JOE HARLOW, MR. and MRS. WILL HARLOW and children, of Cave City; MR. and MRS. R. E. EVANS, MR. EDWARD E. BAKER, MR. and MRS. CARL NICKOLS and daughter, MISS SELMA GOODMAN, MISS BETSY POWELL, of Glasgow; MR. and MRS. SEAY NICKOLS and son, MR. and MRS. G. W. WALTON and son, of Munfordville; MR. and MRS. J. H. STONER, and MR. FRANCIS STONER, of Louisville; MRS.

M. T. NUCKOLS, of Glasgow; MR. and MRS. MORRIS KING, of Hardyville; MR. and MRS. H. M. PEDEN and children, of Mackall, Texas; MR. and MRS. WILL MILLER and daughter, of Loneoak, Hart County, Kentucky; MR. C. PEDEN and daughter, of Glasgow; MR. CLEM PEDEN, of Glendale, Texas; MRS. J. T. MOORE and son, of Woodlawn, Texas; MR. and MRS. LUCIAN PEDEN and children, of Hopkinsville; MR. CHARLIE REDFORD, of Goodnight; MRS. G. H. BAIRD and children, of Elizabethtown; MR. and MRS. R.L. MONTGOMERY of Paducah; MR. and MRS. JOE TOMS and children of Horse Cave; MR. CHARLES R. HARLOW, MR. DAVID HARLOW, of Canmer; MR. JACK STAPLES and son, of Glasgow; MRS. SALLIE BARBOUR, of Goodnight; MR. and MRS. BEN MYERS, of Glasgow; MISS ROSADOU [ROSALEE] PEDEN, MR. and MRS. C. L. PEDEN, MISS LUCINDA PEDEN, and MR. HOWARD PEDEN, of Temple Hill; MRS. LEVI NUCKOLS, MRS. HELEN PEDEN, MR. and MRS. WENDELL NUCKOLS, MR. and MRS. MORRIS SIMMONS and children, and MISS SARAH SIMMONS, of Glasgow; MRS. MARY SMITH, MISS MABEL PEDEN, and MR. and MRS. MOTE PEDEN, of Goodnight; MRS. GEORGIA HARDY, of Horse Cave; MR. and MRS. K. S. PEDEN and children, of Hardyville; and, MR. and MRS. A. L. DOYLE, of Covington, Kentucky, sent enough celery for a bunch to be given to every Peden at the reunion.

PEDEN REUNION--7TH ANNUAL EVENT, 1932: The seventh annual reunion of the **PEDEN FAMILY** was held at the home of MR. WILL MILLER at Loneoak in Hart County, August 23rd [1932]. Next year's event will be held at the old home place of the late MR. HARLAN PEDEN near Canmer, Hart County, fourth Sunday in August. In attendance were: MRS. HELEN PEDEN, MR. and MRS. CARL NICHOLS and daughter, MR. and MRS. CHARLIE PEDEN and two daughters, MR. HOWARD PEDEN, MR. M. C. PEDEN and daughter, MR. and MRS. W. M. SIMMONS and three children, of Glasgow; MR. and MRS. WILL NICKOLS and MR. NAT NICKOLS, of Coral Hill; MR. and MRS. EBLEY PEDEN and three children, of Bon Ayr; MR. J. H. NUCKOLS and daughter, MR. PAUL NUCKOLS, and MRS. SUSIE PEDEN, of Temple Hill; MR. and MRS. WILL BROADY, MR. VOIGE ENNIS and son, MR. HENRY VANCE and son, MR. and MRS. BONNIE PEDEN and son, of Canmer; MRS. MARY G. HARDY, and MR. and MRS. ALLEN ELLIS and two daughters, of Horse Cave; MR. and MRS. JOE TOMS and two sons, MR. and MRS. WILL MILLER and daughter, of Loneoak; MR. and MRS. J. H. STONER and MR. FRANCIS STONER, MR. JOHNNY CAMPBELL, MRS. NELL LEE MILLER and 2 children, MR. and MRS. HARDY PEDEN, MR. and MRS. E. N. DIEFENBACH, and MR. and MRS. KIRBY PEDEN and four children, and MR. and MRS. W. L. MONEYPENNY and two daughters, of Louisville; MRS. A.B. CRADDOCK and granddaughter MISS ANNIE B. CRADDOCK; MR. and MRS. G. W. WALTON and son, MR. and MRS. J. D. GRADY, MR. and MRS. SEAY NICKOLS and son, MR. and MRS. W. H. OWENS and daughter, of Munfordville; MR. and MRS. LUCIAN PEDEN and two sons, MR. and MRS. G. G. PEDEN, and MRS. RUTH WITT, of Hopkins-ville; MR. and MRS. G. H. BAIRD and two children, of Elizabethtown; MR. and MRS. MOTE PEDEN, MISS MABEL PEDEN, MISS FLORENCE REDFORD of Goodnight; MR. and MRS. JOE HARLOW, MR. WILLIAM HARLOW and daughter of Cave City; MRS. LELIA IRVIN and two sons, MR. and MRS. CHARLIE PEDEN, MR. LEE SHACKLEFORD, MR. and MRS. T. J. IRVIN and two sons, of Rowletts; MR. and MRS. MORRIS KING, MR. JACK KING and MR. VICTOR IRVIN, of Hardyville; MR. and MRS. HENRY PEDEN, MR. and MRS. JOE PEDEN and son, of Marshall, Texas; MR. and MRS. A. T. TAYLOR, of Padon, TX; MRS. A. L. DOYLE and three sons, of Covington, KY. Total: 128.

PEDEN REUNION--8TH ANNUAL EVENT HELD AT HOME OF BONNIE PEDEN, 1933: The eighth annual reunion of the **PEDEN FAMILY** was held at the home of MR. BONNIE PEDEN at Canmer, Hart County, Kentucky. on August 7. Next year's reunion will be held at the home of MR. MOTE PEDEN at Goodnight. We want all the kinspeople of the Pedens to be there. Since our last meeting one of our family has passed away, MR. HARDY PEDEN. The oldest person present this year was MRS. BETTIE PEDEN. Those in attendance: MR. NAT NICHOLS, MR. and MRS. WILL NICHOLS and daughter, of Coral Hill; MR. and MRS. KIRBY PEDEN, three daughters and son; MR. G. A. STEWART; MR. and MRS. W. O. ADAIR; MR. and MRS. LELAND MONEYPENNY; MISS LORRAINE ARTT; MRS. T. W. BURKS and son; MISS AGNES CRADDOCK, of Louisville; MR. and MRS. JOE HARLOW; MR. and MRS. WILLIAM HARLOW and two children, of Cave City; MR. and MRS. ELA PARRISH and two children; MR. and MRS. M. J. PARRISH and their two sons; MR. CHARLES REDFORD; MRS. MAGGIE BAIRD; MR. B. L. RICHARDSON; MR. and MRS. MOTE PEDEN and daughter MABEL PEDEN, of Goodnight; MISS MABEL DAVIDSON, of Boyds Creek; MR. and MRS. W. M. SIMMONS and three children; MRS. HELEN PEDEN; MRS. LEWIS PEDEN; MR. and MRS. HADE McGUIRE and two sons; MISS LUCINDA PEDEN; MISS ROSA LEE PEDEN; MR. HOWARD PEDEN, of Glasgow; MR. and MRS. HENRY PEDEN, of Marshall, Texas; MR. CLEM PEDEN, of Crocket, Texas; MR. and MRS. BONNIE PEDEN and son; MR. J. R. KING; MRS. J. L. KING; MR. and MRS. J. M. KING; MISS MATTIE BARTLETT; MR. HERBERT HALL; MR. DAVID RAY HARLOW; MRS. JACK KING; MR. and MRS. J. V. BLAKEY; MISS ELIZABETH RUSH WOODWARD, of Hardyville; MR. J. V. WALTON; MR. H. S. WOODWARD; MR. GEORGE BLAKEY; MISS GERTRUDE BLAKEY; MR. W.A. LAFFERTY and son; MR. HENRY VANCE and son; MR. MURIEL HICKEY; MR. and MRS. W.R. SMITH and daughter, of Canmer; MR. and MRS. THOMAS J. ADKINSON; MR. and MRS. J. W. BLAKEY, daughter and son, of Bowling Green; MR. and MRS. A. B. CRADDOCK and daughter; MR. and MRS. G. W. WALTON and son; MR. and MRS. SEAY NICKOLS and son; MRS. BETTIE PEDEN; and, MR. ANTHONY CARDEN, of Munfordville; MR. and MRS. W. L. KESSLER and daughter, of Center; MR. and MRS. W. H. MILLER and daughter; MRS. MARY G. HARDY, of Horse Cave; MRS. G. H. BAIRD and daughter and son, of Elizabethtown; MR. and MRS. L. W. PEDEN and three sons; MR. JAMES EDWARD PEDEN, of Hopkinsville; MRS. SUSIE PEDEN, of Temple Hill. Total number of people in attendance at this Peden Reunion: 119.

PEDEN REUNION--9TH ANNUAL EVENT HELD AT HOME OF MOTE PEDEN, 1934: The ninth annual reunion of the **PEDEN FAMILY** was held at the home of MR. MOTE PEDEN at Goodnight on August 6th. Thanks was offered by DR. E. F. PEDEN, of Portland, Tennessee. Those who attended the 1934 reunion were: MRS. J. A. GOFF; MRS. C. H. CALLAHAN; MR. and MRS. W. H. PARRISH and daughter SHIRLEY JOAN PARRISH; MR. and MRS. O. P. FREEMAN and daughter ELIZABETH FREEMAN; MRS. PAUL SAUNDERS and son RODGER SAUNDERS; MR. and MRS. NUMIE SMITH and daughter GLADYS SMITH, of Hiseville; MR. and MRS. MOTE PEDEN and daughter MABEL PEDEN; MR. CHARLIE REDFORD; MR. and MRS. WILL JACKMAN and two children; MRS. EUGENE BAIRD; MRS. MARY SMITH; MRS. SALLIE BARBOUR;

MISS BEULAH BARBOUR; MRS. TAYLOR REDFORD; MISS FLORENCE REDFORD; MR. and MRS. JOE HARLOW; MR. WILLIAM HARLOW, of Goodnight; MR. and MRS. JOHN CHAPMAN and daughter LORAINE CHAPMAN; MR. and MRS. WESLEY WELLS and daughters RUTH WELLS and MARY ELSIE WELLS and son FRANCIS WELLS, of Cave City; MR. and MRS. CHARLIE F. PEDEN; MR. and MRS. M. M. PEDEN; MISS BETTIE PEDEN; MRS. J. W. PEDEN; MRS. SUSIE PEDEN; MR. and MRS. A. L. STRINGFIELD; MR. and MRS. RALPH WILKINSON; MR. and MRS. CHARLIE L. PEDEN and daughters LUCINDA PEDEN and ROSALEE PEDEN and son HOWARD PEDEN; MRS. LEWIS PEDEN; MR. KIRBY PEDEN; MR. and MRS. M. R. WILKINSON and daughters VIVIAN WILKINSON and MINNIE RUTH WILKINSON, of Temple Hill; MR. and MRS. JOHN NUCKOLS, daughter MALLIE NUCKOLS and son PAUL NUCKOLS; MR. NAT NUCKOLS of Coral Hill; MRS. JIM MACK PEDEN; MR. SAM PEDEN; MR. and MRS. JOE WILLIAMS; MR. and MRS. W. M. SIMMONS and children SARAH SIMMONS, BLANCH SIMMONS, JAMES SIMMONS and THOMAS SIMMONS; MRS. HELEN PEDEN; MR. and MRS. M. C. PEDEN and daughter MAXINE PEDEN, of Glasgow; MR. WILL PEDEN and daughters MARY PEDEN and DOROTHY PEDEN, and son CLYDE PEDEN, of Lecta; MR. HERBERT BALL; MR. ARNOLD SHORT; MR. JACK KING; MR. and MRS. MORRIS KING; MRS. BONNIE PEDEN and son WILLIAM BURKE PEDEN, of Hardyville; MISS IDA GRACE PEDEN; MR. and MRS. J. H. STONER and son FRANCIS STONER; MISS MARY HOFFELD, of Louisville; MR. J. MARSHALL BRIZANDINE, daughter DELIA BRIZANDINE, son JOHN MAXIE BRIZANDINE, of Franklin; MISS ELIZABETH SLATON, of Davenport, Iowa; MR. W. T. WRIGHT, of Greensboro, N.C.; MRS. ED WINN and granddaughter CAROLYN WINN, of Nashville; MR. W. H. PEDEN; DR. E. F. PEDEN; MR. MOSES PEDEN, of Portland, Tennessee; MR. and MRS. WILL H. DEPP, of Smiths Grove; MR. and MRS. LUCIAN PEDEN and sons WARREN PEDEN, JOE PEDEN, and DONALD PEDEN; MR. ELZIE PEDEN, of Hopkinsville; MR. KIRBY PEDEN and daughter RUTH PEDEN and son KENNARD PEDEN; MISS NOLA JEAN BAIRD of Elizabethtown; MR. and MRS. JOE TOMS and sons WILLIAM TOMS and ELWOOD TOMS; MRS. MARY G. HARDY, of Horse Cave; MR. ROGER WALTON, of Munfordville. Next year's reunion will be held at the home of MR. LUCIAN PEDEN at Hopkinsville, Christian County, on the first Sunday in August. Total in attendance at this Peden Reunion: 129.

PEDEN REUNION--10TH ANNUAL EVENT, 1935: The **PEDEN REUNION** was held at the home of MR. MOSE WILKINSON, near Temple Hill, on August 4, 1935. The crowd began to gather early in the morning with well filled baskets until a large crowd of 300 was present. MR. L. W. PEDEN, of Hopkinsville, made a nice talk and thanks was offered by MR. JOHNNY BLAKEY, of Canmer. Since our last meeting two members of the Peden family had passed away: MRS. JOHN STONER and MRS. HARDY PEDEN. Next year's reunion will be near Salt Petre Cave. We invite all kinspeople of the Peden name to be there. [**My Note:** The article did not contain a list of all the attendees as done previously].

PEDEN SICK NOTICE: **MISS MABLE PEDEN** is at the Maplewood Infirmary for treatment. [**My Note:** Daughter of ELMORE "MOTE" PEDEN].

PEDEN SURPRISE BIRTHDAY DINNER: On October 11th [1934] friends and relatives and neighbors gathered at the home of **MRS. MOTE PEDEN,** of Goodnight, and gave her a surprise 67th birthday dinner. It was a complete surprise to MRS. PEDEN. Present were: MRS. NUMIE SMITH; MR. and MRS. MARTIN HILL SMITH, and daughter WEINEL SMITH, of Owl Spring; MR. and MRS. CLYDE PEDEN, of Lecta; MISS HATTIE THOMAS, of Louisville; MR. and MRS. SEAY NICHOLS. and son CLINT SEAY, of Munfordville; MRS. CLAUD STEEN; MRS. BETTIE MONTGOMERY, and son DAN MONTGOMERY, of Glasgow; MRS. WILL CHURCH and daughter; MRS. MAGGIE BAIRD and son YANCEY BAIRD; MRS. MARY SMITH; MRS. TAYLOR REDFORD; MISS MAGGIE PARKER; MR. CHARLIE REDFORD; MR. and MRS. MOTE PEDEN and daughter MABEL PEDEN; and, MR. WILL PEDEN. [**My Note:** JANIE TERRY ROGERS (MRS. ELMORE "MOTE" PEDEN) was born October 7, 1867].

PEDEN SURPRISE BIRTHDAY DINNER: One of the most enjoyable affairs of the season was the birthday dinner given to **MRS. JANIE PEDEN** at her beautiful country home near Goodnight on October 8th [1925] in honor of her 58th birthday. Present: MR. and MRS. WILL PEDEN and family, MR. and MRS. WILL REDFORD and family, MR. and MRS. PARRISH BOYD and daughter, MR. and MRS. LUTHER WELLS, MR. and MRS. NUMA SMITH and daughter, MR. and MRS. NORRIS KING, of Canmer, MR. and MRS. B. F. MYERS, MR. CHARLEY REDFORD, MR. TOM BAGBY. MR. RUFUS BARBOUR, MRS. EUGENE BAIRD, MRS. ROBERT BARBOUR, MRS. JOHN WOOD, MRS. MARY SMITH, MRS. WILL CHURCH, MRS. DICK McQUOWN, MRS. DURWOOD PEDIGO, MRS. L. A. McQUOWN, MRS. TAYLOR REDFORD, MRS. ANNIE FISHBACK WILMER, of Denver, MISS SETTLE ROGERS, MISS FLORENCE REDFORD, MR. and MRS. MOTE PEDEN and daughter MABLE PEDEN, and others whose names we failed to get.

PEDEN VISITATION NOTICE: **MR. and MRS. MOTE PEDEN and MISS MABEL PEDEN**, and MRS. ELSIE DOYLE and 3 children, of Covington, Kentucky, MR. and MRS. J. H. STONER, of Louisville, and MR. HENRY PEDEN, of Marshall, Texas, visited at the Mammoth Cave Monday afternoon.

PEDEN VISITATION NOTICE AND LETTER: The newspaper clipping stated: "**MISS MABEL PEDEN** is expected home from a 3 weeks visit with MISS WEINEL BURNS, of Paris, Tennessee." The following letter, dated May 30, 1930, which may or may not be pertinent, was found in *Pearl E. Peden's Scrapbook*. Miss Mabel Peden was the sister-in-law of Pearl Eugenia Crenshaw Peden. "Dear Mable, I guess you think I am a long time answering your letter. I kept waiting to talk to Kirby about it and would not think of it. I see him so seldom now they have moved so far away from me they are down in the West end of town and I am in the South end. When it suits the rest it will suit me. I am hoping I will get to come. Francis is in Cincinnati now and I can not depend on him to take me. John has went through with a serious operation at the hospital 5 weeks and sick at home 5 weeks so he is not so strong but he is able to be back at the court house on his job now. I did aim to write more but I find this was all the paper there was in the tablet. Now arrange that reunion to suit yourself and it will be O.K. with me. I hope you are all well and would like for you all to visit us some time this summer. Love to all, Ada."

PEDEN VISITATION NOTICE: **MISS MABEL PEDEN**, of Louisville, KY, is spending some time with her mother, MRS. MOTE PEDEN, at Goodnight, following the death of her father. MISS PEDEN is employed in the alteration department of the Spaulding Dry Cleaning Company, 15th and Breckenridge. [**Note:** ELMORE "MOTE" PEDEN died April 6, 1941].

PEDEN VISITATION ANNOUNCEMENT: **MR. HENRY PEDEN**, of Marshall, Texas, MR. and MRS. J. H. STONER, of Louisville, MRS. ELSIE DOYLE and three children of Covington, KY, who have been visiting MR. and MRS. MOTE PEDEN, returned to their homes last Tuesday.

PEDEN WITH GLASGOW CARRIERS (PAPER BOYS) ON OHIO PLEASURE TRIP: The article (with photograph) included **EWELL PEDEN**, son of WILLIAM HENRY PEDEN and PEARL EUGENIA CRENSHAW. He was born in 1924. The picture was probably taken around 1937. Thirteen boys went on a trip to Cincinnati courtesy of *The Courier-Journal and Louisville Times* by virtue of a recent subscription campaign. The Glasgow carriers who merited the trip were: KENNETH WOOD, JASPER PEDIGO, BILLY ELY, PAUL FOSTER, ELROY BUNCH, RICHARD JONES, LEWIS BISHOP, HAROLD BISHOP, JAMES FOSTER, ELDON LEWIS, ARTHUR COOMBS, MAXIE ERVIN, EWELL PEDEN and HARVEY PEDIGO. J.M. ROACH, District Manager.

PEDEN-FROEDGE AND PAYNE-FROEDGE MARRIAGE ANNOUNCEMENT: Announcement has been made of the marriage of **MISS DOROTHY PEDEN and MR. ROLLIN ORLIN FROEDGE**, Sunday, the ceremony being performed by REV. B. A. SYKES. The bride, a daughter of MR. and MRS. WILL PEDEN and enjoys a wide circle of friends. MR. FROEDGE is a son of the late DR. C. W. FROEDGE, and MRS. FROEDGE is now proprietor of the "Parrott" Cafe. [**My Note:** Written in pencil: "Aug. 6, 1939"]. MISS MARGARET PAYNE, of Temple Hill, and MR. CHARLES ORBIN FROEDGE were married in Jeffersonville, Wednesday. They were accompanied by MR. and MRS. HUGHIE FROEDGE. MRS. FROEDGE is a daughter of the late MR. and MRS. WALTER PAYNE. She is a niece of MR. CHARLES PAYNE of this city, and MRS. TOM BIGGERS, of Temple Hill. MR. FROEDGE, the son of MRS. C. W. FROEDGE, has been living in Detroit a number of years, returning here since the death of his father, DR. FROEDGE. We join their host of friends in wishing for these popular young couples many years of happiness. [**My Note:** Written in pencil is the date "Aug. 9, 1939"].

PEDEN-SAVIEU AND KEYS-COOK DOUBLE WEDDING ANNOUNCEMENT: Announcement has been made of the double wedding in Franklin, KY, of two local couples on May 26 [1944]. **MISS JEAN SAVIEU**, the daughter of MR. and MRS. W. H. SAVIEU, of Louisville, and granddaughter of MRS. CHARLIE BORDERS of this place, was married to **MR. EWELL PEDEN**, son of MRS. WILL PEDEN, of this county. They expect to go to Louisville soon to make their home, where MR. PEDEN will be employed. At the same time, **MISS JESSIE PEARL KEYS**, daughter of MRS. PAULINE KEYS, of this place, was married to **MR. GEORGE COOK**, well known barber with the Vaughn....[Article was clipped without closing sentence].

PEDEN-STEPHENS MARRIAGE ANNOUNCEMENT: **MISS MARY EUGENIA PEDEN**, a daughter of MRS. PEARL PEDEN, of Lecta, and **MR. SHELBY STEPHENS** were married in Bowling Green last Saturday night. SHELBY STEPHENS is a soldier at Fort Knox and his home is at Sulphur Well, KY. [**My Note**: They were married January 31, 1942. Another newspaper article mistakenly wrote she married STANLEY STEPHENS, of Metcalfe County].

PEDEN-WILLIS MARRIAGE ANNOUNCEMENT: **MISS MABEL PEDEN**, daughter of MRS. MOTE PEDEN, of Goodnight, and Staff Sergeant **ERNEST WILLIS** were married at Marl, Arkansas on December 23, ----. MISS PEDEN at present is employed by the Reynolds Metal Company in Louisville. SGT. WILLIS is a native of Pine Bluff, Arkansas, and is stationed at Fort Knox, where he is an instructor. He has been in the Army for 10 years and also lives in Louisville.

PEDIGO DEATH NOTICE: **MRS. A. D. PEDIGO** died on April 21, 1931. Poem "in memory of mother" written by her daughter, MRS. EARL MUNDAY.

PEDIGO DEATH NOTICE: **MRS. W. H. PEDIGO**, age 19, died at the Community Hospital here on Tuesday morning from a complication of diseases. Before marriage she was **MISS ELIZABETH CRENSHAW**, daughter of MRS. THOMAS CRENSHAW. Her mother and a brother survive. She was an amiable lady. The community is shocked at her untimely death.

PEMBERTON-STRADER MARRIAGE ANNOUNCEMENT: **MISS MARY PEMBERTON**, daughter of MR. and MRS. G. T. PEMBERTON, and **MR. U. J. STRADER**, son of MR. and MRS. BRYANT STRADER of Hiseville, were married in Gallatin, Tennessee last Monday. They will live in Hiseville, KY.

PET DOG "BILLIE" DIED IN 1930: This was written by an unknown hand and placed in Pearl's scrapbook: "Our Dog Billie, Our Little Pet Billie, passes away Saturday, May 17, 1930, about 4:30 o'clock. Dear Billie you gone we never see you know more we all miss you and yet we must know you gone and we know we can never see your pretty brown eyes and see you run and play anymore though our heart are sad and our burden is hard to bear as the other dogs gather around our door. Behold the vacant place of Billie. Poor Billie suffer lots that he will never more. We think of poor Billie for the many little thing done that he will do know more and of his chair he love so well. His death has cast a cloud over the family and farmer. The remains laid to rest home burial ground."

PRITCHARD DEATH NOTICE: "Death Of Thomas Pritchard, 86, Hiseville" **MR. THOMAS PRITCHARD**, one of the best, useful men of the Hiseville section, died Wednesday at his home in that place. He was 85 years old. Surviving are his wife and four sons: HERBERT PRITCHARD, of Texas, and WALTER PRITCHARD, JOHN PRITCHARD, and FRED PRITCHARD, of Hiseville. The funeral and burial will be held in Hiseville today.

REDFORD DEATH NOTICE: **MR. FRANK M. REDFORD** died at the home of his niece, MRS. CHARLES J. LEWIS, on East Washington Street, yesterday afternoon, from heart trouble, at the age of 78. MR. REDFORD was a life long citizen of Glasgow and Barren County, and for the past quarter century has been a groceryman. His wife died only a few months ago and his last remaining sister, MRS. PARTHENIA FORD, died Monday of last week. He is survived by 3 sons: MR. HARRY REDFORD, of Cincinnati, MR. GEORGE M. REDFORD and MR. LOUIS P. REDFORD, of this place. He was a member of the Christian Church. The funeral was at the home of MR. L. P. REDFORD on Maple Driveway, conducted by REV. T. H. ALDERSON, assisted by REV. PIERCY and REV. EASLEY. Burial in Glasgow Cemetery. [**My Note:** FRANCIS MARION REDFORD and wife ELIZABETH HODGKINS both were born in 1849 and died in 1927].

REDFORD DEATH NOTICE: "Death Of H. Taylor Redford On Tuesday Night" **MR. HENRY TAYLOR REDFORD**, prominent farmer of the Goodnight section died at home Tuesday night at 11:20 o'clock, following an illness which has extended over a lengthy period. He was 80 years of age and has been bedfast since January 27 of this year. Diabetes and complications were attributed as the cause of his death. A son of the late SAMUEL REDFORD and MARY REDFORD, he was born November 1, 1856, and had lived his entire life in the Goodnight section where he had engaged in farming. On February 10, 1881, he married MISS LIZZIE PARRISH, who survives; also, one son, SAMUEL HENRY REDFORD, of Goodnight; two daughters, MISS FLORENCE REDFORD, at home, and MRS. ASHBY HIGGASON, of Cave City; three brothers, MR. GORIN C. REDFORD and MR. CHARLES C. REDFORD, of Goodnight, and MR. LESLIE W. REDFORD, of Glasgow; and one sister, MRS. ALICE YANCEY, of Glasgow. Funeral service will be conducted this afternoon at 3 o'clock by MR. W. P. COOMBS. Interment will be in the cemetery at this place. [**My Note:** H. TAYLOR REDFORD died in 1936; buried in Glasgow Cem.]

REDFORD SURPRISE BIRTHDAY DINNER: Friends and relatives of **MRS. TAYLOR REDFORD** gathered at her home on August 22th, for a surprise birthday dinner. The guests included MRS. ALICE YANCEY, MR. BEN BRADFORD, MISS LIZZIE BRADFORD, MISS SIS BRADFORD, of Glasgow; MRS. W. J. CHAMBLISS and sons BAIRD CHAMBLISS and BILLIE CHAMBLISS, and MRS. NADINE BARBOUR, of Louisville; MRS. JENNIE COX DAVIS and daughter, of Smiths Grove; MRS. NORVIN WILSON and daughter; H. T. REDFORD, BEN MYERS, HENRY DUFF, R. E. EVANS, J. P. BOYD, G. B. REDFORD, G. F. QUIGLEY, MOTE PEDEN, R. R. BARBOUR, ELA PARRISH, and HENRY REDFORD; MISSES VIRGIE EVANS, CETTIE ROGERS, BEULAH BARBOUR, MABEL PEDEN, FLORENCE REDFORD, MABEL PARKER, WILLIE MAY PARRISH, VIRGINIA BOYD, SARABETH BARBOUR, LOIS BARBOUR, VIRGINIA BARLOW, MARIE BARLOW, **NADINE CRENSHAW**, ALICE REDFORD, MAGGIE BAIRD, SARA BARBOUR, MARY WOOD, **WALLER CRENSHAW**, JAMES BARLOW, ASHBY HIGGASON, YANCEY BAIRD, ROGER HIGGASON, JAMES BOYD, and RAY PARRISH.

REDFORD-GOODMAN MARRIAGE ANNOUNCEMENT: **MISS FLORENCE REDFORD**, of Cave City Rt. 2, daughter of MRS. TAYLOR REDFORD, of Goodnight, and **MR. C. A. GOODMAN**, a native of Monroe County, now of Glasgow, were married in the Baptist Church here last Saturday with DR. J. A. GAINES performing the ceremony. S. H. REDFORD, brother of the bride, and MRS. REDFORD were in attendance.

REDFORD-LEBOEUF MARRIAGE ANNOUNCEMENT: **MISS ELIZABETH REDFORD** and **MR. LEIGHTON LEBOEUF**, of Glasgow, KY, were married last Tuesday in Jeffersonville, Indiana, by REV. LASSITED of the Baptist Church.

REID DEATH NOTICE: **MRS. CECIL REID**, "In Loving Remembrance of Our Dear Mother." Poem written in remembrance of MRS. CECIL REID who departed this life on November 16, 1918. Article indicated the poem was written in 1928 by KIMPTON READ and PAULINE READ.

RICHARDS-HARDIN MARRIAGE ANNOUNCEMENT: **MISS FRANCES RICHARDS and DEWEY HARDIN**, both of Barren County, were married Wednesday by SQUIRE LESLIE WHITE at his courthouse office in Bowling Green.

RICHARDSON DEATH NOTICE: **MR. ALONZO RICHARDSON**, 74 years old, died Sunday night of diabetes, after a lingering illness. He is survived by his wife, who was MISS MARY MAXEY, and 6 sons and 2 daughters: MR. RALPH RICHARDSON, of Hiseville; MR. HERMAN RICHARDSON and MR. B. L. RICHARDSON, of Goodnight; MR. W.H. RICHARDSON and MR. CLINT RICHARDSON of Houston, Texas; and MR. FRANK RICHARDSON, of Detroit; and MRS. ROBERT ADAMS, of California; and, MISS DORA RICHARDSON, of Texas. His surviving brothers and sisters are DR. W. K. RICHARDSON, of Tompkinsville; JUDGE BASIL RICHARDSON, of this place; MR. JOHN RICHARDSON and MRS. PERRY SUMMERS, of Glendale; MRS. LUCY P. HUMBLE and MRS. TABITHA GRISSOM, of this place; MRS. J. T. GILLENWATER, of Cave City. MR. RICHARDSON was born and reared in the extreme north eastern section of Monroe County, on a fine Cumberland River farm, and his father was one of the wealthiest and most influential men of the county. A number of years ago MR. RICHARDSON bought a farm in Goodnight in Barren County. He was a member of the Christian Church and the funeral services were held at the residence by ELDER T. H. ALDERSON, with the remains interred here in the Glasgow Cem.

RODEHEAVER-PARRISH MARRIAGE ANNOUNCEMENT: MR. and MRS. CLYDE A. RODEHEAVER, SR. announce the marriage on July 11th of their eldest daughter, **ELLA LOUISE RODEHEAVER**, to **MR. JESSE L. PARRISH**, by the REV. FRED T. MOFFAT, pastor of the First Baptist Church of Jellico, Tennessee. The bride is a cousin to the famous Evangelistic singer HOMER RODEHEAVER. Best man was MR. O. L. JULIAN and maid of honor was the bride's sister, MISS EVELYN RODEHEAVER. Other members of the wedding party were MARY TOM CLARK, BETSY JANE LLEWELLYN, GLENNA BAIRD, CAROLYN CHAMBERS, SHIRLEY CHAMBERS, and SARA LEVY. Music was provided by MRS. CLYDE A. RODEHEAVER, JR. and MRS. CHARLES E. SMITH. MRS. PARRISH is a teacher and a member of the Jellico City School faculty. MR. PARRISH is connected with the Black Star Coal Company. They will reside in Alva, KY. [**My Note:** Written in pencil is "1932", and then "1931" is written over it].

ROGERS DEATH NOTICE: Last rites for **MR. GEORGE WALTER ROGERS** were held Tuesday afternoon December 12th at 2 o'clock from the Stanley Funeral Home, conducted by REV. WILLIAM ICENOGLE, with burial in the Van Horn Cemetery. MR. GEORGE WALTER ROGERS parted this life Sunday, December 10, at 8:20 o'clock. MR. ROGERS was born January

21, 1871 in Barren County, KY, the son of HENRY LANDON ROGERS and PHOEBE CALDWELL. When a young man he moved with his father to Bowling Green, KY. Soon afterwards, he enlisted in the Spanish-American War and served several years under GEN. JOHN B. CASTLEMAN, of Louisville, KY. He was sent to Porto Rico where he served a year. He lived a few years in Stuttgart, Arkansas and...[obituary torn]...on -- 3, 196 [sic], was united in...[marriage to]...MISS ELLEN CASS. They moved to Carroll County, near Tina, Missouri, and then to a farm three miles north of Carrollton where they resided for almost 30 years. They moved to Carrollton 3 years ago. Besides his widow he leaves three children: GARNETT GRACE ROGERS, of Kansas City; RHOMETTA ROGERS, of Cave City and LANDON ROGERS, at home; three sisters, MISS ELIZABETH GARNETT ROGERS, of Louisville, MISS CETTIE CALDWELL ROGERS, and MRS. LUTHER WELLS, of Cave City; and a brother MR. W. S. ROGERS of Marine City, Michigan. George was a member of the Christian Church, Carrollton, Missouri. [Obituary stated information was abstracted from the Carrollton Democrat].

ROGERS DEATH NOTICE: "Death of Mrs. Charles Rogers Last Saturday." **MRS. CHARLES ROGERS** died at her home here last Saturday morning of paralysis. Death was at eight o'clock. MRS. ROGERS was in her 77th year, and is survived by one son, MR. BYRD ROGERS, of this place, and one daughter, MRS. MOTE PEDEN, of near town. MRS. ROGERS was a member of the Christian Church, and after a short funeral service Sunday the remains were taken to the Rogers burying ground near Goodnight for interment. MRS. ROGERS was a fine type of christian womanhood and a lovely character who had the admiration of all who knew her. Her death will be mourned by large concourse of friends. [**My Note:** MRS. CHARLES ROGERS' maiden name was SARAH MOSS FORBIS. She was a daughter of FELIX GRUNDY FORBIS and ANN ELIZA WOOD, of Barren County. SARAH MOSS (FORBIS) ROGERS died February 5, 1921].

ROGERS DEATH NOTICE: **MR. CHARLIE B. ROGERS** died at his home near Goodnight, Saturday, February 22, about noon, of a complication of diseases. He had been sick two weeks. He is survived by his wife, who was before marriage MISS SARAH FORBIS; a son, MR. J. B. ROGERS; and, one daughter, MRS. MOTE PEDEN, also survive. MR. ROGERS was 78 years old, and a member of the Christian Church of long standing. Funeral services were at the home Sunday afternoon at 2 o'clock, REV. SMITH, of the Cave City Christian Church, preaching, after which interment was in the Rogers burying ground near Goodnight, his Confederate soldier comrades having charge of the burial. As was MR. ROGERS' wish, he was buried in his uniform as a Confederate soldier. MR. ROGERS was one of the best known men of the northern part of the county, and of undisputed honor and influence. He was brave, fearless, and of an uncompromising disposition. During the Civil War he was with GENERAL MORGAN as a chief scout, and was a wonderfully brave and resourceful man. Many tales are told of his daring and bravery on the field of battle. [**My Note:** Died in 1919].

ROGERS LETTER: LETTER ADDRESSED TO MISS JANIE ROGERS, CAVE CITY, KENTUCKY, BARREN COUNTY, AND POSTMARKED AT FOUNTAIN RUN, KENTUCKY,

AUGUST 19TH (2 CENT STAMP): [**My Note:** This letter was written without any punctuation, so I put the periods between the sentences as well as the question marks]. "July 25, 1884. Janie, I have wrote to your papa. Thought this morning I would write to you. I am well this morning. Was sick yesterday. Have quite a crowd here. I like them all very well. Have a very pleasant time. SALLIE FORD and ELLEN SMITH and a good many others were from over there was here yesterday and brought there dinner with them. I eat with them. Had a very nice dinner. Mr. Curd thinks he has improved since has been here. He is going back next week. It is raining very hard this morning but do not think it will rain very long. I want you all to write. Want to know how your all are getting along. Have not heard from home since I left. How is Emma? Want to see her. Tell her she must not forget me. I will look for your papa tomorrow. Hope he will come. I am so anxious to hear from home. Wrote to Aunt Mollie. Thought that she would be sure to write but she has not yet. I want you to write soon. Direct your letters Charlydate [?] Spring. Bird would love to see you. How are you get along since your mama left? Are you going to school yet? Hope you are learning fast. Mrs. Cook said she would love to see you. Says she can not think of you being large enough to wear pants. Told her you was most grown. Bird, you must write if none of them won't. Your mama." [**My Note:** This letter was written to JANIE TERRY ROGERS who was almost 17 years old at the time. Her mother, who wrote the letter, was SARAH MOSS FORBIS, the wife of CHARLES BAGBY ROGERS (1840-1919). Sarah was 51 years old at the time of the letter. "Bird" was Janie's brother, JOHN BYRD ROGERS. "Aunt Mollie" was MOLLIE WOOD, sister of CHARLES B. ROGERS. I do not know who Emma, Mrs. Cook, Mr. Curd, Sallie Ford and Ellen Smith were at this time. Letter found in Pearl E. Peden's scrapbook. She was the daughter-in-law of JANIE TERRY ROGERS. Janie married ELMORE PEDEN and son WILL PEDEN married PEARL E. CRENSHAW].

ROYSE-BAGBY MARRIAGE ANNOUNCEMENT: **MISS ANNIE ROYSE**, a daughter of MR. and MRS. BOB ROYSE, of this place, and **MR. WALTER BAGBY**, son of MR. GENE BAGBY, of Coral Hill, were married on Christmas Day, ----.

ROYSE-BERRY MARRIAGE ANNOUNCEMENT: **MISS FANNIE ROYSE**, daughter of MR. and MRS. W. R. ROYSE, and MR. **GEORGE BERRY**, son of MR. and MRS. HARRY BERRY of Glasgow, married last week and will live in Detroit.

RUDDELL-HIGGASON MARRIAGE ANNOUNCEMENT: **MISS NEVLINE RUDDELL**, daughter of MR. and MRS. E. L. RUDDELL, of Nortonville, and **MR. ROGER TERRY HIGGASON**, son of MR. and MRS. M. A. HIGGASON, of Cave City, were married on February 21, ----, at Hodgenville, KY.

SABENS-BELCHER MARRIAGE ANNOUNCEMENT: **MISS ROSIE SABENS**, daughter of MR. JOE MILLER SABENS, of Laurel Bluff, eight miles south of Glasgow, and **MR. WARDI BELCHER**, of Crawfordsville, Ind., formerly of Barren County, KY, married in Crawfordsville on March 17, ----.

SANDERS DEATH NOTICE: **MRS. ELLEN WILLIAMS SANDERS** died at Deaconess Hospital in Louisville Sunday night following a stroke of paralysis suffered a few hours earlier. She was 80 years old, and was reared in Glasgow. After her marriage to JOHN SANDERS, they went to his home in Kansas and after his death she and her small sons JOHN MILTON SANDERS and IRL SANDERS returned home. JOHN MILTON SANDERS died a number of years ago. MRS. SANDERS was a practical nurse. She was visiting her son, IRL SANDERS, in Louisville, and her brother, M. R. WILLIAMS, at Prospect, when taken with her fatal illness. Her son and 3 grandchildren, IRL SANDERS, JR., of the Canal Zone, JOHN MILTON SANDERS and MISS BETTY SANDERS, of Louisville, KY, and her brother are her only immediate family, but a number of nieces and nephews also survive. MRS. SANDERS was a life-long member of the Christian Church. She was interred in Glasgow Municipal Cemetery.

SAXON DEATH NOTICE: **MRS. MILLIE SAXON** died at the home of CLARENCE BALLARD, Thursday of last week, at the age of 84 years. Before her marriage she was MISS DEFEVERS, and born and reared Barren County. Interment was in Defevers burying ground in the Coral Hill section.

SHAW-ALEXANDER MARRIAGE ANNOUNCEMENT: **MR. HILDRETH ALEXANDER**, son of MR. and MRS. MILLARD ALEXANDER, of the Boyds Creek section, and **MISS ALICE SHAW**, a daughter of MRS. M. J. SHAW, of this place, and a sister of MR. R. W. SHAW and MR. MARCUS SHAW, were married in Louisville a few days ago. They will make their home in Cincinnati.

SMITH-REDFORD MARRIAGE ANNOUNCEMENT: **MISS VERNA SMITH**, daughter of MR. and MRS. L. H. SMITH, of Temple Hill, and **MR. HENRY REDFORD**, son of MR. and MRS. H. T. REDFORD, of Cave City, were married at Mitchellville, Tennessee, on June 23, 1928.

SMITH BIRTHDAY DINNER: "Surprise Birthday For Mrs. Mary Smith." On May 6th, friends and relatives gathered at the beautiful country home of MRS. MAGGIE BAIRD near Goodnight and gave **MRS. MARY SMITH** a surprise birthday dinner. Those present: MR. and MRS. MOTE PEDEN and daughter; MR. and MRS. WILL REDFORD, and daughter; **MR. and MRS. K. CRENSHAW** and children; MR. and MRS. F. PARRISH and children; MR. and MRS. H. W. DUFF; MR. and MRS. JOHN BAGBY, and children; MR. and MRS. PAUL MANSFIELD; MR. and MRS. B. F. MYERS; MR. and MRS. IRBY EUBANK, and son; MRS. MARY WOOD, and daughter; MISS SARAH BARBOUR, and daughter; MRS. TAYLOR REDFORD and daughter; MRS. E. W. DAVIS, and daughter; MISS SMITH; MISS VIRGINIA EVANS; MRS. MARY COX SMITH; MRS. MAGGIE BAIRD; MR. CLAUD STEEN; MR. HENRY REDFORD; MR. TOM BAGBY; MR. T. J. SAMSON; MR. W. K. BAIRD; and, MR. JAMES FISHBACK.

SMITH DEATH ANNOUNCEMENT: "The Sad Death Of Miss Ethel Smith." **MISS ETHEL SMITH** died at the home of her parents, MR. and MRS. CHARLIE SMITH, near Lecta, after six weeks suffering of diabetes. She is survived by her parents, five sisters, MRS. GENIE FRANKLIN and MRS. FRED JAMES, of Lick Branch, MRS. KATE SYRA, of Edmonton, MRS. JIM BOLES, of Rolfe, Iowa, and MISS NANNIE BELLE, who lives at home. MISS SMITH was a member of the Christian Church and she was buried in the cemetery at Lick Branch. [**My Note:** Also included in this obituary is a poem written by her teacher and schoolmates].

SMITH DEATH NOTICE: **DAVID SMITH** died April 25, ---, just before the sun went down...and left his home and mother....We can't understand why one so young should be called from the walks of life. [Words of grief and sympathy followed by a poem signed by MRS. OTHA BRAY].

SMITH DEATH NOTICE: "Death of 'Pete Smith' In Automobile Accident" About 10 o'clock last Saturday, **MR. EUGENE "PETE" SMITH**, 22 years of age, was almost instantly killed in an automobile accident about six miles north of Elizabethtown on the Dixie Highway. Young Smith, who lived in Indianapolis, had been to see his sister, MRS. TOMPY JORDAN, who was sick at her home in Chicago, and was on his way to this place [Glasgow] to take his wife to their home. He apparently fell asleep at the wheel. He is survived by his wife, who was MISS CELESTE ELLIS, of Bruce, KY, his parents MR. and MRS. T. J. SMITH, two brothers, MR. GEORGE SMITH and MR. FRED SMITH, and two sisters, MISS FRANCES SMITH, of Matthews Mills, and MRS. TOMPY JORDAN, of Chicago. Funeral services were held at the residence of his parents on Sunday afternoon, by REV. T. F. GRIDER, who had baptized him ten years ago, and burial was in Glasgow Cemetery. [**My Note:** Written in pencil atop the newspaper clipping is the date of "June 14, 1932."]

SMITH DEATH NOTICE: Funeral services for **MRS. SUSAN BELL SMITH**, 79, widow of the late MR. CHARLIE SMITH, will be conducted at her home near Coral Hill this afternoon, REV. W. DUNAGAN in charge. Burial will be in the family cemetery at the home place. MRS. SMITH died at her home in the Coral Hill section Tuesday around 10 o'clock, following an illness of several months. She had been in declining health some time. She is survived by 3 daughters, MRS. L. M. CHEW, of Jacksonville, Florida, MRS. J. L. EVANS and MRS. CARL SCROGGY, of Coral Hill; 3 sons, FRED SMITH, of Williamson, West Virginia, JACK B. SMITH and RODERICK F. SMITH, of Coral Hill; two brothers, SANFORD BYBEE, of Coral Hill, and W. M. BYBEE, of Louisville. Three grandchildren survive. [**My Note:** SUSAN SMITH died October 4, 1938].

SMITH DEATH NOTICE: "Death Mr. L. D. Smith At His Hiseville Home." Funeral and burial services for **MR. L. D. SMITH** were conducted on Saturday afternoon at 2:30 at Munday Cemetery near Hiseville. He died at his home near Hiseville on Friday night at 8 o'clock, after several months illness. He was 50 years of age, and was a prominent farmer of that section. Surviving are his wife, MRS. DORA SMITH, one sister, MRS. H. B. WORTHINGTON, and four brothers, F. A. SMITH, ELMORE SMITH, N. C. SMITH, and RODDIE SMITH, "R. three" [Route 3?].

SMITH DEATH NOTICE: "Death Of A. L. Smith At His Home Near Lecta." **MR. A. L. SMITH**, age 60, died at his home near Lecta, on Saturday morning of influenza and pneumonia. Surviving are his widow, who before marriage was MISS ADA DEWEESE, and one son. The following brothers and sister also survive: MRS. BENNETT WORTHINGTON, MESSRS. ELMORE SMITH, NUMA SMITH, FRED SMITH, D. SMITH and RODDY SMITH, all of the Owl Springs neighborhood. A. L. SMITH was a member of the Christian Church. Funeral services were at home Sunday afternoon, conducted by BROTHER WARREN DUNAGAN, with interment in the DeWeese burying ground. [**My Note:** A. L. SMITH died on July 7, 1928. Buried next to him is one DAVID L. SMITH (1917-1936), probably his son].

SMITH DEATH NOTICE: "The Death Of Mr. C. R. Smith, 79, At Home In Coral Hill Section Last Tuesday Night." Barren County lost one of its most distinguished and widely known citizens Tuesday at 9:45 p.m. with the passing of **MR. CHARLES R. SMITH** at his home in the Coral Hill community. Death was caused by a series of paralytic strokes and infirmities incident to age. He was 79 years old, and would have celebrated his 80th birthday in September. A member of the Coral Hill Christian Church, "Uncle Charlie" was an ardent Democrat who was born, reared and lived in Coral Hill all his life. He is survived by his wife, MRS. BELL BYBEE SMITH; three daughters, MRS. L. M. CHEW, of Jacksonville, Florida, MRS. CARL SCROGGY, of Route 3, Glasgow, KY, and MRS. L. M. EVANS, of Coral Hill; three brothers, JACK B. SMITH, of Coral Hill, W. F. SMITH, of Williamson, West Virginia, and R. E. SMITH, of Coral Hill; two grandchildren, R. E. RYAN, of Bowling Green, and MISS ANNA KATHERINE EVANS, of Coral Hill; and, one nephew, JACK WATKINS, of Coral Hill. Funeral services will be conducted at his Coral Hill home this afternoon, with REV. T. H. ALDERSON presiding. Burial will be in the family cemetery. [**My Note:** CHARLES R. SMITH died on August 10, 1937].

SMITH DEATH NOTICE: **MRS. SIS SMITH**, widow of the late MR. JULIAN SMITH, died in New York at 82 years of age. MRS. SMITH was born and reared in Barren County. Her father was a brother of MR. JIM SMITH who was one time postmaster at this place, and she is a sister of the late MR. NOAH SMITH, the father of MISS OLIVIA SMITH, MISS NORA SMITH and MRS. BESSIE WHITE, so well known here. She was married to JULIAN SMITH, half-brother of MR. W. B. SMITH of this place and MR. LUTE SMITH and MR. BEN SMITH, of Temple Hill. She and her husband left here for Montana perhaps fifty years ago and were pioneers in the Great West. Her husband was one of the discoverers of Garden of the Gods, and other wonders of the West. MR. SMITH died some twenty years ago, and since then MRS. SMITH has lived with friends in New York, in Warren County, Kentucky, and occasionally at this place. The body was brought to this place Monday and interred in Glasgow Cemetery, after brief services were conducted by REV. B. A. SYKES.

SMITH GOLDEN WEDDING ANNIVERSARY: Poem written by MRS. JAMES BAGBY stated that **CHARLIE SMITH and BELL BYBEE** were married on March 19, 1884, and they had 8 children, 2 of whom had died by the time of their 50th anniversary in 1934. MR. and MRS. C. R. SMITH lived in Coral Hill. MR. and MRS. O. W. ALEXANDER (married 51 years) and MR. and MRS. H. S. SAUNDERS (married 54 years) were in attendance. The music was furnished by CLYDE PACE, ROGER PACE, and BILLY PACE, of Horse Cave and HUGHIE WORTHINGTON, all great nephews of MRS. SMITH. Others in attendance were: MR. and MRS. F. E. ALLEN, and daughter BETTY ALLEN, MR. and MRS. GLENN FISHER and two children, JOHN and FRANCES FISHER of Bowling Green; MR. CHARLIE WARDER, of Louisville; MR. MALCOLM NORRIS, MISS DIXIE PACE, MR. CECIL NORRIS, and MRS. JIM

HOLLOWAY, of Horse Cave; MR. E. L. GOOCH, of Illinois; MISS MOSS McDANIELS, of Hardyville; and, REV. and MRS. OMAR, of Cave City.

SMITH-CHEW MARRIAGE ANNOUNCEMENT: **MISS ZADA SMITH**, daughter of MR. and MRS. C. R. SMITH, of Coral Hill, Kentucky, and **MR. L. M. CHEW**, of Staunton, Virginia, married in Atlanta, Georgia, on September 7th, ----. The ceremony was performed by REV. C. C. HERBERT of the Methodist Church. They will make their home in Jacksonville, Fla.

SOWERS-JONES MARRIAGE ANNOUNCEMENT: **MISS PERNIE SOWERS**, of the Owl Spring section, and **MR. WILLIE JONES** of Coral Hill, were married by REV. B. A. SYKES. MR. JONES is a member of the Jones Brothers firm.

SPEAR DEATH NOTICE: "Aged Woman Found Dead At Beckton." **MRS. MARY M. SPEAR**, 80, widow of the late J. T. SPEAR who died five years ago, was found dead at her home near Beckton on Wednesday. She was evidently a victim of apoplexy. The body was found by her brother, C. W. CHITWOOD. MRS. SPEAR was a member of the Beckton Church of Christ. Services were by REV. ALLEN PHY, with burial in the Smith Graveyard near Coral Hill. [**My Note:** MRS. J. T. "SPEER" died 1937].

SPEER DEATH NOTICE: **MR. J. T. SPEER** died at his home at Beckton, age 76 years, leaving his wife, who was MISS MARY MOSS CHITWOOD, but no children. He leaves two sisters, MRS. WHIT HIGHTREE, of Missouri, and MRS. BETTIE BRANSTETTER, of Oklahoma. MR. SPEER was a former resident of the Coral Hill section, where he grew up. He was a member of the Church of Christ at Beckton, where the funeral was conducted by ELDER ALLEN PHY, of this place, and the remains were then buried at Coral Hill. [**My Note:** He died in 1932].

STAPLES DEATH NOTICE: "Death Of Mrs. Mose Staples Tuesday Morning." **MRS. MOSE STAPLES**, age 63 years, died at her home in the Coral Hill section Tuesday afternoon. Funeral was held Wednesday morning, REV. J. P. BROOKS in charge, and interment was in McCann burying ground near Cave City. Besides hers husband, MRS. STAPLES is survived by one son, SEDDIE STAPLE;, three grandsons, CARL STAPLES, MITCHELL STAPLES, and EWELL STAPLES; one brother, CAPT. DEFEVERS, of this place; and, one sister [name not mentioned] living in Oklahoma.

STEEN-ANDERSON MARRIAGE ANNOUNCEMENT: **MISS MARY CURTIS STEEN**, the daughter of MR. and MRS. CLAUD STEEN, of this place, and **MR. NEIL ANDERSON**, of Lexington, were married in Winchester, KY, May 19th. She has been living in Lexington for the past ten years, where MR. NEIL ANDERSON is also a contractor.

STORY-NUCKOLS MARRIAGE ANNOUNCEMENT: **MISS REBECCA STORY**, of near town, and **MR. WILL NUCKOLS**, of Horse Cave, married in Louisville. MR. NUCKOLS is a former Barren County boy, and MRS. NUCKOLS, a rural teacher of Barren County, taught at Fairview the past year.

TAYLOR-CARY MARRIAGE ANNOUNCEMENT: **MISS EDNA TAYLOR and MR. PAUL CARY** were married Saturday. Both young people are from Lecta, KY.

<u>TAYLOR-TADE MARRIAGE ANNOUNCEMENT</u>: **MISS EULA MAYE TAYLOR**, daughter of MRS. W. E. TAYLOR, formerly of Glasgow, but late of Bowling Green, and **MR. WILLIAM JOSEPH TADE**, were married in Bowling Green by the REV. A. B. HOUSE of the First Christian Church. MR. TADE holds a position with the Louisville & Nashville Railroad Company.

<u>TERRY DEATH NOTICE</u>: **MRS. ELLEN TERRY**, 85, widow of P. E. TERRY, died at her home near Hiseville Saturday night at 9 o'clock. She had been in usual health up to Saturday noon and died suddenly at 9 p.m. MRS. TERRY is survived by one daughter, MRS. J. R. MYERS, of Lancaster, and two sons, THEO TERRY, SONORA TERRY and C. H. TERRY, of Hiseville; a sister, MRS. A. DEPP, near Glasgow and a brother, W. W. BAGBY near Hiseville. Services were at the Christian Church at Hiseville by REV. C. C. OMER, of Bowling Green, and REV. KIRBY SMITH, of Burkesville, with burial in Hiseville Cemetery. [**My Note:** ELLEN BAGBY TERRY died on August 19, 1939].

<u>TERRY DEATH NOTICE: "To The Memory Of William Samuel Terry."</u> On Tuesday night, November 18, 1924, at 10 o'clock and 48 minutes, Father Time called for the immortal soul of **WILLIAM SAMUEL TERRY** to come up higher and help fill the mansion prepared for those who love the Lord. He was devout member of the Hiseville Christian Church. WILLIAM SAMUEL TERRY was the son of JOHN ALFRED TERRY and SALLIE YOUNG and was born at the home of his parents at Bearwallow on May 16, 1847, and spent his entire life in this neighborhood. He leaves his widow, MRS. CARRIE T. TERRY, and one son BILLY SAM TERRY JR., one brother CARTER TERRY, and the following nieces and nephews to mourn his loss: MRS. MAYMIE WARDER, MRS. JOHN WALTHALL, MRS. JIM MYERS, W. A. TERRY, S. E. TERRY, C. H. TERRY, and THEO. B. TERRY. Funeral services were conducted at his late residence by REV. D. A. FRIEND, of Louisville. He was laid to rest in Horse Cave Cemetery.

<u>TERRY DEATH NOTICE: "Edwin Burch Terry, Noble Citizen and Friend."</u> [**My Note:** This is a very long obituary, with a photograph, so only the most significant genealogical information has been abstracted]. A legion of Barren County friends were inexpressibly grieved when news came of the death of **MR. E. B. TERRY** at the Community Hospital here at 10:57 Wednesday morning. The body was removed to the home of his niece MRS. JENNIE BARLOW. The funeral will be at the Baptist Church here tomorrow morning at ten o'clock. Interment will be in the Glasgow Cemetery. MR. TERRY had been ill eleven days. Saturday, June 26, he was removed to the hospital for more treatment. It was apparent from the first that he was in critical condition. Heroic efforts were made to restore him, but the ravage of an illness that developed while on a tour of the Holy Land in 1927 had so weakened him that the fight was a hopeless one. **EDWIN BURCH TERRY** was born August 18, 1869, at Glasgow, the son of REV. NAT G. TERRY and EMILY STARK TERRY. In September, 1875, the family moved near Cave City and he attended school there until 1887. He completed school work at Glasgow Normal School in 1889 and entered Bethel Male College at Russellville where he finished as valedictorian of his class in 1897. His professional work was at National Normal University in

Lebanon, Ohio. With the organization of the Glasgow Graded School in 1901, MR. TERRY began his long and brilliant school work here. In 1925 he entered upon his work as the feature writer and social editor of *The Times*. MR. TERRY was never married. Surviving is one brother, MR. P. L. TERRY, of Cave City, and the following nieces and nephews: MRS. JENNIE BARLOW, MR. R. S. TERRY, of Glasgow; MRS. J. B. GARDNER, MISS BELINDA TERRY and MISS EMILY TERRY, MR. EARLE DICKEY TERRY, MR. EDWIN TERRY, MR. P. L. TERRY, JR., and MR. NAT PARRISH, all of Cave City; REV. A. MACK PARRISH, of Paducah, KY; MRS. W. C. LAWRENCE, of Winchester, VA; MR. NAT TERRY, of Ohio; and MR. W. T. PARRISH, of Louisville. [**My Note**: He died July 7, 1937].

TERRY SURPRISE BIRTHDAY DINNER: The relatives and friends of **MRS. ELLEN BAGBY TERRY**, of Hiseville, gave her a surprise 78th birthday dinner at her home. No finer type of womanhood ever lived than MRS. TERRY. "Her 78 years are like a crown of glory around her head." Present: MR. and MRS. THE. TERRY, and children, THE., JAMES, and ELLEN, of Hardin County; MR. and MRS. S. E. TERRY, SAMUEL TERRY, MR. CARTER TERRY, MR. and MRS. W. A. TERRY, MRS. WILL TERRY, JR., MISS DOROTHY TERRY and MR. WILLIAM TERRY, MRS. MAYMIE TERRY WARDER, MR. and MRS. A. B. BONTA, and MARY W. BONTA of Horse Cave; MISS DOROTHY CONNOWAY and GENE CONNOWAY, MR. and MRS. A. DEPP, MR. and MRS. WALTER DEPP, MISS BETTIE J. DEPP, MR. and MRS. JAMES BAGBY, MR. ROBERT BAGBY, MR. and MRS. GENE BAGBY, MR. and MRS. TED BAGBY, RODDY BAGBY, MR. and MRS. WILL BAGBY, MR. and MRS. JOHN BAGBY, MR. and MRS. JOHN WALTHALL, MISS MARY WALTHALL, MISS DOROTHY WALTHALL, ROGER WALTHALL MR. C. R. SMITH, MR. and MRS. HOWARD GARDNER, MR. and MRS. EDWARD PETERSON, MISS LIZZIE PETERSON, ANNIE PETERSON, MR. EDWARD PETERSON and MR. ROBERT PETERSON, MRS. KATE KING, EUGENIA KING, ANDREW KING, MRS. CHARLES HAYES, MR. and MRS. BURNETT WORTHINGTON, MISS ELIZABETH WORTHINGTON, MISS MAXINE WORTHINGTON, and MR. ORVILLE WORTHINGTON.

TRAVIS DEATH NOTICE: "A Tribute To Mrs. Martha McCoy Travis." The sad death of our departed friend occurred at the Maplewood Infirmary, April 4th, after an illness of flu and pneumonia. She was buried in the Refuge Cemetery, BROTHER RENO conducting the funeral services. **MRS. TRAVIS** was 37 years, 11 months, and 15 days old. She made a profession of religion in a revival held at Lick Branch in the year 1904, joined the church at that place and was baptized. [**My Note:** A long eulogy followed by a short poem by "her girlhood friend" were included in the notice. MARTHA L. TRAVIS died in 1931 and is buried in Refuge Cemetery, Eighty Eight, Kentucky].

TRAVIS-JONES MARRIAGE ANNOUNCEMENT: **MISS PAULINE TRAVIS**, daughter of MR. HUGHIE TRAVIS, and **MR. FLOYD JONES**, son of MR. and MRS. CASSY JONES of Lecta, married ---- [no date].

TUDOR DEATH NOTICE: **PRINCETON P. TUDOR**, departed this life June 23, 1934. Poem written "in loving remembrance of our dear grandfather" by a granddaughter MRS. ORENE HENSLEY, of Center, Kentucky.

<u>TURNER DEATH NOTICE</u>: "The Death Of Dr. C. C. Turner On Feb. 28." Death, with a swift and unsuspected blow, removed one of Barren County's best known and most useful citizens when **DR. CASWELL C. TURNER**, 59, succumbed to a heart attack at his home on East Main Street Sunday morning at 2:30 o'clock. [My Note: A long obituary recounts his life's accomplishments some of which is abstracted as follows]. CASWELL C. TURNER was born July 30, 1883 at Gamaliel, KY, a son of HAYDEN TURNER and ARENA YORK, both of whom were descended from Monroe County pioneer families who took an active part in the early settlement of that section. He was chairman of the Barren County Health Board, charter member of the Board of Trustees of the Community Hospital, a past member of the Glasgow School Board, past chairman of the Board of Trustees of the Glasgow Public Library, an elder in the Christian Church, and a past president of the Barren County Chapter of the Sons of the American Revolution. Survivors are his widow, MRS. FLORENCE HARLIN TURNER, one sister, MRS. HENRY ROBINSON, of Green City, Missouri, and one half-brother, MR. JAMES TURNER, of Hartford, Kentucky. Funeral services were held Tuesday morning at 10 o'clock at the First Christian Church, with the REV. KENNETH McCORKLE conducting the services. Interment was in Gamaliel Cemetery where burial service was conducted at 1 o'clock that day.

<u>TURNER DEATH NOTICE</u>: **MRS. LIZZIE TURNER**, wife of MR. J. R. TURNER, died at the Community Hospital Sunday at midnight, at the age of 63 years, leaving a husband and 7 children: CLYDE TURNER, LEWIS TURNER and PAUL TURNER, of Columbus, Ohio, SEYMOUR TURNER, of Louisville, and HARRY TURNER, of Glasgow, MRS. LOLA DULEY, of Arkansas, and MRS. VELMA HOUCK, of Glasgow. She also left brother, MR. CLARENCE BALLARD and two sisters, MRS. ETHEL ANDERSON, of Burkesville, and MRS. MINNIE SHAW, of Glasgow. The funeral services were conducted by ELDER T. T. ALDERSON, with interment in the Defevers Cemetery.

<u>TURNER-QUIGLEY MARRIAGE ANNOUNCEMENT</u>: **MISS LURA TURNER**, of Akerville, daughter of MRS. CHARLES BRAY, and **MR. HASCAL QUIGLEY**, son of MR. and MRS. G. F. QUIGLEY of Goodnight, were married Sunday night following the services at Salem Baptist Church near the home of the groom, by the REV. MACK J. COLLINS, of Louisville. Best man was MR. GEORGE PARRISH, of Louisville, nephew of the groom, and maid of honor was MISS LOIS BARBOUR. The wedding march, and other songs, were played by MISS SARABETH BARBOUR. One of the most attractive and at the same time most impressive weddings of the season was solemnized last Sunday evening at 8:10 at Old Salem Church in the Barrens when MR. HASCAL QUIGLEY, of Goodnight, led MISS LURA TURNER, of Akersville, to the altar. REV. M. J. COLLINS, of Louisville, officiated. The attendants were MISS LOIS BARBOUR, of Goodnight, and MR. GEORGE T. PARRISH, JR., of Louisville. MRS. QUIGLEY is a cultured, refined young lady, known to many in Glasgow, and MR. QUIGLEY was reared in Goodnight and educated at Bethel College. For several years he has been a popular merchant at Goodnight. Also attending the wedding ceremony were MR. and MRS. TERRY PARRISH and MISS DORA REE PARRISH, of Louisville. [**My Note:** Written in pencil on the clipping was the year "1932"].

<u>VANCE DEATH NOTICE</u>: **MRS. ELLIS VANCE**, My Dear Mother, died February 24, 1935. A poem was written by her daughter, MRS. LOTTIE MORGAN.

<u>VERNON-HUTCHERSON MARRIAGE ANNOUNCEMENT</u>: Announcements have been received of the marriage on Thursday last of **MR. LYON B. HUTCHERSON and MISS LYDIA MAE VERNON**, at Tifton, GA. This was quite a surprise to MR. HUTCHERSON's host of friends here, where he was born and reared. They will make their home at Maple Hill near town.

<u>VINCENT-LESSENBERRY MARRIAGE ANNOUNCEMENT</u>: **MR. and MRS. W. R. VINCENT**, of Hiseville, announce the marriage of their daughter, **SELMA LAWLESS VINCENT**, to **MR. JOSEPH WINLOCK LESSENBERRY**, son of MR. and MRS. J. D. LESSENBERRY, of Hiseville. The wedding was in Jeffersonville [Indiana] on October 15th, ----.

<u>WALKER-WILLIAMS MARRIAGE ANNOUNCEMENT</u>: **MISS ALMA WALKER**, daughter of MR. JOHN WALKER, of the New Salem section, married **MR. GROVER WILLIAMS**, "on the fourteenth." They will live in Bristletown.

<u>WALTON LETTER</u>: <u>FROM HARRY WALTON SERVING IN THE MILITARY IN FRANCE, 1918</u>: The Glasgow Epworth League has received a letter [in part] from **HARRY WALTON**, of this place, now stationed in France: "Somewhere in France, Sunday, February 17th, 1918. Dear Friends: Please accept my thanks for the 'Soldier's Kit' presented by the League and I assure you that every article will come in awfully handy."

<u>WATKINS DEATH NOTICE: "Death Of J. William Watkins In Louisville."</u> One of the saddest deaths of a Barren Countian for many years was that of **MR. J. WILLIAM WATKINS** which occurred in Louisville last Saturday. MR. WATKINS was born November 29, 1889, at the Watkins home near Coral Hill. He held positions at the Citizens National Bank in Glasgow, and similar positions in Louisville. He married MISS IRENE BARTLETT on February 5, 1920, and she survives him. He is also survived by his father, ESQ. W. M. WATKINS, of Coral Hill; a brother, MR. J. S. WATKINS, of St. Louis, Missouri; one uncle, MR. CHARLES R. SMITH, of Coral Hill; and one aunt, MISS BETTIE WATKINS, who has lived with MR. WATKINS since the death of his wife, who was MISS MARGARET E. SMITH and who died about 41 years ago. Miss Bettie too the little orphan boy Willie into her heart and no mother could have been more devoted. WILL WATKINS is buried in Coral Hill. He was a member of the Christian Church and choir].

<u>WATKINS DEATH NOTICE: "Death Comes After Long Illness."</u> **MISS RUTH WATKINS** died at Waverly Hills Sanitarium, June 19th, after a two year illness. She was a member of the Christian Church. Surviving are three sisters: MISS ESTHER WATKINS, of Glasgow, MISS FRANCES WATKINS, of Louisville, and MRS. FRED LUTTERMAN, of Knob Lick; and two brothers, MR. TOM WATKINS and MR. FRANK WATKINS, of Coral Hill. Several nieces and nephews survive. Service was held at the Coral Hill Christian Church by REV. WARREN DUNAGAN, and with burial in the Coral Hill family burying ground.

<u>WATKINS DEATH NOTICE</u>: **MR. ROBERT G. WATKINS**, age 82, died at his home at Coral Hill last Saturday night after several years illness. He had been confined to his bed four months. He is survived by his widow and 3 children: MRS. STANLEY CULVER, MR. FRED WATKINS, and MR. SAM WATKINS, all of Coral Hill. One brother, MR. W. M. WATKINS, and one sister, MISS BETTIE WATKINS, of Coral Hill, also survive. MR. WATKINS was a member of the Christian Church. Services were by BROTHER WARREN DUNAGAN, with burial in the family burying ground.

<u>WATKINS-SHIRLEY MARRIAGE ANNOUNCEMENT</u>: **MISS VIRGINIA WATKINS**, the daughter of MR. & MRS. F. J. WATKINS, and **MR. ALLIE LEWIS SHIRLEY**, son of MRS. LUCY SHIRLEY, both of Coral Hill, married in Jeffersonville, Indiana on October 28th. They will reside at Coral Hill, KY.

<u>WATSON DEATH NOTICE</u>: **MRS. W. D. WATSON**, My Darling Mother, died June 14, 1926. Poem written by her daughter, MRS. EDITH BAILEY.

<u>WHEAT DEATH NOTICE: "Oldest Member of Wheat Family Dies In Monroe."</u> **MR. J. A. WHEAT**, 91 years of age and the oldest of the Wheat family in Monroe County, died at his home near Mud Lick last Sunday at one p. m. His death was due to a complication of diseases due to old age. He had been married twice. His first wife died several years ago. His second wife, who was MRS. LOU SHIRLEY, and the following sons and daughters survive: JAMES WHEAT, JACK WHEAT, BIRD WHEAT, BILLIE WHEAT, and BARNETT WHEAT, of the Mud Lick section, JESSE WHEAT, of Missouri, MRS. BETTIE DAVIS, of Freedom, and MISS COLEY WHEAT, who lives at home. The burial was in the Bethlehem Cemetery. [**My Note:** This notice appeared in *The Glasgow Times*, which noted the information was from *The Tompkinsville News* in Monroe County. An article on the reverse of this notice gave the year as 1925].

<u>WHITE DEATH NOTICE</u>: **MRS. ELIZABETH JANE WHITE**, widow of the late DR. JOHN B. WHITE, of Cave City, died at Maplewood Infirmary here last Wednesday after several weeks illness of a complication of diseases. It will be remembered that DR. WHITE died suddenly while attending services at the Cave City Christian Church after making a professional call. MRS. WHITE was a member of the Baptist Church and is survived by these children: MRS. W. H. FARRIS, MRS. RUFUS BARBOUR, MRS. A. P. YOUNG, MISS MARY WHITE, MR. HENRY J. WHITE, MR. EDWARD R. WHITE, all of Cave City, MRS. H. SCHAAM, of California, and MR. WILLIAM M. WHITE, of Nada, Utah. Services were held in the Cave City Baptist Church, conducted by the REV. T. F. GRIDER, and burial was in the Cave City Cemetery. [**My Note:** ELIZABETH J. WHITE died on February 27, 1929, and DR. WHITE died on January 24, 1926].

<u>WILLIAMS DEATH NOTICE</u>: **MR. RICHARD WILLIAMS** died at his home in the Bristletown section at the age of 75 years. He is survived by his wife and nine children: MISS MAUD WILLIAMS, of this place; MR. J. C. WILLIAMS, of Hiseville; MR. G. C. WILLIAMS, of Coral Hill; MR. H. C. WILLIAMS, MRS. P. H. POWELL, MRS. B. L. WEAVER, MISS BETTIE WILLIAMS, and MISS BESSIE WILLIAMS, all of the Bristletown section.

He is also survived by one brother, MR. JOE P. WILLIAMS, of this place. MR. WILLIAMS was an excellent citizen. Burial was in the family burying ground, after the funeral services by REV. HOWELL.

WILLIAMS DEATH NOTICE: "The Death of Mrs. R. Williams, Bristletown" **MRS. RICHARD WILLIAMS** died at her home at Bristletown on Tuesday afternoon at 2:15 p.m. after six weeks' illness, at the age of 70. Her husband had preceded her to the grave one and a half years ago. Surviving is one brother, MR. WILL SPENCER, of Glasgow, and these children: MISS BETTIE WILLIAMS and MISS BESSIE WILLIAMS, at home; MAUD WILLIAMS, of Glasgow; MRS. PAUL POWELL, of Cedar Grove; MRS. BURFORD WEAVER, of Mt. Pleasant; MR. J. C. WILLIAMS, of Lecta; MR. G. C. WILLIAMS, of Coral Hill; MR. H. C. WILLIAMS, of Laurel Bluff; and, MR. W. C. WILLIAMS, of Bristletown. MRS. WILLIAMS was a member of Boyd's Creek Methodist Church. Funeral service was at the home Wednesday afternoon at 2:15 o'clock with burial at the home place.

WILLIAMS-BECKETT MARRIAGE ANNOUNCEMENT: **MISS HADIE LEWIS WILLIAMS,** of Louisville, daughter of MR. and MRS. MILTON WILLIAMS, of near Glasgow, married **MR. MILIARD D. BECKETT**, of Minneapolis, Minn., in Louisville on May 16th. They will make their home in Louisville.

WILLIAMS-GREER MARRIAGE ANNOUNCEMENT: **MISS JOCILLE WILLIAMS,** the daughter of MR. and MRS. JOE P. WILLIAMS, and **MR. KARL GREER,** son of MR. JAKE W. GREER, were married in Elizabethtown, Kentucky, by REV. S. A. ARNOLD, a Methodist pastor.

WILLIAMS-WOLFE MARRIAGE ANNOUNCEMENT: **MISS CLARA E. WILLIAMS,** thr daughter of MR. and MRS. M. R. WILLIAMS, formerly of this place, and **MR. LEANDER E. WOLFE,** of Louisville, married at the Broadway Christian Church in Louisville on Monday night, March 3, ----.

WINN DEATH NOTICE: **REV. JOHN R. WINN,** life long resident of Barren County, and for a half century a Baptist minister, died at his home on Maple Drive at the age of 77 years. For many years he lived ten miles north of Glasgow on the Jackson Highway where he owned a fine farm, but a few years ago he sold it and moved to Glasgow, where he built a home. He is survived by his wife and four daughters: MRS. SAM CAMPBELL, of Corydon, Indiana; MRS. E. L. CALLAHAN, MISS ESTHER WINN, and MISS RAY WINN, all of Glasgow. BRO. WINN was a prosperous citizen and had accumulated a considerable estate, which is unusual for a minister. He was highly regarded both by his brethren and the citizenry. Funeral services were held at the residence on Monday by REV. J. A. EASLEY, with the interment of the remains in Horse Cave.

WOOD DEATH NOTICE: "Mrs. Mollie Wood Dead." **MRS. MOLLIE WOOD** died at the home of her daughter MRS. GENIE BAIRD, near Goodnight, on Tuesday morning. MRS. WOOD belonged to one of the oldest and most prominent families in the county, being a MISS MOLLIE ROGERS before her marriage. She had been a sufferer from asthma for some time and her death did not come as a surprise to family and friends. MRS. WOOD was 78 years of age, and she is survived by only one child,

MRS. GENIE BAIRD, with whom she spent most of her life. Two brothers also survive her: MR. TOBE ROGERS, of Cave City, and MR. CHARLIE ROGERS, near Goodnight. She was a member of the Christian Church and after funeral services the remains were interred in the burial ground on the WILLIAM B. ROGERS place, near Goodnight. [**My Note:** MOLLIE WOOD died in 1918. TOBE was probably HENRY ROGERS?].

WOOD DEATH NOTICE: "Death Of Jim Wood At His Home, Smiths Grove." **MR. JIM WOOD** died at his home at Smiths Grove last Wednesday night at the age of 64 years. His death was caused by a complication of diseases. He is survived by his widow, two sons, GRAYSON WOOD and HENRY WOOD, three grandchildren, two sisters, MRS. J. H. SHIPLEY and MRS. FLAY PARRISH, of Hiseville, and one brother, MR. JOE WOOD, of Gary, Indiana. MR. WOOD was born and reared in this county. The funeral was at Smiths Grove Christian Church with the burial there.

WOOD DEATH NOTICE: "A Good Man Gone." **MR. SAM WOOD** died at his home in the Hiseville country at the age of 74 years, after a brief illness of pneumonia. MRS. WOOD died about 21 months ago and left no children. He is survived by one half-sister, MRS. EUGENE BAIRD, of Goodnight. Mr. Wood was one of the most successful businessmen of the county, president of Hiseville Deposit Bank, an extensive farmer, and a most excellent citizen. Mr. Wood was a member of the Christian Church, and had a large influence in the religious life of the community. Funeral services will be held at the Christian Church in Hiseville this afternoon at two o'clock, and the burial will follow in the Hiseville Cemetery. [**My Note:** This burial is not recorded in Eva Coe Peden's Barren County Cemeteries, which lists the grave markers in the Hiseville, and other cemeteries, in Barren County. In another article, MRS. OSCAR BOND, of Louisville, attended the funeral and burial of her uncle, MR. SAM WOOD].

WRIGHT DEATH NOTICE: "Mrs. J. L. Wright Expired Monday." **MRS. SARAH EUBANK WRIGHT** died at her home here yesterday evening at six o'clock, after a short illness. She was a daughter of the late FRANK EUBANK, of Coral Hill. Her husband, JAMES L. WRIGHT, passed away last November. She was the last living member of her immediate family and her nearest surviving relatives are the following nieces and nephews: MRS. NANNIE MILLER, of Eighty Eight; JOHN WILKERSON, of Glasgow; MOSE WILKERSON and IKE WILKERSON, of Temple Hill; and, WILL HARLAN, of Roseville. She is survived also by some nieces in California. Funeral services were at the First Christian Church, by the REV. T. H. ALDERSON. Interment was in the Poplar Log Cemetery. [From another obituary: "Mrs. Sarah Wright Dies." MRS. SARAH EUBANK WRIGHT, 80 years old, died in her apartment in the Yancey Apartment Building on Washington Street. She was a daughter of the late FRANK EUBANK who for many years conducted a general store at Temple Hill, but later sold out and moved to near Coral Hill. In addition to the survivors listed above, this notice also named her nephews JOHN and GROVER HARLIN, of Roseville, and also nieces, MRS. J. M. SMITH, of Tulare, California, and MRS. MARY WILKINSON MILLER, of California.

WRIGHT DEATH NOTICE: "J. L. Wright Dies Suddenly." **MR. JAMES L. WRIGHT** died suddenly in the Yancey Apartment Building on Saturday morning. He had been in usual health and around town on Friday at different times. Shortly after dark he and his wife visited MR. and MRS. PATE WALKUP in the same building. His death is attributed to heart failure. MR. WRIGHT who lacked until March next of being 89 years was possibly the best known man in Barren County. He had lived in and near Glasgow for more than a half century and knew more people, and was able to call their names, than any other man. He was the son of the late REV. U. W. WRIGHT, a pioneer Christian preacher, and was born in the Dry Fork section. To his friends he was "Uncle Bud." He is survived by his wife, MRS. SARAH ANDERSON EUBANK WRIGHT, and 3 children by a former marriage: MRS. JOE WOOD, MR. SELBY WRIGHT, and MR. FRANK WRIGHT, all of Los Angeles, Calif. Services will be held Sunday at the First Christian Church by REV. T. H. ALDERSON, with burial in the Glasgow Cemetery. [**My Note:** He died in 1935. His first wife, CHLOE HARVEY WRIGHT, died in 1898].

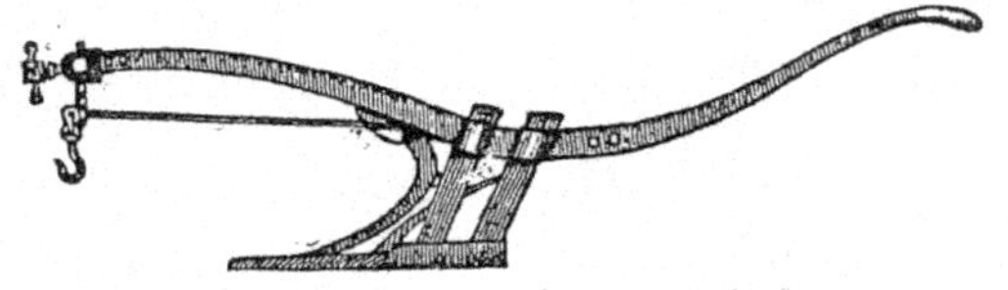

INDEX

-D-

-M-

Heritage Books by Henry C. Peden, Jr. :

A Closer Look at St. John's Parish Registers [Baltimore County, Maryland], 1701–1801

A Collection of Maryland Church Records

A Guide to Genealogical Research in Maryland: 5th Edition, Revised and Enlarged

Abstracts of the Ledgers and Accounts of the Bush Store and Rock Run Store, 1759–1771

Abstracts of the Orphans Court Proceedings of Harford County, 1778–1800

Abstracts of Wills, Harford County, Maryland, 1800–1805

Baltimore City [Maryland] Deaths and Burials, 1834–1840

Baltimore County, Maryland, Overseers of Roads, 1693–1793

Bastardy Cases in Baltimore County, Maryland, 1673–1783

Bastardy Cases in Harford County, Maryland, 1774–1844

Bible and Family Records of Harford County, Maryland Families: Volume V

Children of Harford County: Indentures and Guardianships, 1801–1830

Colonial Delaware Soldiers and Sailors, 1638–1776

Colonial Families of the Eastern Shore of Md.: Vols. 5, 6, 7, 8, 9, 11, 12, 13, 14, and 16

Colonial Maryland Soldiers and Sailors, 1634–1734

Dr. John Archer's First Medical Ledger, 1767–1769, Annotated Abstracts

Early Anglican Records of Cecil County

Early Harford Countians, Individuals Living in Harford Co., Md. in Its Formative Years
Volume 1: A to K, Volume 2: L to Z, and Volume 3: Supplement

Harford County Taxpayers in 1870, 1872 and 1883

Harford County, Maryland Divorce Cases, 1827–1912: An Annotated Index

Heirs and Legatees of Harford County, Maryland, 1774–1802

Heirs and Legatees of Harford County, Maryland, 1802–1846

Inhabitants of Baltimore County, Maryland, 1763–1774

Inhabitants of Cecil County, Maryland, 1649–1774

Inhabitants of Harford County, Maryland, 1791–1800

Inhabitants of Kent County, Maryland, 1637–1787

Joseph A. Pennington & Co., Havre De Grace, Maryland Funeral Home Records:
Volume II, 1877–1882, 1893–1900

Maryland Bible Records, Volume 1: Baltimore and Harford Counties

Maryland Bible Records, Volume 2: Baltimore and Harford Counties

Maryland Bible Records, Volume 3: Carroll County

Maryland Bible Records, Volume 4: Eastern Shore

Maryland Deponents, 1634–1799

Maryland Deponents: Volume 3, 1634–1776

Maryland Public Service Records, 1775–1783: A Compendium of Men and Women of
Maryland Who Rendered Aid in Support of the American Cause against
Great Britain during the Revolutionary War

Marylanders to Carolina: Migration of Marylanders to
North Carolina and South Carolina prior to 1800

Marylanders to Kentucky, 1775–1825

Methodist Records of Baltimore City, Maryland: Volume 1, 1799–1829

Methodist Records of Baltimore City, Maryland: Volume 2, 1830–1839

Methodist Records of Baltimore City, Maryland: Volume 3, 1840–1850 (East City Station)

More Maryland Deponents, 1716–1799

More Marylanders to Carolina: Migration of Marylanders to North Carolina and South Carolina prior to 1800

More Marylanders to Kentucky, 1778–1828

Outpensioners of Harford County, Maryland, 1856–1896

Presbyterian Records of Baltimore City, Maryland, 1765–1840

Quaker Records of Baltimore and Harford Counties, Maryland, 1801–1825

Quaker Records of Northern Maryland, 1716–1800

Quaker Records of Southern Maryland, 1658–1800

Revolutionary Patriots of Anne Arundel County, Maryland

Revolutionary Patriots of Baltimore Town and Baltimore County, 1775–1783

Revolutionary Patriots of Calvert and St. Mary's Counties, Maryland, 1775–1783

Revolutionary Patriots of Caroline County, Maryland, 1775–1783

Revolutionary Patriots of Cecil County, Maryland

Revolutionary Patriots of Charles County, Maryland, 1775–1783

Revolutionary Patriots of Delaware, 1775–1783

Revolutionary Patriots of Dorchester County, Maryland, 1775–1783

Revolutionary Patriots of Frederick County, Maryland, 1775–1783

Revolutionary Patriots of Harford County, Maryland, 1775–1783

Revolutionary Patriots of Kent and Queen Anne's Counties

Revolutionary Patriots of Lancaster County, Pennsylvania

Revolutionary Patriots of Maryland, 1775–1783: A Supplement

Revolutionary Patriots of Maryland, 1775–1783: Second Supplement

Revolutionary Patriots of Montgomery County, Maryland, 1776–1783

Revolutionary Patriots of Prince George's County, Maryland, 1775–1783

Revolutionary Patriots of Talbot County, Maryland, 1775–1783

Revolutionary Patriots of Worcester and Somerset Counties, Maryland, 1775–1783

Revolutionary Patriots of Washington County, Maryland, 1776–1783

St. George's (Old Spesutia) Parish, Harford County, Maryland: Church and Cemetery Records, 1820–1920

St. John's and St. George's Parish Registers, 1696–1851

Survey Field Book of David and William Clark in Harford County, Maryland, 1770–1812

The Crenshaws of Kentucky, 1800–1995

The Delaware Militia in the War of 1812

Union Chapel United Methodist Church Cemetery Tombstone Inscriptions, Wilna, Harford County, Maryland

www.ingramcontent.com/pod-product-compliance
Lightning Source LLC
Chambersburg PA
CBHW080611270326
41928CB00016B/3001
9781585495146